The Teaching Process
&
Arts and Aesthetics

Based on a conference held at Aspen, Colorado, June 25-July 1, 1978.
Co-sponsored by CEMREL, Inc.,
and The Education Program of
The Aspen Institute for Humanistic Studies
with support from **The National Institute of Education**

Gerard L. Knieter and Jane Stallings, *Editors*

Stanley S. Madeja, *Yearbook Series Editor*

CEMREL, Inc., St. Louis, Missouri

Library of Congress Cataloging in Publication Data

The Teaching process, arts and aesthetics.

(Yearbook on research in arts and aesthetic education; 3)

Includes bibliographies.

1. Arts—Study and teaching—Addresses, essays, lectures. I. Knieter, Gerard L., 1931- II. Stallings, Jane. III. Central Midwestern Regional Educational Laboratory. IV. Aspen Institute for Humanistic Studies. Education Program. V. Series.

NX280.T42   700'.7   79-19231

Prepared by CEMREL, Inc., a private nonprofit corporation supported in part as an educational laboratory by funds from the National Institute of Education, Department of Health, Education and Welfare. The opinions expressed in this publication do not necessarily reflect the position or policy of the National Institute of Education, and no official endorsement should be inferred.

Manufactured in the United States of America

CEMREL, Inc.
3120 59th Street
St. Louis, MO 63139

Preface

The yearbooks in this series address themselves to the broad issues of research in the arts and aesthetic education. The series was instituted to provide a platform for scholarly discourse in these fields plus related areas of education and psychology. Thus, the yearbooks provide a means to bring the results of this scholarly discourse to the researcher, the teacher, and the student. We do not intend the yearbooks to be comprehensive reviews of a particular topic, rather they represent a range of views from selected scholars at a given time related to the overall theme. If there were a grand design for the series, it was to bring the scholar, the teacher, the artist, and the arts educator together to speak on issues of concern to all.

The conferences on which the volumes are based themselves represent a novel type of cooperation—that between the National Institute of Education, and the Education Program of the Aspen Institute, and CEMREL, Inc. Each volume has benefited from the kind of discourse generated by the seminar setting provided at the Aspen Institute. Most if not all of the papers published in the yearbooks have been influenced by these discussions and have been altered and revised after their presentation. So not only do the conferences result in a publication, they also broaden the thought and work of those who attend.

Arts and Aesthetics: An Agenda for the Future, the first yearbook, represented an overview of the field and an attempt to set a future course for the arts and aesthetic education. It also influenced the choice of topics for future yearbooks. The second volume, *The Arts, Cognition, and Basic Skills,* was more focused and dealt with the problems of relating the arts to the nature of cognition and the development of basic skills. This, the third yearbook, is concerned with classroom practice and the process of teaching the arts and aesthetics in various settings. A projected fourth volume will treat the content of arts and aesthetic education curricula and instruction. Within the series there is a logical progression from broad topics to the specific concerns of particular arts disciplines.

My hope is that by bringing people from diverse fields together to address a common concern we have provided both a useful contribution to the scholarly literature and a stimulus for inquiry in the arts and aesthetic education as well as other fields of knowledge.

Stanley S. Madeja
Yearbook Series Editor

Acknowledgments

CEMREL would like to acknowledge the National Institute of Education for its support of the conference, and the Education Program of The Aspen Institute for Humanistic Studies for its co-sponsorship of the conference.

Conference Co-Chairmen

Stanley S. Madeja
Vice-President
CEMREL, Inc.
Director
Arts and Humanities Group

Martin Engel
Arts and Humanities Advisor
National Institute of Education

Planning Conference Participants

Anne M. Bussis
Research Psychologist
Educational Testing Service

Joseph F. Dominic
Senior Policy Research Fellow
National Institute of Education

Arthur Efland
Professor of Art Education
The Ohio State University

Martin Engel
Arts and Humanities Advisor
National Institute of Education

Francis Keppel
Director
Program on Education
Aspen Institute for Humanistic
  Studies

Gerard L. Knieter
Dean
The College of Fine and Applied
  Arts
The University of Akron

Virginia Koehler
Assistant Director for Teaching
  and Instruction
National Institute of Education

Stanley S. Madeja
Vice-President
CEMREL, Inc.

Edward Mikel
Coordinator
Aesthetic Education
  Learning Center Network
CEMREL, Inc.

Donald M. Miller
Director of Research
Arts and Humanities Group
CEMREL, Inc.

Sheila Onuska
Program Associate
Arts and Humanities Group
CEMREL, Inc.

Bennett Reimer
Chairman
Music Education Department
Northwestern University

Wade M. Robinson
President
CEMREL, Inc.

Bernard Rosenblatt
Director of Teacher Education and
*   Dissemination*
Arts and Humanities Group
CEMREL, Inc.

Lee S. Shulman
Professor of Educational
*   Psychology and Medical*
*   Education*
Director
Institute for Research on Teaching
Michigan State University

Jane Stallings
Manager of Classroom
*   Process Studies*
Education Research Department
Stanford Research Institute

Patricia Thuernau
Research Specialist
Arts and Humanities Group
CEMREL, Inc.

Yearbook Staff, CEMREL, Inc.

Stanley S. Madeja
Editor

Sheila Onuska
Assistant Editor

Sharon Michel-Trapaga
Production Coordinator

Mary Runge
Secretary

Ted Smith
Designer

Table of Contents

You never enjoy the world aright, til you so love the beauty
of enjoying it, that you are covetous and earnest to persuade
others to enjoy it.

Thomas Traherne
Seventeenth Century Poet

Teaching should be properly classified among the high arts,
classified there with no taint of hyperbole or mere metaphor.

David Hawkins

Gerard L. Knieter and Jane Stallings

Introduction

*Each second we live in a new and unique moment of the
universe. And what do we teach our children in school? We
teach them that two and two make four and that Paris is the
capital of France. When will we also teach them what they are?
We should say to each of them: Do you know what you are?
You are a marvel. You are unique. In all the world there is no
other child exactly like you. And look at your body . . . what a
marvel it is! Your legs, your arms, your cunning fingers, the
way you move!! You may become a Shakespeare, a
Michelangelo, a Beethoven. You have the capacity for
anything. Yes, you are a marvel. And when you grow up, can
you then harm another who is, like you, a marvel?*

Pablo Casals

This book is dedicated to the proposition that the American system of
education can provide an environment wherein students, teachers,
professors, and researchers can experience their own artistic development
and appreciate the artistic product of others.

How to provide this type of environment is the central question of this
book. We have accumulated enough knowledge through research on
teaching basic skills to elementary and secondary students to guide
teaching practice. Nathan Gage and his colleagues at Stanford, and Jane
Stallings and her co-workers at SRI International have successfully
trained teachers to use research findings on instructional processes
related to student gain in reading. Thus, it is hypothesized that similar
carefully focused research on the teaching of the arts could provide
similar findings to guide the teaching of the arts in public schools.

The 1978 Aspen Conference—out of which this book grew—included
participants from research on teaching; music and art professors from
schools of teacher education; practicing public-school music and art

GERARD L. KNIETER is Dean and Professor of Music at The College of Fine and
Applied Arts at The University of Akron, and JANE STALLINGS is Manager of
Classroom Process Studies in the Education Research Department of the Stanford
Research Institute.

teachers; and representatives from government. The questions that guided their discussions were (1) What are the relationships between the body of general research on teaching and the teaching process in the arts and aesthetics? (2) Can methodologies and findings from research on teaching be useful to the teacher in the arts? (3) Are there new or already existing ways of linking the teacher and the researcher to improve the instructional process in the arts or aesthetics? (4) What does the teacher in the arts expect from research? (5) What do the arts contribute to the teaching process?

The papers delivered at the conference, the responses made to them, and the discussions they both generated represent the interaction of the participants and these questions.

Geraldine Jonçich Clifford, Professor and Chairman of the Department of Education at Berkeley, whose paper opened the conference, presents a comprehensive review of the research on teaching emphasizing its perspectives for arts and aesthetic education. After presenting this background information she then explores two polar views: (1) that music education and art education should be aimed toward the talented; and (2) that music education and art education should be for all teachers and all children. The latter view, which focuses education in art and music upon appreciation, hypothesizes that active participation in the arts can lead to the development of increased aesthetic sensitivity while supporting the normal socialization process. School boards and school administrators sometimes focus their criticism on the music and art teachers who appear to give the lion's share of their attention to the few who are talented, while the larger group receives relatively little instruction. As school budgets become more and more limited, such elitist views of education will be harder and harder to defend.

Another problem she discusses is the belief held by some music and art educators that appreciation of the arts is not susceptible to scientific analysis and quantification, that it cannot be taught, that it is something too personal and too intangible to be taught in schools. Clifford maintains this is an intolerable position for an educator since schools are predicated upon a faith in the power to teach. In the last analysis, she believes it unlikely that artist/teachers would seriously maintain that teachers are but talent scouts. She concludes by saying, "However much artists represent a more or less alienated subculture, the teachers among them may indeed share a sufficient measure of the optimism that underlies the American character." This optimism would encourage us all to believe that essential basic education for all people should include both instruction in the appreciation of music and art, and provision of opportunities for all students to experience music and art.

The paper by Virginia Koehler, Assistant Director for Teaching and Instruction at the National Institute of Education, reviews the research on teaching and explores its implications for teaching of the arts. She offers a thorough review and summary of the process/product studies on reading, math, and linguistics. She describes the problems of understanding and documenting both instruction in the arts and the criteria against which outcomes are measured. She concludes that research emphasizing instruction in the arts should be conducted in elementary and secondary schools with initial work taking the form of naturalistic observation of unusually effective programs. Only when the instructional goals are clearly stated and understood by school personnel should process/product studies be conducted to determine effective practices.

The third and fourth papers describe how classroom teachers can collaborate in the conduct of research. The authors of both papers present a strong case for congruity between the researcher's agenda (purposes and method of work) and the teacher's agenda (instructional goals and student needs). Bussis, Amarel, and Chittenden, research psychologists at Educational Testing Service, present two case studies prepared by teachers. The authors describe how the data are collected and analyzed. The information about the children is the sort that is encountered and stored intuitively, but, through this method of study, these data are made available for review and become a basis for decision-making. Tikunoff and Ward, Director of Programs on Schooling and Deputy Laboratory Director at the Far West Laboratory, describe some school-based change as related to teaching personnel. They discuss why change is so difficult to bring about. They present one way of analyzing the teaching/learning process as it is embedded in the classroom and they relate it to bringing change to aesthetic education. They make a good case for giving teachers the opportunity, resources, and support to identify problems, set priorities, and develop procedures for inquiring into and resolving these problems.

Roy Edelfelt, Professional Associate at the National Education Association, focuses upon teachers in the arts and all other teachers who influence the arts. He addresses the elitist problem mentioned by Geraldine Clifford. He comments that unfortunately education in the arts in the United States has been the privilege of the few with the arts narrowly defined by the tastes of the middle or upper class, and arts events populated by comparatively well-heeled people. He sees this situation as the result of our economic system and the restriction of the arts to "serious" works, which eliminates recognition of art that is "of the people." He makes a case for teaching jazz and country music in schools as well as the classics. A wide range of music and art experience should be offered students since students remember schools and teachers more for the kinds of experiences provided than the actual content learned. Human experience and the quality of life should be conceived as aesthetic and artistic dimensions of schooling. Such school experiences should entice the individual to come back for more. Teacher educators should provide teachers with appropriately wide-ranging instruction so they can pursue and provide an improved quality of life for themselves and their students.

Inherent in Edelfelt's concern for the arts is a recognition that something needs to be done about improving the quality of life. The parallels between staff development goals to improve the quality of life and the goals of advocates of aesthetic education for significant, fulfilling experience are clear. There is the possibility that staff development in the arts for all teachers can make living more complete and significant, can provide more intrinsic rewards than most other experiences, and can serve as an antidote to the commercialism, superficiality, and falseness that characterize so much of life. This is because no experience requires more integrity than aesthetic experience.

The paper by Arthur Efland, Professor of Art Education at Ohio State, is a thoughtful exploration of some of the theoretical influences that impinge upon those who teach the arts. He begins by identifying the four elements basic to any theory of art: the *work* of art itself, the *artist* as the work's creator, the *audience* to whom the work of art is addressed, and the *universe* represented in the work, that is, what the work is about. Then, with the aid of a wide historical purview, Efland sketches four orientations of aesthetic theory—mimetic, pragmatic, expressive, and objective—orientations that allow us to consider the arts from earliest times to the present.

In the next section, Efland identifies four orientations to psychology which he relates to the traditional divisions in aesthetic theory:

1. Mimetic Aesthetics with Psychological Behaviorism
2. Pragmatic Aesthetics with Cognitive Psychology
3. Expressive Aesthetics with Psychonanlytic Psychology
4. Objective Aesthetics with Gestalt Psychology.

Although we are invited to consider these relationships, Efland is too much a scholar to suggest that the psychological theories are bound "logically or causally" to the aesthetic orientations. He proposes that there is an obvious compatibility between the way one views the world psychologically and the way aesthetic theories have been traditionally organized.

Efland then relates the four orientations to teaching, asking and answering these questions:

1. If art is imitation and learning is by imitation, what then is teaching?
2. If art is viewed as a transaction between the viewer and the art object, or for that matter, between the artist and the object he or she is making, what then is teaching?
3. If art is the self-expression of the artist and if all behavior is motivated by subconscious drives, what then is teaching?
4. If art is an objective autonomous object with a formal structure capable of being understood directly in perception, and if learning is a

process involving perception of wholes, what then is teaching?
The basic view that we are offered indicates that the four traditional views of aesthetic theory "seem to align themselves with specific orientations in psychology" and "certain teaching practices parallel these orientations."

Hence, the fourth section examines the teaching practices that parallel the orientations and the roles they play in contemporary arts and education. It is a rich unfolding of ideas showing significant relationships among philosophical, psychological, and educational theories from Plato to contemporary educators.

Efland's suggestion that distinctive teaching traditions in each of the arts can be grouped around selected theories of aesthetics which can then be aligned with specific theoretical orientations to psychology provides the reader with one of the most comprehensive examinations of these potential interrelationships found in any literature. However, considerable caution should be observed when aesthetic positions, orientations to psychology, and teaching traditions are aligned. It is true that the author is also aware of this caution, but the danger, as always, is that those among us who are looking for quick solutions, fads, and simple answers will launch the new bandwagon.

In the seventh paper, Laura Chapman, Senior Editor of *Studies in Art Education*, demonstrates the courage seldom seen in most researchers in the arts. She offers us an opportunity for a speculative examination of four orientations to the teaching of the visual arts. We have a theoretical paper, backed by descriptive information, that deals with what teachers hope to accomplish through the teaching process. The author is primarily concerned with how the teacher's belief system—those operative values which are consciously or unconsciously held—influences the rationale for teaching art, the form and content of curricula, and the teaching process. We are provided with "a direction for theory building and further inquiry."

The author presents four options for our consideration: the Idealist, the Realist, the Personalist, and the Experimentalist. She is careful to advise the reader that conclusions drawn from this study are "tentative at best." Yet an inquiry that provides alternative paths for our thinking is useful. Our continuing agenda as a profession should be to seek new ways to identify the assumptions that we bring to the instructional process, to the work of art, and to the sequence of educational experience we call the curriculum.

In the next paper, James Hanshumaker, Professor of Music and Education at the University of Southern California, deals with the problem of determining excellence in the teaching of the arts. He identifies the intricacies involved in rendering a judgment that takes into account the myriad complexities (knowledge of the subject, experience in teaching and in the art form, philosophy, psychology, curriculum, and so on) associated with evaluation of teaching in the arts. Among his most vital observations is the view that much of the aesthetic content of a performance—he views teaching as a performance, too—is not amenable to either verbal or numerical description.

He provides the reader with a review of some of the literature on the characteristics of good teaching, and the opportunity to examine the longheld assumption that only the best performers are the best teachers. He also offers an insightful discussion of the limitations of the competency-based approach to teaching. Finally, he provides a list of the characteristics of excellence in arts teaching which offers an informative basis for further serious discussion.

The final paper by Lee Shulman, Director of the Institute for Research on Teaching at Michigan State, is a review of the conference as seen by an educational psychologist. He succinctly summarizes the conflicts and congruences of the participants' interests and concerns as they related to the five questions posed to the conference. Shulman provides a structure for looking at the conference as an event and as a base from which those committed to teaching and to teaching the arts and aesthetic education can begin to develop a deeper and more fruitful partnership. He links the papers presented with the discussions that followed them.

The conference did provide some answers to the five questions posed to the participants before their arrival. It also made clear some areas for further work. Clifford describes the historic links between the body of general research on teaching and teaching in arts and aesthetics. Koehler relates research on teaching to the arts and suggests that descriptive and collaborative methodologies may be the most useful for further study of teaching in the arts. The Tikunoff and Ward, and Bussis, Chittenden, and Amarel papers suggest ways to link the teacher and researcher to improve the instructional process in aesthetic education. Arts teachers who attended the conference described how they teach and how they answer their own questions about teaching and learning in the classroom. They did not express a felt need for guidance from the research community, but were most interested in the idea of teachers conducting their own research.

The papers by Efland, Chapman, and Hanshumaker address the problems embedded in conducting research in the arts. The principal issue raised is what criteria are to be used to judge the outcomes of programs in aesthetic education. This issue of criteria for judging teaching process or products was not resolved at the conference.

The conference participants did reach general agreement about numerous other issues. They agreed on a need for in-depth case studies of schools with comprehensive arts programs. Along with the quality of the art product itself, such side effects as student pleasure, self-esteem, cooperation, teacher morale, parent participation, attendance (teacher and student), delinquency, and vandalism should be examined. Some have hypothesized that a comprehensive arts program might have a soothing effect upon the school population and might increase a sense of ownership, thus reducing vandalism.

The teaching process in the arts should be studied, using some of the methodology developed to describe classrooms in other fields of studies. The instructional environment and the interactions of teacher and students are easy to document to provide a Gestalt of the classroom. The encouragement and support of teachers can be documented as well as the students' enthusiasm and level of involvement. How well do teachers use their time? How much time is allocated to instruction? How long does it take to get started and to clean up? How much choice do students have? All of these factors have been found to be related to student progress in other subject areas.

Similar studies using the process and outcome data suggested could lead to a better understanding of what is needed to help each child feel unique and, in Pablo Casal's words, "a marvel."

This conference has led us to conclude that not only do we in the arts need to employ some of the newer approaches to educational research in use outside the arts, but we should develop new modes of inquiry that have greater congruity with the aesthetic nature of the individual and the art that is created. Today, the dominant form of research in arts education (most of it in doctoral programs) is based upon the isolation of the single variable—the physical science model. It is an obviously seductive procedure because it invites a relatively high degree of predictability. However, many of the hypotheses selected for this type of examination are often trivial or pedestrian. In addition, the operational reality of teachers, students, and artistic creation in the classroom involves complex interactions among multiple variables—many of which are qualitative rather than quantitative in nature.

One of the dominant themes that emerged from the deliberations was that the organic wholeness of aesthetic education should be studied as an entire process. It is reasonable, therefore, to explore the entire process of ethnographical research, possibly as it is used in cultural anthropology. Societies, for example, are studied—as far as possible—as entire entities. They are viewed in the context of political, economic, religious, and aesthetic traditions. From this orientation, the idea of a group of individuals being labeled "culturally disadvantaged" reveals the ethnocentrism usually associated with any group that holds the view that "their art" is the art for all of the people. The critical idea here is that new programs of research in the arts need to reveal the belief systems of the researchers, as well as of those being studied, in order for all of us to become conscious of our unspoken assumptions.

It is also necessary for us to develop new approaches for the investigation of artistic thinking and problem solving. Such approaches should help us avoid the confusions generated by ever-evolving educational fads. For example, those among us who are looking to brain research as the new solution have accepted the unspoken assumption that analysis of the topography or location equals explanation or meaning. The idea that we can locate where certain processes occur, or appear to occur, has generated considerable joy for many arts educators. Yet, programs to support the fundamental philosophical values of the arts which are basic to human behavior and society are avoided while the illusion of the "new education" (left brain, right brain, split hemispheric adoption, and so on) captures the imagination of the intellectually bankrupt.

The conference also brought us to grips with the question of the criteria for coping with qualitative behavior in artistic creation as well as in teaching and learning. The immediate and the long-range challenge is to chart innovative approaches to research that will allow us to design better ways for studying the several dimensions of expressive human potential through a process that does not oversimplify, distort, or dehumanize.

The 1978 Aspen Conference was a significant event in arts education because it brought together researchers, classroom teachers, and arts educators. It provided an opportunity to examine many of the assumptions that each group held and, therefore, brought us all closer to the "truth." Yet, the differences were important too. The objective researcher who is often characterized as non-feeling was discovered to be deeply concerned with the quality of life in the classroom and in the arts. The arts educator whom some have viewed as emotional and impulsive was observed to be objective and philosophically sophisticated. And, we all observed the classroom teacher as a collaborator in research while engaged in teaching the arts.

However, important issues still remain to be solved. Some of the age-old problems concerning the way we conceptualize value in the work of art are unresolved. Most of our best minds in aesthetic education seem tied to the period between Plato and early Langer, essentially uninformed of alternative ways of conceptualizing either the nature of art or the unique quality of aesthetic reality. State departments of education—activated either by the financial largesse expected from Washington, D.C., or the economic situation—move American education from one mindless fad to another. For example, examine some of the following ideas which have occupied the attention of educators for the past few years: behavioral objectives, competencies, mainstreaming, accountability, and back-to-basics. It is our responsibility to assess the impact of these educational orientations so that as the new "messages" continue to unfold, they will be evaluated *before* they are adopted and then discarded.

The trend to homogenize American society has its counterpart in education where teachers are asked to deal with education as though children and their development were analogous to manufacturing and marketing. The more subtle forms of confusion occur when educators themselves lose sight of the unique qualities of children, teaching, and the arts. While it is reasonable to assume that certain principles of teaching and learning can be applied across all subject matter areas, it is unreasonable to expect that the arts should be viewed as some form of English, math, or science which may be more easily described verbally or numerically.

We need to find those similarities among all subjects that allow us the reasonable generalization. And, we are committed to capturing the unique quality of the arts which enhances and informs the personality so that it can maximize its humanistic potential. The 1978 Aspen Conference acquainted us with one another's truths and realities.

This is the beginning . . .

Akron, Ohio and
Palo Alto, California
May 1979

Geraldine Jonçich Clifford

An Historical Review of Teaching and Research: Perspectives for Arts and Aesthetic Education

Images, usually inspiring and reverential, of the teacher-as-artist ring through history. "But, could we evoke from their classic shades, their Parnassian heights, and their academic groves, the mighty masters of the Teaching Arts, a convocation would assemble such as the earth never saw!" (p. 42) So in 1848 rhetorized the principal of the Classical and Mathematical Institute of Newburgh, New York (Hall, 1848). In the case of teachers of the arts, the conception of artist-teacher is yet more complex. It is the purpose of this paper to suggest how the self-image and experiences of the teacher of the arts, along with other characteristics of the arts as school curricula, relate to the capacity of educational research to influence the teaching process.

This assignment represents an opportunity to extend into the area of arts and aesthetic education earlier investigations (Clifford, 1973, 1978; Jonçich, 1968) into the effects on classroom practice of educational research. In the context of school arts, it is the occasion to examine the optimistic rationality of science, in the form of educational research, in contact or lack of contact with the traditions and sensibilities of artistic expression. This effort may cast more light upon the question of how the internal characteristics of a teaching field and the qualities of a research tradition interface to enhance or frustrate the teaching field's responsiveness to the research enterprise. To anticipate a little, patterns of recruitment, training, and employment of teachers appear in the fine arts that still distinguish these from other teaching fields found in the public schools.

"For most of us, art training in school was a sporadic and haphazard swirl of finger paints, crepe paper, and tambourines" (DiMaggio and Useem, 1978, p. 103). This description recognizes an ignorance of the arts that marks persons like the present author, hence, this is an analysis of arts and aesthetic education as viewed by an outsider. The literature,

GERALDINE JONÇICH CLIFFORD *is Professor and Chairman of the Department of Education at the University of California, Berkeley.*

especially the research literature, on teaching in other arts fields being both small and scattered, this analysis focuses upon arts and aesthetic education solely as represented by the visual arts and music as taught in the public elementary and secondary schools of the United States. It may be that important distinctions between school art and school music are sometimes overlooked in this review.

This paper is in five parts. The first begins with an examination of the predominant teaching mode in America, focusing on the nineteenth century when the present alignment of elementary and secondary schools was moved into place. For purposes of illustration, the reactions of certain art educators to the existence and persistence of verbal domination are indicated. Part Two identifies the ultimate educational objective of public schoolmen and suggests its role in promoting the recitation and textbook method.

Part Three continues the historical analysis by examining the characteristics of the available teaching force, and how these characteristics also shaped the teaching process. This section concludes with a depiction of a two-part division within the body of teachers of the arts— a division that appears to influence the field to the present day.

Part Four accepts the historical fact that education, including arts education, responded to successive pedagogical thrusts—from Pestalozzian theory in the mid-nineteenth century to the disciplinary pressures of the post-Sputnik era. Research began to mix with the philosophical and political influences operating on the teaching process and on theories of art education. Nor were its aims exempt from these influences. This section concentrates on the insufficiency of research pertinent to teaching in the arts and on the reactions of arts educators to tests and measurements.

The intent of the fifth and final part is to advance generalizations about the conditions under which educational research influences schooling—its instructional strategies, curricular arrangements, selection of materials, and instruments of evaluation. The status of research in arts and aesthetic education is assessed using representative statements of arts educators as a base. Then follows an attempt to explain the status of research in this field focusing on four related factors within the public school world of arts education: ambiguous status, internal fragmentation, tensions of elitism, and alienation.

The Teaching Process in America

A literal reading of the title of the first important American treatise on pedagogy, *Lectures on School-Keeping* (Hall, 1829), correctly suggests that instructional methods played only a minor role in nineteenth-century conceptions of teaching. The occupation was widely described as "keeping school," and the teacher's capacity to exercise "good government" was paramount—with a superficial knowledge of the "common branches" (those curriculum fields where all students receive basic-level instruction) as a decidedly secondary qualification. Popular views were slow to change. Nearly a century later O'Shea opened his book *Everyday Problems in Teaching* (O'Shea, 1912) with the opinion that, like parents, "probably nine out of ten trustees and members of boards of education esteem *good order* more highly than anything else in teaching" (p. 1).

A heightened professional consciousness of "teaching" came with the spread of teachers' meetings ("institutes"), normal schools, education journals, and state teachers' associations. Stimulated by European pedagogy, spokesmen for American education debated the relative merits of various methods: Explanatory, Catechetical (question and answer), Synthetical (from parts to wholes), and Analytical (from wholes to parts).

The Recitation

Despite such pedagogical partisanship, the predominant teaching strategy in nineteenth-century America was and continued to be the recitation. In the multi-age rural school and the graded city school alike, the teacher called upon individuals or groups—to recite from their books. Periodic public "exhibitions" allowed parents to determine whether the children were "letter perfect." The recitation extended through the college years, where the typical professor was chiefly neither a lecturer nor a demonstrator, but a hearer of recitations.

In *The Passing of the Recitation* (Thayer, 1928) the author reported that the traditional method was finally being abandoned—since it represented a discredited faculty psychology and notions of a passive pouring-in-of-knowledge, "no longer [in] accord with the fundamental aspirations of democratic citizenship" (p. iii). This obituary for the recitation method was prematurely written, however, for a later survey of 200 secondary-school classes found the recitation method still firmly in place (Dale and Raths, 1945).

Methods used in the basic school subjects tend to shape the whole curriculum. It was observed (Earhart, 1915) that "traditional methods, born of the need to teach a dead language, have been transferred bodily to the teaching of a live mode of speech. . . . What has been used in spelling has been copied in geography" (p. xv). So, too, for the arts. A British school inspector complained in 1915 that verbal methods of teaching appreciation in poetry and music produced reciters and memorizers (Hayward, 1915, p. 127). A New York City principal agreed:

> People outside of school are . . . getting acquainted with the world's best music through the mechanical devices which make this possible. How many schools are still content to do nothing in music except to teach note-reading and such songs as the pupils themselves can render? How many are affected either in material or method by the present great musical movement? (Earhart, 1915, p. 9)

Such borrowing of method was perpetuated by the fact that many books on teaching continued to ignore the arts curriculum. Teachers received no more guidance from a book of the progressive era like *The Technique of Teaching* (Davis, 1924) than they had found in such earlier advice books as *A Treatise on Pedagogy for Young Teachers* (Hewitt, 1884) or *The Eclectic Manual of Methods for the Assistance of Teachers* (1885).

The Word World and the Textbook

Language acquisition has been the aim of school instruction in all ages, and language easily becomes the principal if not exclusive route to all knowing. Arts educators, however, have a history of protest against this tendency. Hayward (1915) inveighed against literature that means only books, and against the music book "thrust between the pupil and the fairy world of sound that might have been his; and every song was henceforward introduced to him through the eye" (p. 127). Powers (1935) protested that "to know art is to feel" (p. 213)—a well-worn theme. The National Survey of Secondary Education analyzed printed courses of study and visited schools, finding that textbooks determined the work in music-reading, that courses in music theory and history placed considerable reliance upon textbooks, and that courses on appreciation, ordinarily taught without textbooks, demonstrated great variations in practice and teacher uncertainity as a consequence (Pierce and Hilpert, 1932). A later analysis (Jones and Evans, 1951) concurred: "The teacher is either floundering or a slavish textbook follower" (p. 23). In the same vein, the use of program music in appreciation classes has been viewed as symptomatic of a failure to understand "music as music." Fowler (1966) cautioned that "music educators need to begin to find methods of teaching music on the nonverbal level—a level indigenous to the art itself" (p. 234).

In 1899 the director of Philadelphia's Public School of Industrial Art had offered *New Methods of Education* (Tadd, 1899) as a protest against the "Old Education" with its overdependence on books and words. The identification of schooling, even in the arts, so closely with textbook learning was known abroad as the "American Method" (Horn, 1937, p. 207). In contrast, European pedagogy relied more upon oral methods; textbooks available in Germany, for example, were largely outlines filled in by the teacher (Hall-Quest, 1918, p. 40; Learned, 1927, pp. 13-14). In 1918, Hall-Quest described American publishers as "among the great educators of the world" (p. 10). And years later it was asserted that, at the least, educational editors and authors were second in influence only to such great "ideological leaders" as John Dewey and E. L. Thorndike (Schramm, 1955, p. 158).

Under the one-book plan found in many late-nineteenth century schools, it was possible for teachers to realize the goal of memorization of the textbook's contents (Earhart, 1915, p. iv). In this century, however, curricular expansion, educational research on vocabulary load and learning, and publishing enterprise caused book size to grow, while supplementary and associated series and workbooks proliferated (Clifford, 1978). Meanwhile, printed courses of study were issued by many local and state boards of education; on August 23, 1931, the *New York Times* reported that in excess of 30,000 courses of study could be found in the Bureau of Curriculum Research of Teachers College, Columbia University. But, an experienced educational leader like Ernest Horn much preferred textbooks; he wrote (1937) that "in comparison with typical courses of study, the average textbook is superior in scholarship, pedagogical arrangement, and the methods of teaching that are recommended" (p. 217). And to assist them in working their way through their word jungle, teachers were gaining the services of expanded and more comprehensive teachers' manuals—detailed maps on how to teach by the "American Method."

Historical Determinants of American Method: I. The Objective of Education

Any discussion of the teaching process must before long be informed by an understanding of the ultimate objective sought through education. In the words of a prominent author of nineteenth-century pedagogical texts (Orcutt, 1885, p. 10), "Instruction, then, is the orderly placing of knowledge in the mind with a definite object."

"The Great Aim of Study Is Character"

In contrasting the formalism of nineteenth-century schools with the supervised study, "socialized recitations," and project method of progressive pedagogy, V. T. Thayer (1928) contrasted the former's primary concern with "the acquisition of information" with the latter's "emphasis upon education for character building" (p. iv). Today's educational theory, he wrote, "no longer makes the mastery of the textbook the chief end of school education" (p. 29).

Thayer's is a misreading of America's educational past—as is often true of reformers. Many generations of American pedagogues shared the vision of Socrates and, among nineteenth-century pedagogical reformers, that of Froebel and Herbart: "The outcome was not so much knowledge of something as becoming something" (Broudy, 1963, p. 39). Character building long remained the ultimate objective of child-rearing manuals and pedagogical tomes. Memorization of the Bible or the textbook, like the emphasis upon achieving exemplary deportment as member of the family or of the school, constituted only a means to that end—and not an end in itself. The formation of good habits, including that of "forming moral judgments," was the responsibility of parents and teachers, and a process to be established early (Morgan, 1890, p. 69).

Writing on *The Recitation,* the Superintendent of the Allegheny County, Pennsylvania schools expressed it thus:

> Discipline is better than knowledge. What a mind can contain is always important but what it can do is far more vital. . . .[Beyond knowledge and discipline] the great aim of study is charac- ter. . . .Manhood is better than intelligence, virtue is above culture, goodness is superior to greatness, and the soul outranks the intellect as the gold outranks the dross. (Hamilton, 1906, pp. 81 and 85)

A normal-school instructor exhorted prospective teachers from Indiana to Rhode Island to "bear in mind that the chief work of the schoolteacher is that of character building. The pupils committed to your care are not so many pitchers to be filled with learning: they are moral beings to be trained for life's duties" (Morgan, 1890, p. 343).

In the event that teachers might be ignorant of elements constituting good character, the author of *School Keeping* (1885) wrote of the teacher:

> He must understand that the object to be gained is "to give wise direction to the moral powers, to encourage virtuous inclinations, sentiments, and passions, and to repress those which are evil; to cultivate habits of truthfulness, obedience, industry, temperance, prudence, and respect for the rights of others, with a view to the formation of character. What a field of action for the educator! (Orcutt, 1885, pp. 14-15)

American schoolbooks concentrated upon this great field of action, doing what the Bible and *New England Primer* had earlier been intended to do: to impress upon pupils accepted principles of morality, piety, and patriotism. The relationship between goodness and beauty was first discussed in literature, not in the fine arts. Considerations of artistic form and style were subservient to ethical content. The exemplary personal moral qualities of the authors represented in schoolbooks were of more importance than was the literary merit of their writings (Elson, 1964).

For these reasons, prevailing American thought found a pedagogical reformer like Herbart to be a congenial influence. Herbart stressed that to attain virtue, a pupil's actions must conform completely to principles, perceptions, and instructions of right and wrong. (See De Garmo, 1895, for a discussion of Herbartianism.) Herbartian innovation lay in his stress on the teacher's appraisal of the pupil's prior knowledge and experiences in order to incite the interest essential to effective teaching, in his wish to break down rigid classifications of subject-matter, and his broad view of those learnings that contribute to character building. Late nineteenth-century American educators, more eager than was public opinion to enlarge the curriculum beyond the "three Rs," welcomed Herbartianism. The opportunities for instruction in the arts widened accordingly.

Character Building and Arts Education

In 1890 the principal of the Rhode Island State Normal School lamented that children's capacities for feeling were not as well studied as their faculties of knowledge, that the laws of desires were less clearly recognized than were the laws of memory (Morgan, 1890). "Even books of model lessons on morals," he complained, "are apt to be devoted to an exposition of teaching moral truth rather than to the mode of awakening right sentiments" (p. 81). He recommended that "color, form, music, drawing, and other subjects that appeal strongly to the sensibility" (p. 93) assume a larger place in courses of study, normal schools, and teachers' institutes. Aesthetic considerations should pervade school design and assist in "school government." Music, for example, "softens the childish asperities, sweetens the temper, and predisposes to obedience" (p. 148).

It is a legitimate complaint that, in the modern school, half the subjects were taught too verbally and the other half too practically; no place was left for contemplation (Hayward, 1915, p. 197). Instruction in the arts and aesthetic education encountered both pressures. Social and ethical outcomes were asked of them, too. If it is an aim of contemporary music education to produce moral, social, and musical uplift and to provide innocent recreation (Britton, 1966, p. 17), this is a long-lived aspiration. In 1890 Morgan espoused school music for its contribution to what the 1918 Commission on the Reorganization of Secondary Education would label the "worthy use of leisure time": "Unlike many of the popular amusements, music leaves no sting behind: its tendency is to refine and ennoble" (Morgan, 1890, p. 150). The public schools of Long Beach, California specified in music courses of study that instruction be aimed to create "a safe emotional outlet for leisure time through establishing high standards in taste and habits in music" (Pierce and Hilpert, 1932, p. 8).

From the perspective of London in 1915, Hayward wrote:

> When we lift our eyes from the classroom and fix them on our emptying rural districts and our swarming urban areas where dull toil is followed by crude and feverish pleasure; when we think of the possibilities of music in public parks and concert rooms, in family circles and national festivals; we realize at once that the question of music appreciation possesses an importance far greater than most questions of pedagogics. (p. 114)

His concerns were echoed by a New York City contemporary, Lida Earhart (1915). She criticized education for neglecting children's emotions "for any purpose than mere suppression of that which is evil" (p. 30); this neglect was also expressed, she was sure, in unattractive schools and in the debased culture of the comic valentine and the ugly picture books that marked children's lives.

When speaking of the functions of arts education, educators made liberal use of moral-sounding words: *ennobling, elevating, pure, lofty, virtuous.* The goal of *social appreciation*—in teaching geography, history, and literature—meant giving attention to creating respect for persistent effort, hardships overcome, and noble suffering. The aims of social appreciation should blend with *aesthetics appreciation* in instruction in music and art—where "good taste, beauty, lofty conception, and the like are involved" (Earhart, 1915, p. 111). Fine sentiment once aroused, moreover, is a social resource not to be "wasted": The emotional state "should be directed into some channel of activity" (p. 127)—perhaps into service clubs, nature study clubs, music clubs, or art leagues.

Sure ethical utilitarianism did not go entirely unchallenged in arts circles, however. If something is beautiful in itself, observed Hayward (1915), "We need not ask for it also to be moral and instructive (;) the artist is neither a preacher nor a teacher (p. 24)." The call "Art for art's sake" was often raised. This challenge, observed Horne (1917), originated in a commitment to *form* over *content,* "a protest against making painting tell a story, against the requirement that art should be narrative, and so ethical in influence" (p. 31).

Historical Determinants of American Method: II. The Teacher

Since educational aims must be realized through the human beings who are the designated agents of educational philosophers and public opinion, the teacher quickly enters into the equation. Thomas Morgan, a Normal School principal, wrote to teachers in 1890, "The chief factor in the great work of character building is your own personality" (p. 347). As the aim of schooling was producing not the scholar but the virtuous man or woman, so the *person* of the teacher was judged more critically than was his or her formal knowledge. Unconscious imitation of teachers by pupils has been long and widely assumed, and no teaching field is perfectly innocent of beliefs about subjective states. "In physics teaching, as in most human endeavors," concluded an editorial in *The Physics Teacher* (Swartz, 1969), "it's the loving that counts" (p. 438).

In arts education this assumption has been expressed by the aphorism that "art is not so much taught as it is caught" (Eisner, 1973, p. 1197). In 1915 those teachers who aimed to realize aesthetic goals were reminded that emotional states are especially communicable and often arise in imitation of the teacher; therefore, "a teacher should keep his own emotional states alive" (Earhart, 1915, p. 126). The teacher who would arouse and marshall sensitivity must himself be a person of feeling (Morgan, 1890, p. 93). Although the Curator of Education of the Cleveland Museum of Art acknowledged that it was not always so presented in schools and colleges, art is nonetheless "a warmly personal subject" whose success "depends to an unusually high degree upon obscure personal factors in the student, the teacher, and the mature artist" (Munro, 1941, p. 249).

The Teacher as Apprentice

It was fortuitous that American theory acknowledged the role of the teacher's largely untrained personal qualities of character and personality, rather than emphasizing technical mastery of subject matter and pedagogical expertness—for American public schools had available far greater numbers of decent and well-intentioned men and women than it had trained and professionalized teachers of the kind known in some European school systems.

Expansiveness has been a key element in the history of American teaching. The fact that the nation built an educational system faster than qualified teachers could be secured, and the additional fact that so many alternative occupations for men existed to compete with and recruit from teaching, had these consequences: American teachers were poorly prepared for teaching careers, women teachers came into numerical dominance, the occupation experienced chronic turnover, and it was impossible to generate public investment in thorough and expensive teacher-training programs. In turn, a pattern developed of providing short-term "survival training" for beginning teachers, and of depending on the stability and professionalism of the textbook, not the teacher.

The president of the State Normal College of Dillon, Montana introduced his book, *The Technique of Teaching* (Davis, 1924) with this distinction: "Principles are recognized by those at home in the educational world; rules are for the apprentices who form so large a proportion of America's teachers" (p. 2). The authors of *The Eclectic Manual of Methods for the Assistance of Teachers* (1885) described their book as "the outgrowth of numerous requests from young and inexperienced teachers of country district schools in nearly every part of the United States for assistance in their work" (p. 2). Teachers using the Eclectic Education Series could thus learn the aim of the textbooks, the plan on which they were constructed, and the principles to which the textbooks conformed. In a related development, which began in 1884, leading music publishers provided summer training schools for teachers, following the teaching methods of the sponsoring textbooks (Poff, 1970, 1976; Tellstrom, 1971).

The Prussian oral teaching method of the mid-nineteenth century—which assumed the existence of teachers trained at state seminaries who had passed a state qualifying examination in academic and pedagogical subjects—reflected a professional level that America could not then meet. Even as late as 1918 a majority of the nation's elementary-school teachers had two or fewer years of academic and pedagogical study beyond high school (Evenden, 1938, pp. 37-38).

Transitory and untrained teachers, proliferating schools, a welter of competing textbooks, and decentralized school administration created confusion, anxiety, and efforts to secure greater stability of practice (Elsbree, 1939). Despite teachers' institutes, courses of study, and pedagogical treatises, the improvement of textbooks and uniform textbook adoptions seemed the most secure path to reform. Thayer (1928) argued that educators' genuine consideration for school children "left no alternative than to prepare a textbook which should offset the teacher's ignorance of subject matter and method"; insuring that schooling provided a modicum of continuity and regularity of instruction meant "insisting upon a loyal adherence to the text" (p. 16). The insistence of nineteenth-century school music on note-reading methods was another indicator of the search for uniform and stable practices (Tellstrom, 1971, p. 89).

Arts Teachers: A Bifurcated Faculty

The search for uniformity of practice and the desire for upgrading teaching skills in a broadening curriculum included providing school supervisors and consultants. A survey in 1960 reported that special assistance—given by supervisors, consultants, special teachers, or aides—reached 90 percent of all elementary-school teachers in music and 52 percent in art education (Dean, 1960). But special subject supervisors were long uncommon in small systems and in rural schools. This was the case even though it was recognized that teaching of the common branches was easier for teachers "due to better instruction in both subject matter and methods which teachers in training are given in these fundamentals" (Kendall and Mirick, 1918, p. v).

Even from the nineteenth-century beginnings of school music and art, it was consistently agreed that the general classroom teacher—responsible for almost all arts and aesthetic education prior to the elective courses offered in the high school—was woefully untrained for and insecure in the task (Horn, 1941; Horner, 1965, p. 211; Mitchell, 1965; Reimer, 1966). Earhart (1915) probably spoke for many: "The very word aesthetics is foreign to our tongues and we feel that the things for which it stands are beyond our endeavor . . ." (p. 111). It was reported in 1941 (Ziegfeld, p. 807) that prospective elementary-school teachers were more likely to have had foreign-language training that art courses. Small wonder, then, that a teachers' handbook in instructional methods (McDonald and Nelson, 1958) felt it necessary to reassure teachers that they could indeed learn to draw simple diagrams on the blackboard—just as they had earlier learned to write words there. Because of inadequate teacher preparation, Pauline Johnson (1965, p. 55) described art as possibly the least understood, most difficult, and frequently the poorest taught subject offered by the elementary school.

In music education the classroom teacher was often expected to supply a general music experience with elements of vocal and instrumental performance, listening, and music theory; yet, in only one-third of schools sampled in a national survey was ability to teach music considered a qualification for being hired (Broudy, 1966, p. 183). Connett

(1942) in examining the opinions of administrators drawn mainly from smaller school districts of the Midwest and Southwest found general satisfaction with teachers' interaction with elementary-school students but the acknowledgment that too many general classroom teachers were poorly trained to teach music. "Half of our eighteen grade [school] teachers," reported one superintendent, "know practically nothing about music" (Connett, 1942, p. 265).

Given minimal art and music education requirements in teacher-training institutions, it was unlikely that many elementary-school teachers could come to feel at home with the arts—drawn as these teachers were from the middle stratum of a utilitarian and non-intellectual American culture. Teachers of the arts do not represent, moreover, a unitary profession. Their ranks have also included former students of music conservatories and independent art schools, as well as graduates of college and university art departments where the emphasis in their training has sometimes been placed neither on performance nor pedagogy, but on a rather bookish curriculum in theory and history (Munro, 1941a, p. 23). In this century special teachers and supervisors for elementary and junior high school arts programs have been recruited from this group, as have been many high school teachers. This segment of arts teachers, while secure with the arts, has often been found ill at ease with or even resistant to the general pedagogical currents which press insistently against American public education. Early on in this century, for example, it was reported that the "first principle" of academic, analytical art teaching was prior learning to draw with accurate representation. This, the method adopted from the professional art school, was in conflict with the proposition that "the true purpose of art education is the education of the whole people for appreciation," with learning to draw a secondary or tertiary objective (Dow, 1908, pp. 1, 2).

Visits made to high school music classes early in the decade of the Great Depression as part of the National Survey of Secondary Education (Pierce and Hilpert, 1932, p. 24), found teachers to be competent music specialists; their teaching weaknesses stemmed primarily, instead, from what was described as inappropriate selection of subject matter and insufficient knowledge of classroom techniques. Similar results came later, from Connett's sample of 879 school administrators who made the following observations largely about this group of America's music teachers: (1) Their greatest satisfaction was with their teachers' musical abilities, and their smallest was with their teaching abilities; deficiencies in psychological areas were singled out for comment. (2) Their teachers' chief positive personal and professional trait was described as a willingness to use their talents in community performance, while their outstanding negative rating concerned lack of understanding of and inability to command the respect and cooperation of high school students. In the words of one exasperated administrator, "High school music teachers cause more grief than all the rest of the teachers on the faculty" (Connett, 1942, p. 267).

Along with whatever differences in temperament and other personal qualities might distinguish the two major subgroups of teachers assigned responsibility for teaching school arts, historical data show pronounced variations in training (Hastie, 1965) that might explain much about such observations as those made above. Ege, the head of teacher training at the Cleveland School of Art and a professor of art education at Western Reserve University, characterized the art school atmosphere as "apt to create teachers who are more interested in skill and production of art than in the broader aspects of the art program" (Ege, 1941, p. 722). While art schools resisted giving more than a quarter of their curriculum to non-art courses, art education students in teachers colleges took one-half to two-thirds of their units in non-art courses (Ege, 1941; Munro, 1941a).

Some other observers have linked the art teacher's pedagogical inadequacies to the artist's drive to perfect his or her skills. In 1918, Gebhard, a professor of music at George Peabody College for Teachers, went so far as to assert

> Good singers and pianists are generally poor teachers in the schoolroom. They almost always are inclined to take too much of the time in displaying their own abilities. They do too much singing or playing with the children, and in this way interfere with their natural growth in independence. (p. 94)

And a music supervisor for Louisiana's State Department of Education contended that the time and energy devoted by musicians to the development and maintenance of their musicianship left little time for matters like educational research (Funchess, 1949).

Although art institutes no longer have the direct influence on the training of school arts teachers that they had a half century ago, the National Society for the Study of Education's latest Yearbook on Art Education suggested that their ethos has a persisting effect:

> Perhaps to a greater degree than for other fields, the individual who elects to become an art teacher feels that he is making a decision between two alternatives, that of a producing artist and that of a teacher. He often feels...that the two roles are irreconcilable or incompatible. (Hastie, 1965, p. 247)

A Science for Teaching: Educational Research and Arts Education

Despite an eroding of the nineteeth century's great expectations about the contribution of science to improving the human condition, educational research has continued to be looked to for reliable information to guide purposeful change and for protection from sudden shifts in the educational wind. Arts educators, too, have expressed hope for educational research, especially from its core discipline of psychology. When writing of the problems of teaching adolescents, for example, a prominent art educator characteristically affirmed that taking the avenue of psychology must surely be the way to resolve the dilemmas of art education (Munro, 1935, p. 31). In the interest of improving music education, Bennett Reimer (1966) argued more recently:

> At almost every point in the process of teaching and learning about music, accurate information concerning the results being obtained could keep the process free from wasted effort and insure that maximum benefits were being gained. Decisions as to proper methods of teaching, materials to be employed, types of experiences to be stressed, and curricula to be developed, all could be made intelligently and accurately if based on clear-cut knowledge of how the teaching-process actually affects the learner. (p. 461)

Research on the Teaching Process

Instructional emphasis in the arts has shifted markedly over the past century, leaving behind in practice many remnants of once powerful convictions (Henry, 1958; Keel, 1965; Logan, 1955; Tellstrom, 1971). Yet there is general agreement that such shifts in objectives and teaching strategies have occurred with minimal contributions from educational research. This seems to be so not by reason of any lack of awareness of the main lines of educational research (Beittel, 1960; Eisner, 1969, 1973; Jones and Evans, 1951; Madsen, Greer, and Madsen, 1975; Moore, 1941; Mursell, 1936; Pierce and Hilpert, 1932; Prince, 1974; Schneider, 1969; Zinar, 1976).

It is rather that traditionally only a small part of educational research has been directed at the teaching process. Even during the 1960s, when methodological innovations and unprecedented research funding raised new research possibilities, the advance in substantive knowledge of teaching was described as disappointing (Travers, 1973, p. vii). A yet smaller fraction of research examines, observationally or experimentally, teaching situations that obtain in the arts, or probes the dynamics of classroom activity in terms of teacher behavior (Eisner, 1969, p. 84; Horner, 1965). Although it was reported in 1950 (Schultz, Roos, and Moore, p. 64) that the period since World War I was one of "renewed stress" on discovering methods of teaching art, the results were meager indeed; of only seven investigations identified, one was a study of the biographies of one hundred artists so as to locate significant influences in their lives which the schools might henceforth provide (Triplett, 1943). There was no section on the teaching of music in either the first or second *Handbook of Research on Teaching* (Gage, 1963; Travers, 1973) and, in number of pages, the briefest subject-matter articles in both volumes were those on teaching the visual arts. With respect to research on and for teachers, the situation does not appear profoundly unlike that described in 1915, when Hayward observed that despite available books on aesthetics and popular guides to pictures and music, "books intended to help the teacher. . .have hardly been produced by the educationists of any land" (p. v).

In 1932 a national music education survey reported that a "lack of thoughtful and objective studies for this field of instruction renders the teacher and specialist dependent chiefly on their own initiative (Pierce and Hilpert, p. 16). Perhaps as a consequence, practices varied considerably. Compared to music, art education has even fewer courses of study to standardize practice (Pierce and Hilpert, 1932, p. vi), and two generations later, Eisner (1973) contended that art educators lacked even careful descriptions of the teaching practices employed in the visual arts: "Thus no one, I believe, knows with confidence what teachers of art do in the classroom beyond those general practices that are obvious (p. 1207)."

In this century, much attention in school arts was redirected toward teaching for aesthetic appreciation. Experimental research in this area remains rare, however (Eisner, 1973, p. 1201), as does research on the later "allied arts" enterprise (Reimer, 1970). Time allotments are a critical concern when so much is asked of the arts curriculum—performance, appreciation, social learnings, creativity, historical and theoretical understanding—yet time allotments, like grade placements, vary greatly and appear to have arbitrary or logical, not "scientific" bases (Pierce and Hilpert, 1932, pp. 50; 67).

The most influential of music educators of the second quarter of this century, and a devoted exponent of teaching methods conforming to developmental psychology, was James Mursell. He once characterized as "a breach of developmental continuity and, in all probability, an educational failure" a series of common music teaching practices: teaching notational symbols of music as an abstract code, teaching music theory as a formal grammar, teaching techniques divorced from actual music making (1958, pp. 144-147). Nowhere in his extended discussion, however, is any music research cited. This appears symptomatic.

A survey conducted by the National Education Association in 1962 reported that 70 percent of the larger elementary schools and 47 percent of the smaller provided instrumental instruction; among secondary schools the figures were 46 percent and 27 percent for the larger and smaller schools respectively. Teachers of instrumental music had little research to assist them, however. It was claimed (Thorpe, 1958, p. 166) that a teacher doing ensemble work would have to move entirely outside the music education field to obtain research guidance on the question of whether a player should listen to the complete composition before or after any practice of his or her part. Contentions about the relative merits of grouped or individualized instruction for beginning violin students were not supported by evidence; neither was there research indicating whether bowing techniques or fingering techniques should be emphasized first (Petzold, 1964). Teachers of singing also lacked research on many aspects of their duties (Horner, 1965, p. 113).

Research of all kinds, including historical research, has neglected the viewpoints and experiences of the agents of formal education. Hence there have been few efforts to design research from the perspective of the teacher's concerns and agenda, which include "relational" as well as instructional outcomes (Lortie, 1975). Of whatever curriculum field we speak, it is undoubtedly true that more research, psychological or otherwise, concerns *learning* than *teaching*. Since most classrooms, and perhaps studios, remain teacher-centered and teacher-directed, the available research is inadequate on its face. It may well be that this is more the case in arts and aesthetic education than it is elsewhere.

Arts Educators and Test Makers

The response of arts educators to the primacy of quantification and measurement in educational research appears to be a key element in understanding the past, and probable future, relationship between the science of research and the teaching of the arts. Regardless of their limited use in the diagnosis of individual or group instructional needs, or in the assignment of pupils to different arts programs, aptitude and achievement tests are instruments of research. Without usable measuring devices to determine learning outcomes, conventional research on teaching will hardly be possible. The fact that individual researchers in learning in the arts frequently construct their own instruments makes the correlation and cumulation of research virtually impossible.

That available tests are both few in number and of questionable validity is not much disputed. In 1961 about 1.5 percent of recognized tests were fine arts instruments, and tools for assessing artistic learning are scarce compared to the situation in other teaching fields (Eisner, 1969, p. 79). The appreciation area was notable for having inspired very little experimentation in test development relative to its curricular importance (Greene, Jorgensen, and Gerberich, 1953, pp. 536-537). Despite recent developments in music aptitude testing, most music tests lacked wide employment in research, thereby acquiring little validation beyond the criterion measures of music grades, teacher ratings, or performance rankings (Schneider, 1969, p. 896). One influential art educator flatly asserted that the claims of tests and scales were "unwarranted" (Munro, 1956, p. 193).

Test construction for school or research use in arts and aesthetic education has probably been inhibited less by the admitted difficulties involved than by the conspicuous lack of support for or belief in the possibilities of the effort. A quarter of a century ago it was observed (Greene, et al., 1953) that there remained "an echo of protest from a small group of artists that artistic production does not lend itself to objective evaluation" (p. 526). While it has been acknowledged that "precision, objectivity, uniformity, and overt demonstration" are desired outcomes of arts education—as well as of the sciences, languages, and mathematics—

they are often peripheral where what is sought is unpredictability, subjectivity, inwardness (Reimer, 1971, p. 73). A probably representative view of the larger scientific model in which test construction is embedded is Munro's (1941b): "The extreme subdivision and simplification of problems that is necessary for exact experiment and measurement substitutes artificial arrangements of a few lines, dots, or colored papers for the rich complexity of art, and artificially simplified questions of yes-or-no preference for the intricate relativities of esthetic taste" (p. 267).

Test makers were characterized (Logan, 1955) as seeming to possess "only the most meager interest or background in art"; in consequence their tests "fail miserably in not being aware of a tenth of the aesthetic qualities they are supposedly measuring" (p. 236). Criticisms of the McAdory Art Test on the basis of the poor quality of many of the sample items (Schultz, et al., 1950, p. 69) reminds one of the reaction that many teachers of literature would make to the passages in many standardized reading tests. Available tests in music have been dismissed as covering only very limited aspects of music, especially music understanding (Leonhard, 1958, p. 325). The Seashore tests were labeled by their critics as being *acoustical* rather than *musical* measures (Hendrickson, 1960, p. 907). And Mursell's disdain for Carl Seashore's approach to determining musical aptitude—which he labeled atomistic and mechanistic—inhibited test making until very recently (Leonhard and Colwell, 1977, p. 82).

Educational Research and Teaching Practice

It is extraordinarily difficult to acquire evidence of the effects of research on teaching practice. Even in a field such as reading, where published research studies number in the thousands, diffusion and implementation reports are absent, and most assertions about impact rely on soft or nonexistent data (Clifford, 1973, pp. 4-6). Moreover, demonstrable changes in instructional research, accompanied by explicit attributions of responsibility to "science," cannot be taken at face value (Clifford, 1978). As was illustrated in a survey of art and music practices (Pierce and Hilpert, 1932), such "tangible evidence" as courses of study are not necessarily reliable indicators of modal classroom behavior—much less of possibly large variations in practice.

Despite the growth of research on arts education, especially during the 1960s, the statements of many prominent arts educators force the conclusion that research has had little impact upon teaching practices in music and the visual arts. A logical analysis of the social-psychological and sociological structure reported to characterize school arts teaching supports that assumption. It is unlikely that research affects school practice when it has had little apparent impact upon the literature of the field (Horner, 1965, pp. 3; 217). Rusk's *Methods of Teaching the Fine Arts* (1935) did not report research and, except for one guide to teaching published in 1951, Hendrickson as late as 1960 could still fault music education texts for providing teachers with poor introductions to research (1960, p. 905). The research organs founded to report on the growing body of dissertations, federally-funded research, and conference proceedings of the 1960s spoke of issues concerning arts educators, "but few are aware of the existence of these journals" (Hoffa, 1977, p. 76). Whether first blame belonged with researchers or teachers, there was "no question" that a research-classroom gap existed in music education (Williams, 1975). Unlike workers in most curriculum fields, arts educators themselves barely participated in the widespread movement of this century (Clifford, 1978) to analyze textbook content and to propose improvements (Ernst, 1955; Petzold, 1960; Smiley, 1955).

In 1932 Hilpert examined courses of study and classroom operations, observing close imitation of art school practices, teacher opposition to objective testing and measurement, and the absence of "professional attitudes toward educational research" (Pierce and Hilpert, 1932). He concluded that

> art education has not kept abreast with the other subjects in secondary education in scientific investigations. There is need on the part of art teachers for tolerance and understanding of research and for cooperation with trained investigators who have done so much to improve the curriculum in other fields. (p. 68)

The chairman of the first Yearbook Committee on Art Education of the National Society for the Study of Education made a similar assessment a decade later (Munro, 1941a):

> In comparing this volume with previous yearbooks on the Society, the reader may find it relatively unscientific and unobjective, lacking in experimental detail, full of unsupported generalizations. To a large extent, these criticism are justified. But they are true, not of this *Yearbook* alone, but also of most current thinking and writing on art and art education. (p. 8)

Even granted that political events and federal funding—especially between 1963 and 1970—have created something of a real research boom in arts and aesthetic education (Eddy, 1977; Hoffa, 1977), there is little evidence to indicate that the *values and assumptions* of the last quarter century of the research tradition of American education have infected thinking, writing, and practice in art and art education.

A Framework for a General Theory of Research Influence

Explanations of the conditions favoring incorporation of research findings into school practices often emphasize *characteristics of the research*. Discrete and isolated studies, for example, have less opportunity of successfully competing for the schools' notice than does research having some cumulative continuity, some paradigmatic status conferred perhaps by a unifying psychological theory. By all accounts (Eisner, 1977; Hastie, 1965; Horner, 1965, p. 2; Jones and Evans, 1951, p. 27; Michael, 1964; Schneider, 1969, p. 899), the piecemeal, one-shot unpublished investigation characterizes the histories of both art and music research. Recognizing this, art education spokesmen have called for more organized and systematic basic-research efforts such as Harvard's Project Zero (Eddy, 1977). The multi-disciplinary character of arts research has eventual potentialities, but it has contributed to research fragmentation and definitional uncertainty. "A rather frustrating undercurrent" at the Fifth International Seminar on Research in Music Education in 1975 was the issue of whether the papers presented "truly represented research either in their orientation, design, or execution" (Standifer, 1975, p. 60).

While there is satisfaction in knowing that influential research is also "good research" and "conclusive research," these are not necessary conditions. Apart from and probably much more important than qualities inhering in the research are *conditions existing within the receptor*—in this case, within the educational world. Educational research cannot be insulated from the world of education. Its findings must be "thrown into and filtered through the marketplace of ideas"—far more so than medical or engineering research it appears (Clifford, 1973; McDonald, 1964, p. 3). There seems to be considerable truth in the proposition that "A research conclusion which people are willing to accept will be something they already know" (Wold and Hastie, 1965, p. 329). Where research contradicts personal or group "experience"—as for instance, the research on the effects of class size—it is least able to be influential. Its chances improve greatly where research speaks to neutral issues or, better yet, where it substantiates existing opinion. Therefore, while efforts to determine research impact have primarily searched for evidence of change, it must be remembered that research also exists to confirm and retain practices already in place.

Recognition of this *legitimation* function of research (Clifford, 1973, pp. 27-28), encourages one to consider the several ways in which the character and implications of research "fit" the field. Research findings may fit by being timely. Vocabulary research fit nicely into existing trends toward meaningfulness and simplification of school readers, as did the teaching and curricular reforms advocated by early progressive theorists (Clifford, 1978). Another dimension of "fit" is logical fit or *obvious applicability*. However much teachers sympathize with larger educational goals, or with the need to understand phenomena, research is more eagerly received if it appears to supply answers to perceived teaching questions; the research activity should "make sense." Much extant educational research makes little sense because it does not promote obvious action or intervention. Status or descriptive research is of this kind—and it constituted a large part of the research in arts education

(Eisner, 1969; Hastie, 1965, p. 284; Schneider, 1969, p. 895). Such research is easy to do, noncontroversial, and often functions as window dressing.

Finally, any theory of research influence has to consider how *status variables*—of school level or subject matter, of teachers, of students— might condition receptivity to research (Clifford, 1978). It could be argued that the "common branches"—those curriculum fields taught by nonspecialists which must accept all students for basic-level instruction—will be more receptive to innovative or "pupil-oriented" influences. There is relatively lesser status in such teaching, it is more open to public scrutiny, and the incumbents have only weak claims to esoteric scholarship; and if their pedagogical problems are not greater, they are at least more visible.

Many high school teachers, however, have lived in a rather different, more sheltered environment. In 1930 only half the youngsters aged fourteen to sixteen enrolled in high school; the Depression accelerated the rate to two-thirds. But high drop-out rates after age sixteen and curricular and tracking arrangements meant that many teachers escaped the *full* consequences of universal schooling. High-school teachers of the arts were among them. In 1965 it was reported (Silverman and Lanier, 1965, pp. 116-117) that less than 10 percent of American senior high schools made art a requirement and that under a quarter of high school students enrolled in one or more art electives; a somewhat higher proportion took music courses. While elective status or prerequisites or screening procedures did not "freeze out" all the problem students, some kinds of pupil variability were considerably attenuated—and with this, perhaps, teacher interest in new ideas.

Following this line of reasoning, elementary-school, general-classroom teachers of the arts would have been more receptive to research than would high-school art teachers. They were, however, so ill-prepared for, and insecure in, the subject matter of music or art that their needs for pedagogical help brought forth, at best, the experientially based assistance of the arts supervisor. Elementary-school teachers, then, would be more likely to be influenced by spelling or arithmetic research—via their teacher training, textbooks, and teacher manuals—than by arts research.

High-school arts teachers bore more resemblance to teachers of algebra or chemistry, teachers whose self-image was as mathematician or scientist, as well as teacher. Such outside allegiances shield teachers from some of the influences of the public-school culture. In similar, perhaps more extreme fashion, the high-school drama teacher, orchestra or band teacher, art teacher, even the teacher of appreciation classes, to a greater or lesser degree considered himself or herself an *artist* as well as a teacher. And, of what obvious and indisputable importance is scientific inquiry to an artist?

The Case of Public-School Arts Education

When analyzing the research estate in arts and aesthetic education, and regretting its imperceptible impact upon the teaching process, arts educators frequently identify factors not yet discussed here. These include the late appearance of doctoral programs in the fine arts and the few mechanisms existing for the dissemination of research. The first means that a prime impetus for producing educational research has only recently come into being for arts education, and the second means that completed research has more difficulty in reaching its potential consumers. The present analysis, however, considers these as symptoms rather than as causes—symptoms of a persisting mind-set that remains highly skeptical of research for arts purposes, including those of arts education.

Ambiguous Status. The arts have had a marginal and uncertain status in the schools as in American culture. They are "a hostage of private consumption and public suspicion" (DiMaggio and Useem, 1978, p. 106). Enrollments in arts electives are low, and art teachers complain that administrators assign them students who are discipline problems, candidates for therapy, and in academic difficulty—a consequence, it is believed, of cultural stereotypes of an effete and unmanly subculture, irrelevant to practical pursuits, presided over by a suspiciously high proportion of female teachers (Ege, 1941, p. 723; Hastie, 1965, p. 136; Roach, 1973, p. 38; Silverman and Lanier, 1965). Despite significant increases in the population exposed to galleries, film festivals, orchestras, and drama, and despite high consumption of prints, records, and art books, public opinion remains disposed to consider arts education a luxury, vulnerable to every "back-to-basics" competition from remedial reading to science education. Despite art educators' protests—that the arts are "the rice and beans of the teaching and learning process," not the frills (Zinar, 1976, p. 74)—the fundamental appeal of aesthetic response, to "know by feeling," places the arts in perpetual jeopardy, assigned to the last hour on Friday afternoon (Johnson, 1965, p. 56). That arts teachers are easily called upon for distracting and time-consuming school service and community entertainment duties may be less a sign of their influence than of their marginality.

The visual arts have had some place in the curriculum for a century, and music longer still. Nevertheless, their ambiguous curricular status and the divided responsibility for initial teacher preparation has retarded graduate studies and the research activity accompanying them. Before 1930 only five doctoral dissertations in music were reported (Lanier, 1962, p. 6), with appreciable growth, especially in experimental research, appearing only after 1950, the same period when graduate degrees in art education made their modest appearance (Eisner, 1965a; Funchess, 1949; Schneider, 1969). Despite some early research in art and music, this late development put arts education a third to a half century behind most other fields. Significantly, while the Music Supervisors (Educators) National Conference took form in 1907, the *Journal of Research in Music Education* was begun only in 1953; and *Studies in Art Education,* initiated in 1959, is not exclusively a research organ.

Internal Fragmentation. Beginning in 1872, certain states and school districts employed supervisors and directors to improve and unify practices in arts education (Bealmer, 1965). In *The Art in Teaching Art* (Keiler, 1961), however, it was argued that the foundation of all teaching is "sincere conviction," and that teacher discretion should not yield before some rigid course of study: "Only basic directions can ever be advocated or meaningfully stated; setting goals and organizing procedures must remain the responsibility of each individual art teacher" (p. 5).

Although common curricular patterns do exist, it has proven difficult for arts educators to agree on objectives, nomenclature, standards, or procedures. To the divisions between elementary and secondary school teachers in music can be added those between vocal and instrumental teachers. Perhaps as a reflection of their different roots, band teachers and orchestra teachers reportedly diverge in important ways: the former are group and entertainment oriented; the latter, individual and "art" oriented (Britton, 1966, p. 25). Music and art educators have quarreled internally about process and product. While arguing that music classes should be "saturated" with musical experiences, Prince (1974, p. 31) regretted that many teachers taught *about* music by having pupils study the orchestra's instruments and the biographies of musicians. Each of the shifts in emphasis of the past century has left its residue, and its partisans. Lacking a consensus of opinion, and even more a body of definitive research, many matters of content and method remained unsettled.

A reason given for the absence of adequate evaluation research was the "lesser agreement on standards and desirable outcomes of education than there is in the more academic fields" (Horner, 1965, p. 174). Such variation in standards was thought virtually to foreclose measurement possibilities, "especially when creative art suggests deviation rather than conformity to set rules and beliefs" (Schultz, et al., 1950, p. 70). A federal regional laboratory official could find little likelihood of devising "behavioral objectives" in music education, given specialists' failure to agree on the common outcomes desired (Williams, 1975, p. 41). Such observations recall Thomas Munro's old complaint (1941b):

In contrast with the representatives of other subjects, especially the exact sciences, art teachers often seem to the administrator to be tiresomely incapable of making up their own minds as to what they want to teach and how, or even to the materials and equipment they need to teach it with. (p. 259)

Tensions of Elitism. America's is a mass and comparatively undifferentiated educational system. Many teachers, in many fields, have had difficulty with the working out of the commitment to schooling "all of the children of all of the people" into the late adolescent years. The literature in arts education makes it appear that tensions between universalistic educational goals and the development of the possibly innate talents of an elite are more important in or, at least, closer to the surface of the arts teaching fields.

The potential leavening effect of arts education has been an argument for its inclusion in the public schools' curriculum. Long ago a normal-school advocate of "training the imagination" and "cultivating the capacities for feeling" put the matter in this fashion (Morgan, 1890):

> The public school levels up. Cultivation in music plays a large part in this leveling-up process. It is in its nature aesthetic, it reaches the taste, cultivates a love for beauty in all its forms, and opens to the child some of the rarest pleasures which otherwise might be the sole prerogatives of the rich. (p. 151)

Art, it has since been argued, belongs neither to an economic aristocracy nor to an elite of the talented. The director of drawing of the Newton, Massachusetts schools (Daniels, 1918) disputed the "somewhat widespread belief that the methods of teaching drawing belong in a realm to which the elect have admittance" (p. 163). Art education, he argued, was the business of all teachers and their clients were all children. As nature drawing could open all children's eyes to some new beauty, singing is also universal: All can participate—"monotones can be cured"—and singing promotes cooperative experiences and "exemplary social and civic attitudes" (Earhart, 1918, p. 37; Pierce and Hilpert, 1932, p. 17). In a variation on the nineteenth-century promise that "To open a school is to close a prison," certain twentieth-century music educators pledged that "If you teach a boy to blow a horn, he'll *never* blow a safe!"

The stress upon the appreciation goal in school art and music appeared early in the progressive era, and it was explicitly universalistic (Horner, 1965, p. 84). "The true purpose of art teaching is the education of the whole people for appreciation," wrote a professor at Teachers College in 1908 (Dow, p. 1). The objectives of mass education, however, coexisted with a persistent drive to find and realize talent, to perfect performance and polish product. Of "general art" courses in the high schools, Hilpert observed that they are "really designed for the few pupils who have some talent" (Pierce and Hilpert, 1932, p. 48). Elementary school teachers of art, most of whom have probably judged themselves deficient in artistic ability, were reportedly disposed to believe that art ability is a specific, hereditary endowment (Schultz, Roos, and Moore, 1950, p. 64). It was disclosed that art appreciation tests were, in fact, constructed in order to discover art talent and advise pupils about training and vocational possibilities (Schultz, et al., 1950, p. 70)

School administrators were understandably critical of music teachers for appearing to divide their attention inappropriately "between the few who are musically talented and the larger group of average and below-average musical ability" and for their inability to keep foremost in their minds the musical development of students rather than the display that music can make. Accordingly it was reported that there was "a lack of well-balanced teachers who have a sympathetic attitude toward *all* pupils" (Connett, 1942, pp. 261, 263). More recently it has been stated that the growing band and orchestra movement in secondary schools—and the associated concerts and festivals—often leads to highly selective music programs. Concern for polished performance meant both considerable drill and insufficient instructional attention to "knowledge of music as an art" (Prince, 1974, p. 28).

Alienation and Resistance. "To treat a nocturne as if it were a problem in arithmetic to be solved in consecutive steps is as stupid as it is futile" (Baldwin, 1936, p. 94). By this sentence, this supervisor of music in the Cleveland Public Schools voiced an apparently widespread and persisting belief among educators in the arts—that the essence of art may be inexpressible. Before a genuine testing movement existed, Morgan (1890) made the distinction between feats of memory and cultivation of the feelings: The results of the former can be tested, but the latter "becomes more difficult, less subject to rules and routine and impossible of mathematical measurement" (p. 90). That attitudes of skepticism, disinterest, even hostility towards research continue to exist is commonly reported (Beittel, 1960; Eisner, 1965b, 1973; Reimer, 1966).

Along with the conviction that aspects of art education, like appreciation, are not susceptible to scientific analysis and quantitication, there has sometimes been the belief that they cannot even be taught, that they are "something too personal and intangible to be susceptible to actual training in schools or other institutions" (Hayward, 1915, p. 2). Therefore, Hayward reported of British educators that, "At any meeting of teachers or educational officials it would be easy to raise a cheer by proclaiming that the child 'unconsciously' perceived beauty or goodness and by protesting against systematic attempts to educate the aesthetic or moral judgment" (p. 190).

This is, however, an intolerable position for any educator to pursue consistently. Schools are after all predicated upon a faith in the power *to teach.* Research, too, aims *to teach.* In the last analysis, it appears unlikely that artist-teachers would seriously maintain that teachers are but talent scouts. And when more researchers are also artists, it may be that artist-teachers will come to accept that artist-scientists also have something to teach. However much artists represent a more or less alienated subculture, the teachers among them may, indeed, share a sufficient measure of the optimism that underlies the American character. Out of that optimism this society has built a vast system of schools. And, Hayward's British educators to the contrary, these schools have consistently been devoted to the development of the moral, if not the aesthetic, judgment of a whole people.

Berkeley, California
July 1978

NOTES

The author is indebted to George C. Kyme for many helpful suggestions about sources and trends in the teaching of school music.

REFERENCES

Baldwin, L. L. Listening. In G. M. Whipple (Ed.), *Music education*. Thirty-fifth yearbook of the National Society for the Study of Education, Part II. Bloomington, Illinois: Public School Publishing Co., 1936, 91-98.

Bealmer, W. J. The role of the state art supervisor: Leadership and the improvement of instruction. In R. W. Hastie (Ed.), *Art education*. Sixth-fourth yearbook of the National Society for the Study of Education, Part II. Chicago: University of Chicago Press, 1965, 201-220.

Beittel, K. R. Art. In C. W. Harris (Ed.), *Encyclopedia of educational research*. New York: Macmillan, 1960, 77-87.

Britton, A. P. Music education: An American specialty. In B. C. Kowall (Ed.), *Perspectives in music education: Source book III*. Washington, D.C.: Music Educators National Conference, 1966, 15-28.

Broudy, H. S. Historic exemplars of teaching method. In N. L. Gage (Ed.), *Handbook of research on teaching*. Chicago: Rand McNally, 1963, 1-43.

Broudy, H. S. Educational theory and the music curriculum. In B. C. Kowall (Ed.), *Perspectives in music education: Source book III*. Washington, D.C.: Music Educators National Conference, 1966, 173-184.

Clifford, G. J. A history of the impact of research on teaching. In R. M. W. Travers (Ed.), *Second handbook of research on teaching*. Chicago: Rand McNally, 1973, 1-46.

Clifford, G. J. Words for schools: The applications in education of the vocabulary researches of Edward L. Thorndike. In P. Suppes (Ed.), *Impact of research on education: Some case studies*. Washington, D.C.: National Academy of Education, 1978, 107-198.

Commission on the Reorganization of Secondary Education. *Cardinal principles of secondary education*. Washington, D.C.: 1918. Bureau of Education Bulletin, 1918, No. 35.

Connett, E. Administrative criticism of music teaching. *Journal of Educational Research*, 1942, *36*, 254-268.

Dale, E. and Raths, L. E. Discussion in the secondary school. *Educational Research Bulletin*, 1945, *24*, 1-6.

Daniels, F. H. Drawing and applied art. In C. N. Kendall and G. A. Mirick (Eds.), *How to teach the special subjects*. Boston: Houghton Mifflin, 1918, 163-254.

Davis, S. E. *The technique of teaching*. New York: Macmillan, 1924.

Dean, S. E. *Elementary school administration and organization: A national survey of practices and policies.* Washington, D.C.: United States Government Printing Office, Department of Health, Education, and Welfare, 1960.

DeGarmo, C. *Herbart and the Herbartians.* New York: Scribners, 1895.

DiMaggio, P., and Useem, M. Review of American Council for the Arts in Education, Coming to our senses: The significance of the arts for American education. *Harvard Educational Review,* 1978, *48,* 103-106.

Dow, A. W. Training in the theory and practice of teaching art. *Teachers College Record,* 1908, *9,* 1-54.

Earhart, Lida B. *Types of teaching.* Boston: Houghton Mifflin, 1915.

Eclectic manual of methods for the assistance of teachers. Cincinnati: Van Antwerp, Bragg, 1885.

Eddy, J. *Arts education 1977—in prose and print: An overview of nine significant publications affecting the arts in American education.* Washington, D. C.: United States Government Printing Office, 1978. (Prepared for the Subcommittee on Education in the Arts and the Humanities of the Federal Interagency Committee on Education).

Ege, O. F. Some problems of aim and method in training art teachers. In G. M. Whipple (Ed.), *Art in American life and education.* Fortieth yearbook of the National Society for the Study of Education. Bloomington, Illinois: Public School Publishing Co., 1941, 721-726.

Eisner, E. W. Graduate study and the preparation of scholars in art education. In R. W. Hastie (Ed.), *Art education.* Sixty-fourth yearbook of the National Society for the Study of Education, Part II. Chicago: University of Chicago Press, 1965, 274-298. (a)

Eisner, E. W. American education and the future of art education. In R. W. Hastie (Ed.), *Art education.* Sixty-fourth yearbook of the National Society for the Study of Education, Part II. Chicago: University of Chicago Press, 1965, 299-325. (b)

Eisner, E. W. Art education. In R. L. Ebel (Ed.), *Encyclopedia of educational research.* (4th ed.). New York: Macmillan, 1969, 76-86.

Eisner, E. W. Research on teaching the visual arts. In R. M. W. Travers (Ed.), *Second handbook of research on teaching.* Chicago: Rand McNally, 1973, 1196-1209.

Eisner, E. W. Thoughts on an agenda for research and development in arts education. In S. S. Madeja (Ed.), *Arts and aesthetics: An agenda for the future.* St. Louis: CEMREL, Inc., 1977, 411-422.

Elsbree, W. S. *The American teacher: Evolution of a profession in a democracy.* New York: American Book Co., 1939. (Republished by the Greenwood Press of Westport, Connecticut, 1970.)

Elson, R. M. *Guardians of tradition: American schoolbooks of the nineteenth century.* Lincoln: University of Nebraska Press, 1964.

Ernst, K. D. A study of certain practices in music education in school systems in cities over 150,000 population. Unpublished doctoral dissertation, University of Oregon, 1955.

Evenden, E. S. Contributions of research to the education of teachers. In G. M. Whipple (Ed.), *The scientific movement in education.* Thirty-seventh yearbook of the National Society for the Study of Education, Part II. Bloomington, Illinois: Public School Publishing Co., 1939, 33-52.

Fowler, C. B. The discovery method: Its relevance to music education. In B. C. Kowall (Ed.), *Perspectives in music education: Source book III*. Washington, D.C.: Music Educators National Conference, 1966.

Funchess, L. V. Research is needed in music education. *Phi Delta Kappan,* 1949, *30,* 349-350.

Gage, N. L. (Ed.). *Handbook of research on teaching.* Chicago: Rand McNally, 1963.

Gebhard, D. R. Music. In C. N. Kendall and G. A. Mirick (Eds.), *How to teach the special subjects*. Boston: Houghton Mifflin, 1918, 36-99.

Greene, H. A., Jorgensen, A. N., and Gerberich, J. R. *Measurement and evaluation in the elementary school*. New York: Longmans, Green, 1953.

Hall, B. R. *Teaching a science. The teacher an artist*. New York: Baker and Scribner, 1848.

Hall, S. R. *Lectures on school-keeping*. Boston: Richardson, Lord, and Holbrook, 1829.

Hall-Quest, A. L. *The textbook: How to use it and judge it*. New York: Macmillan, 1918.

Hamilton, S. *The recitation*. Philadelphia: J. B. Lippincott, 1906.

Hastie, W. R. The education of an art teacher. In W. R. Hastie (Ed.), *Art education*. Sixty-fourth yearbook of the National Society for the Study of Education, Part II. Chicago: University of Chicago Press, 1965, 243-273.

Hayward, F. H. *The lesson in appreciation*. New York: Macmillan, 1915.

Hendrickson, G. Music. In C. W. Harris (Ed.), *Encyclopedia of educational research*. New York: Macmillan, 1960, 905-913.

Henry, N. B. (Ed.). *Basic concepts in music education*. Fifty-seventh yearbook of the National Society for the Study of Education, Part II. Chicago: University of Chicago Press, 1958.

Hewitt, E. C. *A treatise on pedagogy for young teachers*. Cincinnati: Van Antwerp, Bragg, 1884.

Hoffa, H. The history of the idea. In S. S. Madeja, (Ed.), *Arts and aesthetics: An agenda for the future*. St. Louis: CEMREL, Inc., 1977, 61-80.

Horn, E. *Methods of instruction in the social studies*. Report of the Commission on the Social Studies, Part XV. New York: Charles Scribner's Sons, 1937.

Horn, E. Inequalities in opportunities for art development. In G. M. Whipple (Ed.), *Art in American life and education*. Fortieth yearbook of the National Society for the Study of Education. Bloomington, Illinois: Public School Publishing Co., 1941, 491-498.

Horne, H. H. *The teacher as artist*. Boston: Houghton Mifflin, 1917.

Horner, V. *Music education: The background of research and opinion*. Hawthorne, Victoria: Australian Council for Educational Research, 1965.

Johnson, P. Art for the young child. In W. R. Hastie (Ed.), *Art education*. Sixty-fourth yearbook of the National Society for the Study of Education, Part II. Chicago: University of Chicago Press, 1965, 51-85.

Jončich, G. *The sane positivist: A biography of Edward L. Thorndike*. Middletown, Connecticut: Wesleyan University Press, 1968.

Jones, A. H., and Evans, G. K. Areas of needed research in music education. *Education,* 1951, *72,* 23-27.

Keel, J. S. Art education, 1940-64. In W. R. Hastie (Ed.), *Art education.* Sixty-fourth yearbook of the National Society for the Study of Education, Part II. Chicago: University of Chicago Press, 1965, 35-50.

Kendall, C. N., and Mirick, G. A. *How to teach the special subjects.* Boston: Houghton Mifflin, 1918.

Keiler, M. L. *The art in teaching art.* Lincoln, Nebraska: University of Nebraska Press, 1961.

Lanier, V. *Doctoral research in art education.* Los Angeles: University of Southern California, 1962.

Learned, W. S. *Quality of the educational process in the United States and Europe.* Carnegie Foundation for the Advancement of Teaching, Bulletin No. 20. New York: The Foundation, 1927.

Leonhard, C. Evaluation in music education. In N. B. Henry (Ed.), *Basic concepts in music education.* Fifty-seventh yearbook of the National Society for the Study of Education, Part I. Chicago: University of Chicago Press, 1958, 310-338.

Leonhard, C., and Colwell, R. J. Research in music education. In S. S. Madeja (Ed.), *Arts and aesthetics: An agenda for the future.* St. Louis: CEMREL, Inc., 1977, 81-108.

Logan, F. *The growth of art in American schools.* New York: Harper & Brothers, 1955.

Lortie, D. C. *Schoolteacher: A sociological study.* Chicago: University of Chicago Press, 1975.

Madsen, C. K., Greer, R. D., and Madsen, C. H. (Eds.). *Research in music behavior: Modifying music behavior in the classroom.* New York: Teachers College Press Co., 1975.

McDonald, B. M., and Nelson, L. *Methods that teach.* Dubuque, Iowa: William C. Brown Co., 1958.

McDonald, F. J. The influence of learning theories on education (1900-1950). In E. R. Hilgard (Ed.), *Theories of learning and instruction.* Sixty-third yearbook of the National Society for the Study of Education, Part I. Chicago: University of Chicago Press, 1964, 1-26.

Michael, W. B. A short evaluation of the research reviewed in language arts and fine arts. *Review of Educational Research,* 1964, *34,* 249-254.

Mitchell, C. The art education of elementary school teachers. In W. R. Hastie (Ed.), *Art education.* Sixty-fourth yearbook of the National Society for the Study of Education, Part II. Chicago: University of Chicago Press, 1965, 221-242.

Moore, J. E. Art education. In W. S. Monroe (Ed.), *Encyclopedia of educational research.* New York: Macmillan, 1941, 58-65.

Morgan, T. J. *Studies in pedagogy.* Boston: Silver, Burdett, 1890.

Munro, T. Adolescence and art education. In W. S. Rusk (Ed.), *Methods of teaching the fine arts.* Chapel Hill: University of North Carolina Press, 1935, 25-58.

Munro, T. Introduction. In G. M. Whipple (Ed.), *Art in American life and education.* Fortieth yearbook of the National Society for the Study of Education. Bloomington, Illinois: Public School Publishing Co., 1941, 3-25. (a)

Munro, T. The psychological approach to art and art education. In G. M. Whipple (Ed.), *Art in American life and education*. Fortieth yearbook of the National Society for the Study of Education. Bloomington, Illinois: Public School Publishing Co., 1941, 249-288. (b)

Munro, T. *Art education: Its philosophy and psychology*. New York: Liberal Arts Press, 1956.

Mursell, J. L. The application of psychology to the arts. *Teachers College Record,* 1936, *37,* 290-299.

Mursell, J. L. Growth processes in music education. In N. B. Henry (Ed.), *Basic concepts in music education*. Fifty-seventh yearbook of the National Society for the Study of Education, Part I. Chicago: University of Chicago Press, 1958, 140-162.

Orcutt, H. *School keeping: How to do it*. Boston: N. E. Publishing Co., 1885.

O'Shea, M. V. *Everyday problems in teaching*. Indianapolis: Bobbs-Merrill, 1912.

Petzold, R. G. The perception of music symbols in music reading by normal children and by children gifted musically. *Journal of Experimental Education,* 1960, *28,* 271-319.

Petzold, R. G. Directions for research in music education. *Music Educators Journal,* 1964, *50,* 39-42.

Pierce, A. E., and Hilpert, R. S. *Instruction in music and art*. National Survey of Secondary Education, Monograph No. 25. Washington, D.C.: United States Government Printing Office, United States Office of Education, Department of the Interior, Bulletin No. 17, 1932.

Poff, D. G. Summer schools of music sponsored by publishing companies, 1888-1920. Unpublished doctoral dissertation, University of Michigan, 1970.

Poff, D. G. The national summer school of music sponsored by Ginn and Company, 1888-1919. *Contributions to Music Education,* 1976, *4,* 94-103.

Powers, H. H. The teaching of art. In W. S. Rusk (Ed.), *Methods of teaching the fine arts*. Chapel Hill: University of North Carolina Press, 1935, 213-220.

Prince, W. F. Music education's split personality. *Music Educators Journal,* 1974, *61,* 27-33.

Reimer, B. Effects of music education: Implications from a review of research. In B. C. Kowall (Ed.), *Perspectives in music education: Source Book III.* Washington, D.C.: Music Educators National Conference, 1966, 461-483.

Reimer, B. *A philosophy of music education*. Englewood Cliffs, New Jersey: Prentice-Hall, 1970.

Reimer, B. Aesthetic behaviors in music. In *Toward an aesthetic education.* Washington, D.C.: M.E.N.C. 1971, 65-87.

Roach, D. W. Contemporary music education: A comprehensive outlook. *Music Educators Journal,* September 1973, *60,* 36-40.

Rusk, H. H. (Ed.). *Methods of teaching the fine arts*. Chapel Hill, North Carolina: University of North Carolina Press, 1935.

Schneider, E. H. Music education. In R. L. Ebel (Ed.), *Encyclopedia of educational research*. (4th ed.). New York: Macmillan, 1969, 895-907.

Schramm, W. The publishing process. In L. J. Cronbach (Ed.), *Text materials in modern education*. Urbana: University of Illinois Press, 1955, 129-165.

Schultz, H. A., Roos, F. E., and Moore, J. E. Art education. In W. S. Monroe (Ed.), *Encyclopedia of educational research*. (Rev. ed.). New York: Macmillan, 1950, 64-72.

Silverman, R., and Lanier, V. Art for the adolescent. In W. R. Hastie (Ed.), *Art education*. Sixty-fourth yearbook of the National Society for the Study of Education. Chicago: University of Chicago Press, 1965, 115-152.

Smiley, Edna. *A study of musical configurations, symbols, terms, and words found in basic music texts at the fourth-grade level*. Unpublished doctoral dissertation, Indiana University, 1955.

Standifer, J. A. A report on ISME's research seminar in Mexico City. *Music Educators Journal*, 1975, *62*, 59-60.

Swartz, C. E. The Hawthorne effect and other mysteries. *The Physics Teacher*, 1969, 7, 429, 438.

Tadd, J. L. *New methods in education: Art, real manual training, nature study*. Springfield, Massachusetts: Orange Judd Co., 1899.

Tellstrom, A. T. *Music in American education, past and present*. New York: Holt, Rinehart, and Winston, 1971.

Thayer, V. T. *The passing of the recitation*. Boston: D. C. Heath, 1928.

Thorpe, L. P. Learning theory and music teaching. In N. B. Henry (Ed.), *Basic concepts in music education*. Fifty-seventh yearbook of the National Society for the Study of Education, Part I. Chicago: University of Chicago Press, 1958, 163-194.

Triplett, N. L. Influences in the adolescent years of artists. *School Review*, 1943, *50*, 300-308.

Travers, R. M. W. (Ed.). *Second handbook of research on teaching*. Chicago: Rand McNally, 1973.

Williams, D. B. The research-classroom gap. *Music Educators Journal*, 1975, *61*, 41-44.

Wold, S. G., and Hastie, W. R. From research and theory to teaching practice. In W. R. Hastie (Ed.), *Art education*. Sixty-fourth yearbook of the National Society for the Study of Education, Part II. Chicago: University of Chicago Press, 1965, 326-346.

Ziegfeld, E. Preparation of the general classroom teacher for teaching art. In G. M. Whipple (Ed.), *Art in American life and education*. Fortieth yearbook of the National Society for the Study of Education. Bloomington, Illinois: Public School Publishing Co., 1941, 801-819.

Zinar, Ruth. Reading language and reading music: Is there a connection? *Music Educators Journal*, 1976, *62*, 70-74.

Virginia Koehler

Research on Teaching: Implications for Research on the Teaching of the Arts

Introduction

Effective classroom teaching has been the subject of interest to a relatively small group of educational psychologists for the last fifteen years. These researchers have attempted to describe the process of instruction and to identify effective processes with respect to some criterion of effective teaching such as student achievement. All work in this area has involved either observation in naturalistic settings or experimentation in simulated classroom settings. For many years, the goal of this research was to identify teaching behaviors that are effective across subject matters, grade levels, geographic locations, or types of students. While a relatively general model of effective instruction in the basic skills for elementary grades has emerged, there is now cognizance that contexts, such as subject matter or grade level or type of student, are crucial mediating factors in the relationship between teaching process and student learning.

Recently, therefore, researchers have developed new approaches and methods both to describe and to control for the contexts in which teaching takes place. One very crucial context is subject matter. To date, most research efforts have focused on the teaching of basic skills (reading and mathematics) in the elementary grades and on differences in the effectiveness of behaviors in different basic skills settings. Very little research has focused on the teaching of the arts. It is the purpose of this paper to summarize the two dominant approaches toward classroom process research, to discuss the results, and to draw implications from these findings for a research program on the teaching of the arts.

Classroom Process Studies

Classroom process studies have played an important role in research on teaching. Knowledge gained from classroom research serves two purposes: it leads to an understanding of classroom processes; and it increases the effectiveness of education. In relation to these two purposes,

VIRGINIA KOEHLER *is Assistant Director for Teaching and Instruction at the National Institute of Education.*

two types of teaching-process studies have evolved: those which attempt to describe or define the process, and those which attempt to determine which teaching processes are effective in relation to desired outcomes, such as student achievement. The latter type, process/product research, has dominated research on teaching for ten years. However, interest in descriptive classroom research is increasing, and it has attracted researchers from many disciplines to the study of classrooms—linguists, ecological psychologists, cognitive psychologists, and sociologists.

Process/Product Studies

Process/product studies are designed to delineate causal relationships between classroom processes—such as teacher behaviors—and outcomes—generally student achievement. The purpose of these studies is to provide information on effective teaching skills, behaviors and/or competencies to be used in teacher training, licensing, and selection.

Examples of two major process/product studies are Phase II of the California Beginning Teacher Evaluation Study and the Correlates of Effective Teaching Project at the University of Texas R&D Center for Teacher Education. The BTES was originally designed as a five-year study to provide the California Commission for Teacher Preparation and Licensing with information on measurable teacher competencies known to be related to student achievement in reading and mathematics. This information was to be used in devising a new teacher licensing system. Funded by the National Institute of Education, administered by the Commission, and conducted by Fred MacDonald at Educational Testing Service, Phase II was a hypothesis-generating phase involving intensive observation and testing of fifty Grade Two and fifty Grade Five California teachers and their students. (See Koehler, 1974, for original design; and MacDonald, 1976, and MacDonald and Elias, 1976, for results.)

The Correlates of Effective Teaching Program, at the University of Texas R&D Center for Teacher Education, included a number of projects related to teacher effectiveness. The major effort was a two-year study of teaching effectiveness involving examination of the classroom behaviors of second-grade and third-grade teachers who consistently produced student learning gains. From a large sample of teachers, thirty-one were selected who were both experienced and consistent across time in terms of the amount of academic learning their students achieved. These teachers were observed extensively over a two-year period. The researchers found that, for many variables, teacher behaviors which were identified as effective in low socioeconomic status (SES) schools were different from those which were effective in high SES schools (Brophy and Evertson, 1974). Program personnel are now analyzing data from the junior high school process/product study.

The results of process/product studies of the late sixties and early seventies have been summarized in different ways (for example, Dunkin and Biddle, 1974; and Medley, 1977). Probably the most significant synthesis of the results was written by Berliner and Rosenshine (1976) and resulted in a description of the Direct Instructional Model. This model provides a framework for describing and analyzing teacher activity which is consciously directive and is related to elementary school students' learning of the basic skills. "Basic skills" is defined as reading and mathematics, generally measured by standardized achievement tests. In this model, the teacher supervises lessons and workbook activity, allows little free time or unsupervised student desk work, and clearly communicates the goals of the lessons to the students. The teacher decides what activities will take place, but the students are actively involved in the lesson. Content coverage is extensive, and questions tend to be focused and at a low cognitive level. These questions are geared to information that should already be known rather than to that which can be deduced or guessed. Teacher reinforcement rapidly follows most answers. Learning is organized around questions posed by the teacher or materials provided by the teacher. Teacher-student interactions are direct and academically oriented.

In addition to providing information on effective teacher behaviors, the processes/product paradigm has strongly influenced evaluation designs. Leinhardt (1978) has recently described the ways in which she combined teacher effectiveness research and evaluative research in a study of individualized instruction. Stallings and Kaskowitz (1974) and Soar (1973) utilized the paradigm in evaluating Follow Through programs. Cooley and Lohnes (1978) developed an evaluation process/ product model. More recently, process/product models have been utilized in the NIE study of compensatory education programs (*The Effects of Services on Student Development,* 1977), and in the summative evaluation of the NIE-funded Response to Educational Needs Project which is being conducted by Gibboney and Associates.

While the results of process/product studies have been extremely important to our understanding of effective teaching, they have also generated several negative reviews (for example, Heath and Nielson, 1974). Berliner (1976) also outlined many of the problems with conducting process/product studies in his article "The Impediments to the Study of Teacher Effectiveness"; and researchers associated with The Evaluation of Teaching Program at the University of Texas R&D Center for Teacher Education have conducted a number of methodological studies on these and other problems. Several types of problems associated with process/ product studies are described in the paragraphs below.

Lack of Reliability and Validity of Observation Measures: While interrater reliability of observation measures is generally extremely high, test-retest reliability is low. This indicates a lack of stability or inconsistent teacher behavior from one lesson to another. (See Barr, 1929;

Shavelson and Dempsey, 1975; Calkins, Borich, Pascove, Kugle, and Marston, 1978.)

The lack of reliability obviously affects the validity; but Borich and Malitz (1976) are also examining construct validity across a number of observation measures. They are finding that the relationship between supposedly similar constructs (such as "warmth") across several measures is generally very low.

Outcome Measures: In general, standardized tests have been utilized in process/product studies. These are seen as highly unsatisfactory for two reasons: they do not necessarily reflect what the teachers are trying to teach; and there are many other outcomes besides cognitive achievements which are deemed to be important. Further, it has been found that the stability of teacher effects on student achievement measures over several years is quite low. (See Rosenshine, 1970; Shavelson and Dempsey, 1975.)

A number of researchers have suggested that shorter measurement periods, such as one or two weeks, are preferable to long periods, such as one year; and that the measures should assess knowledge of the content of instruction. (See Borich, 1976; Conference Series No. 1, IRT, 1977, pp. 57-70.)

Statistical Problems: Major statistical problems are related to difficulties in reducing masses of data into manageable units; to the unit of analysis issue—individual student or classroom average (Glendenning and Porter, 1976); to attempts to discern causal relationships with correlational data; and to a host of problems related to the use of regression techniques. For example, Godbout, Marston, Borich, and Vaughan (1977) pointed out that seemingly "significant" correlations in studies with many variables and many nonsignificant correlations may, in fact, be random occurrences.

Unidirectionality of Effect: The process-product paradigm assumes a unidirectional causal relationship: teachers' behaviors cause students to learn. However, those of us who have taught and/or observed classrooms understand that student responses affect teacher behavior. This may, in fact, explain why some teachers can be effective one year and not the next; that is, there is a different set of students. Unfortunately, while this problem is recognized by many process-product researchers, our technology does not yet allow us to explore this interaction within the process/product paradigm.

◻◻◻

There have been two major types of reactions to the problems with process/product studies. The first is to attempt to improve upon the paradigm, and the second is to abandon it entirely and seek other ways of thinking about and conducting research on classroom processes. We will first review attempts at improvement, and in the subsequent section consider the alternatives.

Better Observation Procedures: Two approaches have been taken to respond to the various reliability and validity problems related to observation measures. In Phase III of the Beginning Teacher Evaluation Study, Berliner and his colleagues at Far West Laboratory controlled for subject matter by introducing the experimental teaching unit which provided a group of teachers with common subject matter for a period of several weeks. By pre- and post-testing students, more and less effective teachers were identified and observed by ethnographers (Berliner and Tikunoff, 1976).

A second approach to dealing with observation measure problems is to combine teaching behaviors and determine which are effective in relation to the instructional settings in which they occur. It was hypothesized that certain combinations of behavior are more appropriate units to relate to student achievement than the single or micro behaviors that had been utilized in the past. Also, it is hoped that by controlling for context variables, the measures of teacher behaviors will be more reliable. (See Doyle, 1978(b); Good, 1978; Soar, 1978; Stallings, Cory, and Fairweather, 1978; Wiley and Harnischfeger, 1977.)

Improving Outcome Measures: Many researchers have pointed to the desirability of utilizing actual student behaviors as product measures in teacher effectiveness studies (Conference Series No. 1, IRT, 1977). One such measure is student time on task. This measure is important for two reasons: it is a student behavior that teachers have more control over than achievement on a standardized test; and it is an immediate measure which teachers understand and can utilize while teaching. Furthermore, it is related to student achievement on standardized tests. Berliner, Fisher, Filby, and Marlieve (1976) have developed and are using a construct called Academic Learning Time (ALT). ALT is time spent by a learner engaged in a task that is within an intermediate range of difficulty and is related directly to an academic outcome. This construct is being utilized as both an independent and a dependent measure in Phase IIIb of the California Beginning Teacher Evaluation Study (Berliner et al., 1976). (See also Rosenshine, 1978.)

Research Design Improvements: A major problem with classroom process/product studies is that they are correlational. Very complex statistical models and procedures have been developed to test causal relationships utilizing correlational data, but many of the assumptions upon which these models depend are not consistent with the type of data and the ways in which it is collected (that is, using volunteer teachers) in process/product studies. Correlation models simply cannot take the place of experimental designs. Therefore, several researchers have turned to the experimental mode to test relationships between teacher behaviors and student outcomes. The Correlates of Effective Teaching Program at the University of Texas R&D Center for Teacher Education is completing the analysis of data on a First Grade Teaching of Reading experiment in which teachers received a publication listing a number of principles of effective teaching of reading taken from past correlational studies. Preliminary results indicate that students of teachers who received the material achieved more than the students of teachers who did not (Odgen, Brophy, and Evertson, 1977). Gage, at Stanford University's Center for Educational Research, has developed a teacher training program for Title I elementary school teachers of basic skills on the basis of numerous correlational reports of effective teaching behaviors. Teachers will be trained with this material, and their students' achievement gains will be compared with the gains of students of teachers not receiving the treatment. In these two studies, the teachers' behaviors will be closely observed to determine exactly which behaviors were changed by the treatment. The second year of Jane Stallings' process/product study of junior high schools will be experimental in that information from the first year will be turned into a feedback program for the teachers in her sample to determine whether this information changes the teachers' behaviors and, thereby, their students' achievement gains (Stallings, Cory, Fairweather, and Needels, 1978). Finally, Wang (1976) has utilized experimentation in studying various instructional means for maximizing students' time utilization and task completion rates.

While process/product research has fallen short of delivering a complete set of principles of effective teaching which can be utilized in selecting teachers and improving practice, it has made recent contributions to our understanding of how basic skills should be delivered in elementary school classrooms. However, a number of crucial factors which would be of value to teachers applying the direct instructional model have not yet been the subject of research. For example: How should teachers motivate different types of students to stay on task? Since there are only six hours in each school day, on what basis should teachers decide to spend more time on one subject area and therefore less on another? And, is there a point beyond which more time on one subject area would actually reverse the instructional effect? Future research will have to concentrate on these types of issues, but there is some question as to whether the process/product paradigm can, at this point, provide the answers. We will now turn to a very different approach which promises to increase our understanding of the teaching process, and to provide some answers to the kinds of questions listed above.

Descriptive Research

The limitations of the process/product paradigm in answering many questions related to effective teaching have focused the limelight on a very different approach to classroom research. For want of a better term, it will be called descriptive research. While it has been around for quite some time (see, for example, Gump, 1967, and Jackson, 1968), descriptive research has only recently received the stamp of approval from the research community at large. Last summer, the NIE requested a number of experts to write papers suggesting future research directions. (See *Report of the Teaching Learning Task Force*, 1977.) Those who wrote specifically on instruction included David Berliner, Courtney Cazden, Robert Davis, Robert Dreeben, Robert Glaser, Walter Doyle, David Hawkins, Roger Shuy and Peg Griffin, and David Wiley and Annagret Harnischfeger. While there were different emphases presented in the papers, there were few disagreements about the direction future research should take. Research should be descriptive, with attention paid to the ecology or environment of the classroom. It should consist of small sample, in-depth, longitudinal and naturalistic observations. Classroom research should be conducted by researchers from disciplines such as sociology, linguistics, and anthropology, rather than just psychology. The education system as it exists today should be studied. And teachers should become collaborators in the effort.

The descriptive approach focuses on what is rather than what should be. There is, therefore, less concern with desired outcomes and "effective" teaching and more with defining and understanding existing classroom procedures. Cronbach (1975) describes it as "intensive local observation [which] goes beyond discipline to an open-eyed, open-minded appreciation of the surprises Nature deposits in the investigative net." Because the emphasis is on understanding the classroom—or, as Doyle (1978a) describes it, developing an indigenous theory of classroom activities—much of the work is qualitative in nature, and it is all observational. A growing number of descriptive studies are being conducted. Several types of these are described in the following paragraphs:

Teaching as Clinical Information Processing. The report from Panel Six of the National Conference on Studies in Teaching (*Teaching as Clinical Information Processing,* 1974) called for a new approach to the study of teaching—one which attempts to describe the mental life of the teacher, taking advantage of the wisdom of the practitioner. Shavelson (1973, 1976) also called for research in this area. In response to a Request for Proposals for research in teachers' decision-making, Lanier and Shulman (1976) responded:

> The essential features of this view are that the study of teaching must take account of the purposes or goals which the teacher seeks in any setting; the characteristics of the environment which define the teacher's task and sets limits to his/her alternatives; and the invariant information processing capacities of the teacher which require that he/she respond selectively to the elements of the task

environment, treating some as relevant cues and others as irrelevant, some as figure and others as ground. (p. B-I-4)

Important features of the research at the Institute for Research on Teaching include interdisciplinary work and collaboration with practicing teachers who teach one-half time and work on research projects one-half time at the IRT. A number of the projects are described in a recent issue of the *Journal of Teacher Education* (Shulman and Lanier, 1976).

Ecological Research. Ecology is the study of the relationships between organisms and their environment. Barker (1968) applied the discipline to the study of psychological phenomena. Research in ecological psychology, Baker explained, attempts to determine the interaction among individual behaviors, the psychological environment (that is, perceptions), and the ecological environment (the real-world settings). Bronfenbrenner (1976) pointed out the potential utility of the paradigm in educational research, and the approach is exemplified in Jackson's *Life in the Classroom* (1968). Ecological classroom researchers, then, view the classroom as an ecological unit in which students and teachers interact with each other as well as with the setting. This approach is particularly helpful in explaining behaviors of individuals in such settings, especially for determining the effects of setting variables on individual behavior. For example, the ecological perspective would point out that the fact that there are thirty students in a classroom undoubtedly causes teachers to behave in certain ways. A logical analysis indicates that the ways to change those behaviors significantly would be to reduce the number of students, to add more adults to the classroom, or to alter the structure of the classroom by, for example, introducing computer-assisted instruction. Inservice teacher training would not be particularly useful in changing these behaviors. A review of this approach and its relationship to research can be found in Far West Laboratory's Five Year Plan (1977, pp. IV-61-138) by Ward and Tikunoff.

Walter Doyle (1977 a and b) is building a theory of classroom processes which combines two paradigms: the mediating process paradigm and the classroom ecology paradigm. The mediating process paradigm is useful in understanding how the task structure of the classroom is processed by the student. In this view, the relationship between teacher behavior and student achievement is mediated by a number of processes which require elucidation. In Doyle's words, "[student] attending and processing ... depend not on the discrete dimensions of an instructional treatment but on the task structure defined by that treatment" (1977b, p. 38). Doyle pointed out, however, that much of this work has been conducted in laboratory settings (for example, Rothkopf, 1965, 1976). He feels this is probably not generalizable to natural educational settings; consequently, he has turned to the ecological paradigm to describe the mediating classroom processes and task structures which affect student learning in natural classroom environments. Ponder and Doyle (1977) have utilized the ecological research model to explore the effects of the teachers' relative isolation and functional autonomy on their acceptance and utilization of curricular innovations. Doyle is presently developing the mediating process/ecological paradigm in greater depth.

Activity Structures: The Sociological Perspective. A growing number of sociologists are beginning to utilize their constructs in the description of classroom processes. They are particularly interested in the importance of the structure of activities and the patterns of behavior within those activities. Meyer, Cohen, Brunetti, Molnar, and Salmon (1974), for example, have looked extensively at the ways in which teams of teachers (in team-teaching programs) plan, structure their instructional activities, and make instructional decisions. Meyer et al. utilized *a priori* measures and large sample sizes in their study.

Mehan (1978) and Bossert (1978) have utilized small sample ethnographic research to analyze activity structures. Mehan looks for classroom phases or events and breaks them into their constituent parts in order to assess whether or not individual students have learned the "rules" of the various activity structures and can therefore effectively participate. Bossert, on the other hand, investigates the relationship between activity structures and the development of activity-specific skills and norms. He reports, for example, that students that he observed developed different norms of peer cooperation and competition in different instructional activities.

Teaching as a Linguistic Process

The use of linguistic constructs and methodologies to describe verbal and nonverbal classroom interactions is a recent development in classroom process research. In the mid-sixties and early seventies, sociolinguists applied participant field-study techniques to describe both language usage by urban subgroups of the population and differences in usage among the subgroups (Baratz and Baratz, 1970; Labov, 1966; Shuy, Wolfram, and Riley, 1966). For the sociolinguist, the social context is the most powerful determinant of verbal behavior. Differences in language usage by subgroups of the population became a topic of concern as linguists considered what happens to children as they enter the classroom context. Subsequently, a number of linguists began to assess differences between communication patterns in the homes of certain cultural groups and those used in the schools. For example, Philips' (1972) study on the Warm Springs reservation in Oregon indicated that there were distinctive patterns of social etiquette or appropriateness governing interaction in community life which differed from those Anglo teachers used and expected children to use at school. Erickson and Mohatt (1977) found the same phenomenon among Native Americans in Ontario, Canada, and also found that Native American teachers used Native American communication etiquette, while the Anglo teachers employed Anglo communication etiquette in their classrooms.

A major concern of educational linguists, then, is that the differences between communication patterns of teachers and pupils may cause educational failure—although the relationship is complex and may be mediated by the attitudes of the teachers (Stubbs, 1976). The fact that there are differences between home and school discourse rules for some students, and that teachers seldom explicate their classroom rules, leaves these children at a disadvantage. The "mismatch" model suggests that inadequate learning of classroom discourse rules can lead to misunderstandings in both referential and social meanings. Thus, the effects of a student's language on teacher judgment can be critical—affecting the ways in which the teacher interacts with the student (Hamersley, 1974). These interaction patterns may have a strong impact on student achievement.

Methodology. Descriptive research requires an approach to collection and analysis of data that is different from the quantitative procedures most generally used in process/product research. In descriptive research, the phenomena are many, their interactions are complex, and the context is important; while in process/product research, parsimony is a desirable goal. The approach generally advocated by descriptive researchers is qualitative. Understanding of what is going on develops from many hours of sensitive observation in a particular setting. (See Glaser and Straus, 1967; and Miller, 1977.) If statistics are employed, they are typically nonparametric.

Ethnographic research is a particular form of qualitative methodology. The purpose of ethnographic research is to describe a particular culture such as an individual classroom, as seen through the eyes of the participants. In any event, ethnography is becoming extremely popular in educational research. In fact, most research which is nonquantitative and involves some observation—such as "hanging around the halls"—is defined, many times incorrectly, as ethnographic research. Enthusiastic newcomers to ethnographic research collect copious field notes and then encounter numerous problems in deciding what to do with them. Very often, distinctions among the five stages of ethnographic research— determination of focus, collection of data (field notes), data reduction, data analysis, and interpretation—break down. The focus is not clarified prior to data collection, and the field notes quickly become interpretive statements.

But as Dell Hymes (1977) has pointed out, ethnographic research can and should be as rigorous as quantitative research. Erickson (1977), for example, has worked out a complex and systematic procedure for data reduction which involves participation of the observed teachers. And

Tikunoff, Berliner, and Rist (1976) described a very lengthy, multi-step approach to collection, reduction, and analysis of their ethnographic data. A rigorous approach is crucial to descriptive research. Rigorous methodology increases the reliability and validity of the results, and admits the possiblilty of replication.

There are two major elements distinguishing descriptive studies from process/product research: (1) the lack of explicit student learning criteria and (2) the lack of *a priori* observation process measures. And yet, a focus for descriptive research must be chosen. A discipline can provide that focus, and this has happened in a number of the linguistic studies. Educational settings are utilized for capturing teacher/student and student/student dialogues since the classroom is a relatively formal and accessible setting. But the choices of which dialogues to analyze, and the ways in which the dialogues are analyzed (that is, the structural coding schemes), are often derived solely from various linguistic subdisciplines rather than from educational concerns. These results, therefore, are of greater interest to linguists than to educators.

Other descriptive researchers have focused on subjects which appear to be educationally important. For example, they consider topics such as the use of time and how students interact on academic topics during "independent learning situations." Walter Doyle (1978a) argues, however, that we should use descriptive research to *develop* constructs which are indigenous to classrooms because we will eventually find that constructs borrowed from other disciplines are inadequate to an understanding of classroom phenomena. To Doyle, Erickson (1978), and others, a major goal of descriptive classroom research over the next several years is the development of a theory or theories which explain classroom processes.

Two Contexts: Subject Matter and Grade Level

A number of contexts, or setting variables, have emerged as mediators in the relationship between teacher behaviors and student learning. Two contexts of extreme importance to arts educators are subject matter and grade level.

The importance of subject matter and grade level in modifying the effectiveness of teacher behaviors was first pointed out in the Texas Teacher Effectiveness Study results (Brophy and Evertson, 1974). It was further highlighted by MacDonald (1977; and MacDonald and Elias, 1976) in reports on the findings of Phase II of the California Beginning Teacher Evaluation Study. MacDonald found that no individual teaching skill, as he defined it, was significantly related to student learning across grade levels (in this instance, grades two and five) and subject matter (reading and mathematics). His findings, for example, indicated that the organizational pattern for Grade Two reading should combine group instruction with individual monitoring of performance and a variety of materials, but effective Grade Two mathematics instruction emphasized more indi-

Table 1

Common Dimensions of Effectiveness Across
Grade Levels and Subject Matters

Grade Level		Subject Matter		Common Effective Behaviors
2	5	Reading	Math	
X	X	X	X	21
X		X	X	45
	X	X	X	24
X	X	X		35
X	X		X	28

vidual monitoring and less group work. For Grade Five reading, a variety of instructional materials was a negative predictor, and in Grade Five mathematics, group instruction was more effective than individual instruction. When individual skills are combined into patterns of teacher behaviors, however, there were several commonalities across all four quadrants. These patterns, of course, are related to the Direct Instructional Model: direct teaching, monitoring of individual student behavior, and high levels of focus and goal-directedness.

In Phase III of the Beginning Teacher Evaluation Study, Berliner and Tikunoff (1976) explored the Phase II findings in greater depth by utilizing ethnographers in the Grade Two and Grade Five classrooms of twenty more effective and twenty less effective teachers (as defined on the basis of student learning in reading and mathematics). The protocols were analyzed, and sixty-one classroom process dimensions were identified as significantly distinguishing between the more and less effective teachers in at least one of the comparisons. *Table 1* indicates the number of dimensions which were common across subject matter and grade level.

Twenty-one of the sixty-one dimensions were common across all four quadrants. These included teacher lack of abruptness, teacher attending to students, teacher lack of belittling, and student engagement. The largest number of common dimensions were found across Grade Two reading and math, while a much smaller number were found across reading and math in Grade Five—indicating that effective instruction at the Grade Two level looks about the same for reading and math, but looks very different in Grade Five.

Such results have changed the ways in which researchers think about and conduct studies of teaching. Process/product researchers now control for context either by conducting their studies within one type of context or by analyzing their data within single contexts. For example, Good (1978) has conducted a major process/product study in Grade Four mathematics classes, and is now conducting an experiment to determine whether or not changing teachers' mathematics instructional strategies in the directions suggested by the correlational study affects students' mathematics achievement. Tikunoff and Ward (1977) are also looking at teachers' instructional strategies in Grade Four mathematics classes, and work is being conducted at the Institute for Research on Teaching on the planning of reading lessons. All this research, however, utilizes general instructional theories within the context of one subject matter. In other words, the primary focus is on instruction, not on the subject matter.

A second approach looks particularly at the relationship between the subject matter and the teaching/learning process. Porter, Schmidt, Floden, and Freeman (1977), for example, have developed a taxonomy of Grade Four mathematics tasks, and have analyzed items on three standardized tests in that taxonomy. The next step will be to analyze the content of math instruction and to determine the factors which influence teachers' decisions regarding the content they choose to teach. Susan Florio, who is also at the Institute for Research on Teaching, is conducting a two-year ethnographic study of a nationally renowned Grade Two teacher's teaching of writing (Florio, 1978). One goal of her research is to determine how that teacher integrates the teaching of writing into other subject areas. Chittenden and Amarel (1978) have studied, and are continuing to study, children's learning of reading skills within an open-school instructional model. They observe how children's development in a number of different subject matter skills, such as art, relates to their learning of reading.

The only natural-setting subject matter instructional observational study that focuses on the arts of which I am aware is the 1972 Smith and Schumacher study. They spent many hours observing teachers and students in aesthetic education classes as one aspect of an evaluation of CEMREL's aesthetic education curriculum. They analyzed teachers' approaches and student responses to various types of tasks within the curriculum. Smith (1977) noted in an article on the criterion issue that a teacher and his or her students could do well in some types of tasks, but the class could fall apart in others.

For reasons which I will explicate later, research on the teaching of the arts—particularly in elementary schools—would benefit from this latter research approach: that is, it would benefit from naturalistic observations of arts content and activities from the standpoint of the tasks students engage in and of the ways in which the teacher structures the class around those activities.

Research on teaching has focused primarily on the elementary grades. Since there appears to be a difference between the effectiveness of teacher behaviors in Grades Two and Five, one would assume that a study of teacher behaviors in junior and senior high school would identify effective behaviors that are very different from those identified in the elementary grades. Knowledge of subject matter, for example, may become more important in secondary school. Interestingly, two junior high school process/product studies of basic skills instruction (Stallings, et al., 1978; and Evertson, Anderson, and Edgar, 1977) indicate that the Direct Instructional Model is as effective at the junior high school level, as in elementary school. A direct comparison of effective teaching of reading skills in junior high and elementary schools has not yet been made. Obviously, there is a need for both process/product and descriptive studies at the secondary school level.

Research on the teaching of the arts will probably also produce very different results at the secondary school level. The arts become separable and distinct subject matters at the secondary school level. Production is emphasized and arts teachers critique student products. The teachers are trained differently and the classes are voluntary. For all of these reasons and more, findings from research on the teaching of the arts in elementary school will not be generalizable to secondary schools, and vice versa.

Implications for Research on Teaching the Arts

The Criterion Issue

One of the most crucial issues facing us as we contemplate a research program in arts education is the identification of the criterion or criteria of effective teaching. In basic skills process/product studies, we have utilized such student learning measures as standardized or criterion-referenced tests or even correctness of homework as criteria of effectiveness. While none of these is totally satisfactory, we have had at least some sense of what skills students should be learning in the basic skills. We now have an even better, more proximate measure of effectiveness: student time on task. This is a student process variable that we know is related to student learning outcomes. But what do we want children to learn in the arts—performance skills, appreciation, concepts?

On second thought, however, it may not be necessary to define learning goals as criteria of effective teaching before embarking on a research program. In fact, it may be desirable not to. I think we have erred in the basic skills area by defining/identifying goals which may, in fact, be unattainable given the realities of schools and classrooms. Assuming that the educational system is susceptible to rationality and rational-actor norms—which suggests that we can develop goals and adjust processes to meet these goals—has led many states into developing competency-based testing programs. There is a great amount of controversy about these programs, and it certainly is not clear that they will improve instruction.

Learning goals must be developed in full cognizance of the realities of classroom life, including the multiple classroom agenda. Many scholars now reject the rational-actor assumption that teachers attempt to maximize instructional time with the sole aim of increasing student achievement. "Filling time," or achieving more immediate goals, may be a more accurate description—at least for some teachers. This is not to say that teachers do not act rationally. They may—but their goals may be different from our own. Philip Jackson (1968, p. 162) described the difference between the teacher's primary concern—"the thoughts and practices dominating his immediate actions with students"—and the teacher's ultimate concerns—"his hopes and expectations concerning the long-term achievement of individuals within his class":

> Teachers, particularly in the lower grades, seem to be more activity-oriented than learning-oriented. That is, they commonly decide on a set of activities which they believe will have a desirable outcome and then focus their energies on achieving and maintaining student involvement in those activities. Learning is important, to be sure, but when the teacher is actually interacting with his student it is at the periphery of his attention, rather than at the focus of his vision. (p. 162)

Cusick (1978) reviewed a number of ethnographic studies of effective teachers and found that these teachers spend a lot of time attempting to build communities with common social norms in their classrooms, and therefore much activity was devoted to monitoring social behavior of children to ensure that all the children became a part of the community. In discussing goals with the teachers, the community-building process and social behavior goals were paramount in their responses, although they were also interested in student learning. Cusick contrasts this *gemeinschaft* approach with the *gesellschaft* approach which lays individual learning goals on education systems and holds teachers accountable for them.

An understanding of the realities of classrooms is crucial in thinking about the goals of arts instruction. At this point, art may be one of the biggest time fillers in the American elementary school curriculum. For example: In a study of eleven grade one and grade two classrooms, Wiley and Harnischfeger (1977) found that art was the subject matter which received the most attention after the basic skills. In personal communication with Harnischfeger, however, it was determined that there was little, if any, direct instruction in art—it was just a fill-in activity. Ward and Tikunoff (1976) also talk about art as a fill-in in their ethnographic studies of the development of instructional programs.

Art is also used in conjunction with other subjects. For example, in the kindergarten classroom in which I observe, the teaching of letter sounds revolves around pictures of objects that begin with the various sounds. Students are then asked to draw pictures of six objects that begin with the day's sound. This allows the teacher (who has no aide) to work with a small reading group while the other children are engaged in drawing pictures. There seems to be more cooperation and "sanctioned" student interaction in this drawing activity than in any other activity. One student, for example, is known for being able to draw a rat, and he will help other children draw rats on R days. But the teacher feedback is related to the number of correct words, not the art work—although the children themselves seem to be aware of who can "draw well."

Interestingly enough, two of the more perceptive discussions of the criterion issue are concerned explicitly with arts education. Smith (1977) developed a set of criteria of effective teaching of the arts which relies on extensive observation:

> (1) a defensible conception of the program and its priorities exhibited in the teacher's actions; (2) a quality of improvisation in the teacher's behavior; (3) a responsiveness to pupils' suggestions; (4) an involvement and participation by students; and (5) a varied set of changes in pupil personality which accent the multiplicity of possible goals and experiences suggested in Figure 1 and Table 1 [which are matrices of art forms (theater, music, dance . . .) and pupil roles (creator, recreator/performer, implementor, appreciator, critic)]. (p. 132)

Elliot Eisner (1975) has developed the notion of evaluation through connoisseurship and criticism. Connoisseurship refers to an appreciation of the art of teaching, and criticism is disclosure, or, as Eisner defines it, "a rendering in linguistic terms of what it is that he or she has encountered in such a way that others not possessing his level of connoisseurship can also enter into the work" (p. 9). The connoisseur, then, would observe a classroom, and reveal his or her set of criteria through the written critique. Both these notions of evaluation and criteria rely heavily on process observations.

In further establishing criteria of effective teaching of the arts—particularly those relating to product or learning goals—it is essential that the concerns, goals, and strategies of practicing classroom teachers be taken into account. To be sure, some of these strategies are changeable. Over the next several years, for example, we will see a greater emphasis placed on basic skills subject matter, and larger amounts of instructional time will be devoted to them. With public pressure, it is possible to increase the amount of attention given to the arts. But certain elements of classroom behavior are probably relatively invariant. As long as there are twenty to forty students in a classroom, teachers will spend time building communities and molding social norms which govern individual behavior. Art, music, and drama may be taught in such a way as to instill norms of cooperation. The activity structures chosen for math, on the other hand, emphasize individual behavior. And these differences may be due to the subject matter itself, and possibly to teachers' theories about the subject matter. It will be up to the classroom ecologists to describe and explain these seemingly invariant behaviors. Setting goals prior to understanding such realities could be a wasteful activity and one which would only frustrate teachers more than they already are.

Recommendations for Research on the Instruction of the Arts

Richard Feynman described "Cargo Cult Science" in his Commencement Address at the California Institute of Technology in June 1974:

> I think the educational and psychological studies I mentioned are examples of what I would like to call Cargo Cult Science. In the South Seas there is a Cargo Cult people. During the war they saw airplanes land with lots of good materials, and they want the same thing to happen now. So they've arranged to make things like runways, to put fires along the sides of the runways, to make a wooden hut for a man to sit in, with two wooden pieces on his head like headphones and bars of bamboo sticking out like antennas— he's the controller—and they wait for the airplanes to land. They're doing everything right. The form is perfect. It looks exactly the way it looked before. But it doesn't work. No airplanes land. So I call these things Cargo Cult Science, because they follow all the apparent precepts and forms of scientific investigation, but they're missing something essential, because the planes don't land.

Now, while I would not like to think of past work in research on teaching as Cargo Cult Science, it certainly has been plagued by two interrelated problems:

1. The development of criteria of effective teaching—such as learning goals—in the absence of an understanding of the structural limitations of schools and classrooms, and of the concerns and objectives of classroom teachers.

2. Inquiry into effective teaching processes which ignores such contexts as subject matter and grade level.

The second problem is being remedied in process/product research. The first problem has led to a paradigmatic shift.

A research program on instruction in the arts presents an opportunity to avoid many of the errors made in classroom process studies in the past. Accordingly, recommendations for a research program fall under three broad research objectives: understanding present practices in arts instruction; determining effective processes in the instruction of the arts; and increasing the emphasis placed on the arts.

Understanding Present Practices in Arts Instruction: We have very little baseline information on arts instruction in our schools. Therefore:

- We need broad descriptive data on such topics as: the incidence of regular teacher vs. special arts teacher arts instruction in elementary school classrooms, and projections for the future; state and local requirements for arts instruction; and so on.
- We need small-scale in-depth descriptive research on arts instruction by elementary school teachers. How much instruction in the arts do elementary students receive? Are the arts used as "fill-ins"? Are the arts used to teach other subjects? Does the regular teacher interact

with the arts teacher in cases where there is an arts teacher? What are the attitudes of classroom teachers towards the arts and arts instruction? What socialization goals are pursued with arts instruction? What types of peer group interaction take place during arts instruction?

- In secondary schools, we need to determine who chooses to take arts classes, and why. What are the standard modes of instruction in the various types of arts classes? Do "non-arts" teachers (that is, science teachers or English teachers) instruct students in the arts? And so on.

This research will provide us with baseline information we need for considering how to change the existing system. For example, if we find that elementary school teachers utilize art as a fill-in activity, curriculum materials can be developed to provide for more structured fill-ins, and teacher training programs can be designed to give teachers a sense of the degree to which they can use the arts in the instruction of other subject matters.

Determining Effective Processes in the Instruction of the Arts: Findings from research in this area will feed into teacher training programs and into materials development which in turn will improve instruction in the existing system. Therefore:

- We need process/product studies in secondary schools. Of crucial importance is the interrelationship among what a teacher knows about the subject matter and the teaching of the subject matter, his or her ability to perform in that subject matter, and the effectiveness of instruction. That is: Is it necessary for a teacher to be able to sing in order to teach singing? Or to play an instrument well in order to teach it? Also important are the relationship between how a teacher critiques a student's production and his or her effectiveness, and what criteria teachers use. Are there effective grouping practices or peer group critiquing practices in arts instruction?
- We need experimental studies that test the correlational findings in the process/product studies.
- We need small case studies of elementary school teachers who are reputed to "be creative" in teaching the arts and of teachers who are known to integrate the arts into other subject matters. These case studies should keep track of student productions in the arts, as well as in other basic skills areas.

Increased Emphasis on the Arts: John Meyer (1978) suggested that major changes in schooling come about by changes in institutions—in the norms regarding the structure and function of the school system—rather than by changes in the organization of schools and classrooms. If this is the case, research cannot change the relative emphasis our school system places on the arts. These changes must come about through changing the attitudes of the public toward the arts in our schools and, thereby, through political processes. Nonetheless, research can be utilized by those who are intent upon changing the system. Therefore:

- We need continued research on the relationships between the learning of various symbol systems, such as musical notations, and the learning of literacy skills and mathematics.

In addition, should the arts become a high priority either nationally or locally, the research community should be prepared to offer advice on effective instruction. Therefore:

- We need to conduct research in elementary and secondary schools where instruction in the arts is emphasized. Initial work should be descriptive in nature, with naturalistic observation of unusually effective programs. Should the instructional goals be clearly enunciated and understood by school personnel, process/product studies should be conducted to determine effective practices.

What has driven the logic of this particular organization of a research agenda in the instruction of the arts is a firm belief that an understanding of present practices and school/classroom processes is absolutely necessary prior to a determination of the degree to which the system can change and of how that change can be brought about.

Washington, D.C.
October 1978

REFERENCES

Baratz, S., and Baratz, J. Early childhood interaction: The social science base of institutional racism. *Harvard Educational Review*, 1970, 40, 29-50.

Barker, R. G. *Ecological psychology: Concepts and methods for studying the environments of human behavior.* Palo Alto, California: Stanford University Press, 1968.

Barr, A. *Characteristic differences in the teaching performance of good and poor teachers of the social studies.* Bloomington, Indiana: Public School Publishing Co., 1929.

Berliner, D. Impediments to the study of teacher effectiveness. *Journal of Teacher Education*, 1976, 27(1), 5-13.

Berliner, D., Fisher, C. W., Filby, N., and Marlieve, R. *Proposal for Phase III of Beginning Teacher Evaluation Study.* San Francisco: Far West Laboratory for Educational Research and Development, 1976.

Berliner, D., and Rosenshine, B. *The acquisition of knowledge in the classroom* (BTES Technical Report, IV-1). San Francisco: Far West Laboratory for Educational Research and Development, 1976.

Berliner, D., and Tikunoff, W. The California Beginning Teacher Evaluation Study: Overview of the ethnographic study. *Journal of Teacher Education*, 1976, 27(1), 24-34.

Borich, G. Sources of invalidity in measuring classroom behavior. *Instructional Science,* 1976, 6, 283-318.

Borich, G., and Malitz. *Convergent and discriminant validation of three classroom observation systems: A proposed model.* Austin, Texas: The University of Texas Research and Development Center for Teacher Education, 1976.

Bossert, S. T. *Activity structures and student outcomes.* Paper prepared for the National Institute of Education Conference on School Organization and Effects. San Diego, 1978.

Bronfenbrenner, U. The experimental ecology of education. *Teachers College Record,* 1976, 78(2), 159-204.

Brophy, J., and Evertson, C. *Process-product correlations in Texas Teacher Effectiveness Study. Final Report.* Austin: University of Texas Research and Development Center for Teacher Education, 1974.

Calkins, D., Borich, G. D., Pascove, M., Kugle, C. L., and Marston, P. T. Generalizability of teacher behaviors across classroom observation systems. *Journal of Classroom Interaction,* 1978, 13(1), 9-22.

Cazden, C. *How knowledge about language helps the classroom teacher, or does it: A personal account.* Invited address, American Educational Research Association, San Francisco, 1975.

Cazden, C. Teaching as a linguistic process. In *Report of the teaching learning task force.* Washington, D.C.: National Institute of Education, 1977.

Chittenden, E., and Amarel, M. *Formulations about reading from classroom documentation.* Paper presented at the annual meeting of the American Educational Research Association, Toronto, 1978.

Conference Series No. 1. *Current directions in research on teaching.* East Lansing, Michigan: The Institute for Research on Teaching, 1977.

Cooley, W. W., and Lohnes, P. R. *Evaluation research in education.* New York: Irvington Publishers, Inc., 1976.

Cronbach, L. Beyond the two disciplines of scientific psychology. *American Psychologist,* 1975, 30, 116-127.

Cusick, P. *A study of value/belief patterns of teachers and those administrators who are engaged in attempts to influence teaching.* Proposal to Extend NIE Contract 400-76-0073. East Lansing, Michigan: Institute for Research on Teaching, Section II J, 1978.

Devault, M. L., Harnischfeger, A., and Wiley, D. *Schooling and learning opportunity—Interim report.* Chicago: CEMREL, October, 1977.

Doyle, W. Classroom research. In *Report of the teaching learning task force.* Washington, D. C.: National Institute of Education, 1977.(a)

Doyle, W. Paradigms for research on teacher effectiveness. In L. Shulman (Ed.), *Review of Research in Education* (Vol. 5). Itasca, Illinois: Peacock, 1977. (b)

Doyle, W. *Classroom ecology.* Paper presented at the annual meeting of the American Educational Research Association, Toronto, 1978. (a)

Doyle, W. *Task structures and student roles in classrooms.* Paper presented at the annual meeting of the American Educational Research Association, Toronto, 1978. (b)

Dunkin, M. S., and Biddle, B. J. *The study of teaching.* New York: Holt, Rinehart and Winston, Inc., 1974.

The effects of services on student development. Washington, D.C.: The National Institute of Education, 1977.

Eisner, Elliot. *Applying educational connoisseurship and criticism to educational settings.* A Proposal to the Spencer Foundation, 1975.

Erickson, F. *The communication of social meaning in subject matter instruction.* Paper presented at the annual meeting of the American Educational Research Association, Toronto, 1978.

Erickson, F. When is a context? Some issues and methods in the analysis of social competence. *Quarterly Newsletter of the Institute for Comparative Human Development.* The Rockefeller University, 1977, 1(2), 5-10.

Erickson, F., and Mohatt. J. *The social organization of participation structures in two classrooms of Indian students.* Paper read at American Educational Research Association, New York, 1977.

Evertson, C., Anderson, L., and Edgar, D. *Investigations of stability in junior high school math and English classes: The Texas Junior High School study.* Austin, Texas: R&D Center for Teacher Education, 1977.

Far West Laboratory for Educational Research. *Five year plan.* San Francisco, California, 1978.

Feynman, Richard P. *Commencement address.* California Institute of Technology, June, 1974.

Fisher, C. W., and Berliner, D. C. *Quasi-clinical inquiry in research on classroom teaching and learning* (BTES Technical Report). San Francisco: Far West Laboratory for Educational Research and Development, 1977.

Florio, S. *Classroom studies of the teaching and learning of writing.* Proposal to Extend NIE Contract 400-76-0073. East Lansing, Michigan: Institute for Research on Teaching, Section III L., 1978.

Gage, N. L. Paradigms for research on teaching. In N.L. Gage, (Ed.), *Handbook of research on teaching.* Chicago, Illinois: Rand McNally and Company, 1963.

Gage, N. L. Research on cognitive aspects of teaching. In *The way teaching is.* Washington, D. C.: Association for Supervision and Curriculum Development and National Education Association Center for the Study of Instruction, 1966.

Glaser, B., and Strauss, A. L. *The discovery of grounded theory: Strategies for qualitative research.* Chicago: Aldine Press, 1967.

Glendenning, L., and Porter, A. *Independence and selecting the appropriate unit of analysis.* Paper presented at the Conference on Methodology for Aggregating Data in Educational Research. Stanford, California, 1976.

Godbout, R., Marston, P. T., Borich, G., and Vaughan, C. *The problem of spurious significance in classroom education research.* Austin, Texas: The Research and Development Center for Teacher Education, 1977.

Good, T. *An examination of teachers' effects on high, middle, and low aptitude students' performance on a standardized achievement test.* To appear in *American Educational Research Journal* 1978.

Gump, P. V. *The classroom behavior setting.* Washington, D. C.: Office of Education, 1967.

Hammersley, M. The organization of pupil participation. *Sociological Review,* 1974, *22,* 355-368.

Heath, R. W., and Nielson, M. A. Performance-based teacher education. *Review of Educational Research,* 1974, *44,* 463-84.

Hymes, D. Linguistic method in ethnography. In P. Garvin (Ed.), *Method and theory in linguistics*. The Hague: Mouton, 1970, 249-311.

Hymes, D. Critique: Assessing language development—Written and/or oral. *Anthropology and Education Quarterly*, 1977, *8*(2), 91-92.

Jackson, P. W. *Life in classrooms*. New York: Holt, Rinehart and Winston, 1968.

Koehler, V. The California Beginning Teacher Evaluation Study. *Performance Based Teacher Education*, 1976, *2*(9), 8-9.

Labov, W. *The social stratification of English in New York City*. Washington, D.C.: Center for Applied Linguistics, 1966.

Lanier, J., and Shulman, L. *Institute for Research on Teaching: Technical proposal*. East Lansing, Michigan: Michigan State University, 1976.

Leinhardt, G. Applying a classroom process model to instructional evaluation. *Curriculum Inquiry*, 1978, in press.

MacDonald, F. Report on Phase II of the Beginning Teacher Evaluation Study. *Journal of Teacher Education*, 1976, *27*(1), 39-42.

MacDonald, F., and Elias, P. *Beginning Teacher Evaluation Study, Phase II Technical Summary*. Sacramento and Washington, D.C.: California Commission for Teacher Preparation and Licensing, and the National Institute of Education, 1976.

Medley, D. *Teacher competence and teacher effectiveness*. Washington, D.C.: American Association of Colleges of Teacher Education, 1977.

Mehan, H. et al. Students' interactional competence in the classroom. *Quarterly Newsletter of the Institute for Comparative Human Development*. The Rockefeller University, 1977, *1*(1).

Mehan, H. *The structure of classroom events and their consequences for students' performance*. Paper prepared for Ethnography and Education Conference. Philadelphia, Pennsylvania. Research for Better Schools and Graduate School of Education, University of Pennsylvania, 1978.

Meyer, J. W. *Levels of the educational system and schooling effects*. Chicago, Illinois: Finance and Productivity Center, 1978.

Meyer, J., Cohen, E., Brunetti, F., Molnar, S., and Salmon, E. L. The impact of the open space school upon teacher influence and autonomy: The effects of an organizational innovation (Stanford Center for Research and Development in Teaching, Technical Report No. 21). Stanford University, October 1971.

Miller, D. B. Roles of naturalistic observation in comparative psychology. *American Psychologist*, 1977, *32*(3), 211-219.

Ogden, I., Brophy, J., and Evertson, C. *An experimental investigation of organization and management techniques in first grade reading groups*. Austin, Texas: University of Texas R&D Center for Teacher Education, 1977.

Philips, S. *Acquisition of rules for appropriate speech usage*. In C. B. Cazden, et al. (Eds.), *The functions of language in the classroom*. New York: Teachers College Press, 1972.

Ponder, G., and Doyle, W. *Teacher practicality and curriculum change: An ecological analysis*. Paper presented at the meeting of the American Educational Research Association, New York, 1977.

Porter, A. C., Schmidt, W. H., Floden, R. E., and Freeman, D. J. *Impact on what? The importance of content covered* (Technical Report No. 2). East Lansing, Michigan: Institute for Research on Teaching, 1977.

Report of the teaching learning task force. Washington, D.C.: National Institute of Education, 1977.

Rosenshine, B. *Academic engaged time, content covered, and direct instruction.* Unpublished manuscript, 1978.

Rosenshine, B. The stability of teacher effects upon student achievement. *Review of Educational Research,* 1970, *40,* 647-662.

Rothkopf, E. Z. Some theoretical and experimental approaches to problems in written instruction. In J. D. Krumboltz (Ed.), *Learning and the educational process.* Chicago: Rand McNally, 1965.

Rothkopf, E. Z. Writing to teach and reading to learn. A perspective on the psychology of written instruction. In N. L. Gage (Ed.), *The psychology of teaching methods.* Seventy-fifth yearbook of the National Society for the Study of Education, Part 1. Chicago: University of Chicago Press, 1976.

Shavelson, R. What is the basic teaching skill? *Journal of Teacher Education,* 1973, *24,* 144.

Shavelson, R. Teachers' decision-making. In N. L. Gage (Ed.), *The psychology of teaching methods.* Seventy-fifth yearbook of the National Society for the Study of Education, Part 1. Chicago: University of Chicago Press, 1976.

Shavelson, R., and Dempsey, N. *Generalizability of measures of teacher effectiveness and teaching process.* (BTES, Technical Report 75-42). San Francisco: Far West Laboratory for Educational Research, 1975.

Shulman, L., and Lanier, J. The Institute for Research on Teaching: An overview. *Journal of Teacher Education,* 1976, *28*(4), 44-49.

Shuy, R., Wolfram, W., and Riley, W. K. *Field techniques in an urban language study.* Washington, D.C.: Center for Applied Linguistics, 1966.

Smith, L. M. and Schumacher, S. *Extended pilot trials of the Aesthetic Education Program: A qualitative description, analysis, and evaluation.* St. Louis: CEMREL, 1972.

Smith, L. M. Effective teaching: A qualitative inquiry in aesthetic education. *Anthropology and Education Quarterly,* 1977, *8*(2), 127-139.

Soar, R. S. *Follow Through classroom process measurement and pupil growth (1970-71). Final Report.* Gainesville: College of Education, University of Florida, 1973.

Soar, R. S. *Setting variables, classroom interaction, and multiple pupil outcomes. Final Report.* Submitted to the National Institute of Education, June, 1978.

Stallings, J. A., and Kaskowitz, D. *Follow Through observation evaluation 1972-1973.* Menlo Park, California: Stanford Research Institute, 1974.

Stallings, J., Cory, R., Fairweather, J., and Needels, M. *A study of basic reading skills taught in secondary schools.* Palo Alto, California: SRI International, 1978.

Stubbs, H. *Language, schools, and classrooms.* London: Methuen, 1976.

Teaching as clinical information processing. Panel Six of the National Conference on Studies in Teaching. Washington, D. C.: National Institute of Education, 1974.

Teaching as a linguistic process in a cultural setting. Panel Five of the National Conference on Studies in Teaching. Washington, D. C.: National Institute of Education, 1974.

Tikunoff, W. Berliner, D., and Rist, R. *An ethnographic study of the forty* classrooms of the Beginning Teacher Evaluation Study known sample (BTES Technical Report). San Francisco: Far West Laboratory for Educational Research and Development, 1976.

Tikunoff, W., and Ward, B. Effective teacher education program–Some selected findings from three studies. San Francisco: Far West Laboratory for Educational Research and Development, 1977.

Wang, M. C. Maximizing the effective use of school time by teachers and students. Paper presented at the meeting of the American Educational Research Association, San Francisco, April, 1976.

Wiley, D., and Harnischfeger, A. Research on teaching and learning: Standpoint and pointers. In Report of the teaching learning task force. Washington, D. C.: National Institute of Education, 1977.

64

Elizabeth Steiner / *A Response to Koehler*

A Platform for Research on the Teaching Process in Arts and Aesthetics

> *Knowledge enormous makes a God of me.*
> John Keats, *Hyperion*

A platform, if well constructed, is made up of planks which support our feet. And so I shall propose one for research on the teaching process in arts and aesthetics. My approach will be through the extension of V. Koehler's recommendations for a research program which in her words "fall under three broad research objectives: understanding present practices in arts instruction; determining effective processes in the instruction of the arts; and increasing emphasis placed on the arts."

In the past, the research objectives of understanding processes and of determining effective processes, as Koehler rightly notes, produce two types of studies: the descriptive, directed toward understanding teaching; and the process/product, directed toward determining effective teaching. The process/product studies dominated the field, even though problems have been associated with them. One problem that Koehler sees as inherent to process/product study arises from the assumption of "a unidirectional causal relationship: teachers' behaviors cause students to learn." Interaction, the affect of student responses upon teacher behavior, is not treated. Through a systems approach, however, such studies can be formulated within a configuration rather than an effects paradigm. G. Maccia and myself (1977) have done just that. Two problems that Koehler sees as particularly plaguing the process/product studies are developing criteria of effectiveness in the absence of an understanding of classroom realities, and studying effective teaching processes without taking into account contexts such as subject matter and grade level.

Descriptive research is seen as a solution to the problem of realistic learning goals. As Koehler says: "Learning goals must be developed in full cognizance of the realities of classroom life." What students can learn in classroom settings should be determined through naturalistic observations by researchers in collaboration with teachers. These determinations

ELIZABETH STEINER *is Professor of Philosophy and Research Methodology at the School of Education, Indiana University.*

should be the source of learning goals as criteria of effective teaching.

If effective teaching is reduced to what is feasible teaching in U.S. classrooms of the seventies, then two fallacies are committed. The first, the fallacy of schooling, makes classrooms the only teaching site. The second, the naturalistic fallacy, makes what is, what necessarily ought to be. It is patent that there are alternatives to the school setting for the teaching-studenting process. Also it is equally patent that what is possible in a given setting is not necessarily all that is possible. The *status quo* is not necessarily what is of most worth, and change in the direction of excellence is possible. Surely of such stuff are goals made. Where there are no steps, there can be no climbers. Learning goals must be developed in full cognizance of the psychical development open to any person. Plank 1 of the Platform for Research on the Teaching Process in Arts and Aesthetics, therefore, is as follows:

> *Aesthetics and Arts Educational Objectives: Do conceptual analytic studies which explicate the excellencies which are aesthetic appreciation, criticism, and production and/or performance in the arts, and psychological studies of stages in the development of these excellencies.*

This plank should provide the inquiry stand for essential knowledge as to criteria of effective teaching processes in the arts and aesthetics.

Descriptive research is also seen by Koehler as providing understanding of present practices in arts instruction: "This research will provide us with baseline information to use in considering how to change the existing system." She gives an example of finding out that elementary teachers use art as a fill-in activity, and then changing the practice so that art becomes a more structured fill-in and art is also taught with other subject matters. Obviously, descriptive research will give us essential information about the constraints which do operate upon the teaching process directed toward the excellencies which are aesthetic appreciation, criticism, and production and/or performance in the arts. Having to fill-in is one such constraint, and one that is as intolerable in the arts as it is in any subject matter so central to our psychical development. This constraint must be done in. Yet descriptive research cannot be of help in effecting the change. Only experimental research can, for it gives ways of loosening constraints through knowledge of the interdependence of factors.

Descriptive research, of course, can accomplish more than information of constraints; it can provide knowledge of significant factors or properties of processes. This natural history stage of research has long been recognized in other fields, but neglected in the study of the teaching process and recently rediscovered and rechristened—'ecological,' 'ethnographic,' 'qualitative,' 'naturalistic,' 'anthropological,' and so on. Take your pick of name. Since an aesthetics and arts teaching-studenting process (AE) includes at least one aesthetics and arts teacher (AT), at least one aesthetics and arts student (AS), aesthetics and arts to be taught and learned (AC), and a setting (G), what is required is to form general ideas representing the instances of AT, AS, AC, and G so that the general ideas constitute exclusive classes which are exhaustive of the teaching-studenting process in arts and aesthetics education. The upper portion of the map of aesthetics and arts educology (*Figure 1*) depicts in set theoretic notation the schema for the descriptive portion of knowledge of aesthetics and arts education. Plank 2 of the Platform for Research on the Teaching Process in Arts and Aesthetics can now be stated:

> *Descriptive Research on the Teaching Process in Arts and Aesthetics: Do descriptive studies to provide information about constraints and to provide knowledge about significant factors of the teaching process in arts and aesthetics.*

Figure 1

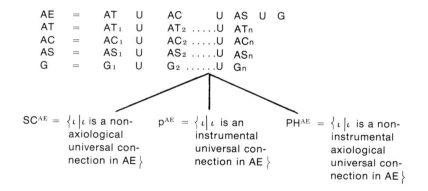

$$AE = AT \cup AC \cup AS \cup G$$
$$AT = AT_1 \cup AT_2 \ldots \cup AT_n$$
$$AC = AC_1 \cup AC_2 \ldots \cup AC_n$$
$$AS = AS_1 \cup AS_2 \ldots \cup AS_n$$
$$G = G_1 \cup G_2 \ldots \cup G_n$$

$SC^{AE} = \{\iota | \iota$ is a non-axiological universal connection in AE $\}$

$p^{AE} = \{\iota | \iota$ is an instrumental universal connection in AE $\}$

$PH^{AE} = \{\iota | \iota$ is a non-instrumental axiological universal connection in AE $\}$

'AE'	stands for aesthetics and arts education
'AT'	stands for aesthetics and arts teacher
''AC'	stands for aesthetics and arts to be taught and learned
'AS'	stands for aesthetics and arts student
'G'	stands for setting
'SC^{AE}'	stands for science of aesthetics and arts education
'p^{AE}'	stands for praxiology of aesthetics and arts education
'PH^{AE}'	stands for philosophy of aesthetics and arts education

This plank should provide baseline information as well as essential knowledge of factors needed to move to relational studies.

Among the relational studies, Koehler recognizes those that function to determine effective processes in the instruction of the arts. She states the needs in this area as

- Process/product studies in secondary schools.
- Experimental studies that test correlational findings in the process/ product studies.
- Small case studies of elementary school teachers who are reputed to "be creative" in teaching the arts, and teachers who are known to integrate the arts into other subject matters.

Because most process/product studies were conducted in elementary schools, Koehler's call for studies in secondary schools is on target. But, even though consideration be extended to schools at various levels, this would not suffice. In the light of the schooling fallacy discussed earlier in this response, consideration must extend beyond school settings. Koehler's statement of the second need also hits the mark. Knowledge of associations between factors is not enough. We need to know how factors depend upon one another. Experiments are called for. Through reference to case studies of not just teachers but teachers of arts, Koehler points to the inclusion of content factors, the subject matter of the arts, in relational studies of effective teaching in aesthetics and arts. I should think, however, that small case studies would be of more use in descriptive studies.

Provided process/product studies of effective teaching include setting and content factors, as well as teacher and student factors, and provided they are experimental and configural, these studies could give us knowledge of instrumental universal connections in aesthetics and arts education. That is to say, what could be made available to us are principles for organizing the behavior of aesthetics and arts teachers and students, the subject matter of aesthetics and arts, and the setting as effective means to bring about the ends of aesthetic appreciation, criticism, and production and/or performance in the arts. Nevertheless, to stop with relational studies that are praxiological is to commit the fallacy of practical discipline; that is, that a discipline consists only of principles of effective processes or practices. Theoretical aesthetics and arts educology, or principles of aesthetics and arts education, consists not only of praxiology of aesthetics and arts education but also of science and philosophy of aesthetics and arts education. Two more kinds of relational studies need to be conducted.

Scientific relational studies are non-axiological insofar as the dependencies of factors are studied without reference to instrumental or inherent value of any factor. A major difficulty with praxiological studies of teaching has been conducting them without understanding how teacher, student, content, and setting factors interrelate. Such understanding is a requirement if one is to study the effective organization of teaching-studenting factors. Scientific studies provide such understanding through establishing universal non-axiological connections between factors.

Philosophical relational studies are axiological for they study the inherent value of factors. Of course, it is not enough to study factors from an instrumental standpoint. The ends toward which the means are directed must be justified. Principles of worthwhileness with respect to the aesthetics and arts teaching-studenting process, universal non-instrumental axiological connections in aesthetics and art education, must be established. For example, aesthetic appreciation, criticism, and production and/or performance in the arts must be justified as human excellencies to be developed through the aesthetics and arts teaching process.

It follows from what has been stated above that Plank 3 of the Platform for Research on the Teaching Process in Arts and Aesthetics is

Explanatory Research on the Teaching Process in Arts and Aesthetics: Do scientific studies of how factors of the teaching process in arts and aesthetics are interrelated, praxiological studies of how these factors can be organized effectively, and philosophical studies of the worthwhileness of the factors.

This plank should provide the inquiry stand for knowledge of principles of aesthetics and arts education, that is, scientific, praxiological, and philosophical principles of the teaching-studenting process in arts and aesthetics.

V. Koehler's final recommendation to increase the emphasis placed on the arts is not taken by her to be a recommendation for research. She recognizes that "research cannot change the relative emphasis which our school system places on the arts." And surely she is right. Also she is right when she states that "these changes must come through changing the attitudes of the public toward the arts in our schools." She goes on to place the locus of change of attitude in political processes. But consider the fallacy of public power which takes the locus of power to be public not private. Political forces, not psychical forces formed through education, are erroneously taken to be the primary factors. Is it not the case that education can change attitudes and so affect political processes? An affirmative answer leads to Plank 4 of the Platform for Research on the Teaching Process in Arts and Aesthetics:

Research on Aesthetics and Arts Education of Adults: Do descriptive and explanatory studies of the teaching process in arts and aesthetics in which the student is an adult.

This plank should provide an inquiry stand to develop a knowledge base for educating adults in aesthetics and arts and thereby changing their attitudes. Who could but support that which is found to bring the highest quality to each moment as it passes?

Bloomington, Indiana
July 1976

REFERENCES

Maccia, G., and Steiner, E. *Uses of SIGGS in educational research.* Paper presented at the annual meeting of the American Educational Research Association, New York City, April 1977.

Anne M. Bussis,
Edward A. Chittenden, and Marianne Amarel

Collaborative Research*

The term "collaborative research" in this paper refers to the central involvement of practitioners in all phases of a research study—from planning and instrument development through data collection and analysis.

It should be noted at the outset that the ETS collaborative study is not unique in seeking a more substantial role for teachers in research. A number of investigators have recently come to view the teacher as a critical source of knowledge about classrooms and instruction and have engaged the practitioner's active cooperation in their research in order to tap that knowledge (for example, Doyle, 1977b; Lortie, 1975). Another research strand enlisting practitioner assistance has emphasized the decision-making process in instruction and has sought to map out different teacher perspectives on the nature of curriculum and children's learning (for example, Bussis, Chittenden, and Amarel, 1976; Shulman, 1977). Other researchers have involved the teacher extensively in exploring the potential of ethnographic techniques (for example, Florio and Walsh, 1976); and still others have undertaken a direct study of the effects of research participation on teachers (Kennedy, 1977; Tikunoff, Ward, and Stacy, 1977).

Collaboration as conceived here differs somewhat in both form and intent from the studies mentioned above, being closer to a research strategy advocated by Hawkins (1966). Drawing on precedents in the history of physical science, Hawkins argues that the psychologist interested in children's learning would do well to seek out experienced

ANNE M. BUSSIS, EDWARD A. CHITTENDEN, and MARIANNE AMAREL are research psychologists who constitute the professional staff of the Early Education Group at Educational Testing Service in Princeton, New Jersey.

*Portions of this article are planned for inclusion in forthcoming publications describing the ETS Collaborative Research Project on Reading.

teachers and vigorous learning situations. Thus, the collaborative research described here has been undertaken not for its own sake or for the primary purpose of studying teachers and teaching, but in the interest of studying children's learning. More specifically, the background for this paper is three years of classroom-based research (still continuing) that has focused on the ways that children enter into the skill of beginning reading and progress toward reading proficiency. Although "reading" is therefore a specific referent in much of the discussion that follows, the general methodological considerations are applicable to virtually all areas of school learning.

This paper is organized in two sections, dealing first with the methodology and then with its results. Part One begins with some basic premises and narrows to a rationale for the research and a description of the study. Part Two addresses the nature of the research outcomes of the study (what we are beginning to find out about learning to read) as well as outcomes that pertain to collaborating practitioners (what we are beginning to discover about professional development by doing the research).

Part One: Rationale and Description

Space limitations prohibit a full discussion and justification of the basic philosophical premises we hold. Nonetheless we will state those premises and go on to discuss the research rationale we have derived from them.

Premise 1. Learning is an active and constructive process. All learners (including children learning how to read) actively select, interpret, shape, and integrate the "facts" of the world they encounter so as to construct a working knowledge of that world.

Premise 2. Human beings strive above all else to make sense of experience—to make it as meaningful and purposeful as possible. In the former instance (making experience meaningful), we tend to think of interpretative processes that construe information in ways that are sensible to the person. In the latter case (making experience purposeful), we tend to think of expressive processes by which people convey their meaning and intention to themselves and to others. Whatever way one thinks of it, making sense and stating sense (meaningful interpretation and intentional expression) are two sides of the same coin.

Premise 3. The theoretical aims of educational research are best served at this point in time by descriptive data that capture the full complexity of learning phenomena as faithfully as possible.

These premises have led us to further assumptions and methodological decisions about how to study children learning to read. As mentioned previously, we believe these conclusions would hold for the study of children's learning in other school areas as well. On the other hand, they are not the only set of inferences that could reasonably be drawn from our philosophical position. Other colleagues who share our basic premises are engaged in different (though compatible and often complementary) forms of research.

Learning to read, in the literal sense of acquiring the mechanics and technical skill, is best understood when placed within the broader framework of the child's understandings, intentions, and styles of functioning. Seen in this light, learning to read is subsumed in the more comprehensive process of becoming a reader—a process that begins well before the child's entry into first grade and continues long thereafter. Such a view raises questions about multiple routes to reading acquisition and about the different meanings reading may hold. Do different understandings and intentions lead to different strategies of mastery? What purposes of the child does reading serve? How is learning to read connected to other interests and expressive style? Stated another way: We assume that the child's overall functioning will influence to a large extent how and when (and, in some classrooms, whether) the transition through meaningful decoding to reading is accomplished.

These assumptions about learning to read imply a research focus on the reader as opposed to a focus on skills that readers acquire. There are several methodological consequences of this. A study of readers (in contrast to reading skills) suggests the need for documentation of evidence of a child's interests, styles, and strategies. It requires a study over time so that patterns of change may emerge from the documentation and the relationship of reading to the broader purposes of the reader may become evident. A focus on the reader also calls for intensive study of relatively few learners in contrast to gathering limited data on a great many children.

In short, attention to readers means a case history approach. Thus, the first and foremost objective of our research is to construct carefully documented case histories of individual children's classroom learning over time. Such histories are rare (if not totally absent) in the research literature on reading,[1] and, as far as we can ascertain, this is also true of educational research on teaching and learning in general. This is not to say that naturalistic case history approaches are an anomaly in all of psychology or in related research areas. They have long been utilized to good advantage in comparative and clinical psychology, anthropology, sociology, linguistics, and medicine; they have been advocated for more general use in psychological research (for example, Stake, 1978; Willems and Raush, 1969); and they are now the rule rather than the exception in the new fields of sociolinguistics, ethnography, and ethnomethodology (for example, Doyle, 1977a and b; Erickson, 1977; Garfinkel, 1967; Mehan, 1974). With some important exceptions (Labov, 1977), however, the majority of case history work has focused on classrooms or other socially defined groups such as institutions and speech communities as the unit of analysis. We believe there exists a complementary need to study the individual learner.

Our long-range aim in constructing case histories is the advancement of theoretical formulations about learning to read. Detailed examination and comparison of even a few histories reap an interesting yield of observations and hypotheses that can be checked further in the documentary records of other children. This type of exercise has already produced some tentative formulations that we have begun to share with researchers and practitioners outside of the study. Equally important, formal dissemination of case histories will provide public access to descriptive information that can then be reexamined by others. The potential significance of minimally reduced records and case histories as "data banks" in the social sciences is only beginning to be acknowledged (Bloom, 1974; Stake, 1978) and has yet to be realized.

There is an additional advantage that should be mentioned as a footnote to the approach we have chosen. Carefully abridged case histories are a powerful medium for communicating research results in a manner that extends understanding. Stake (1978) is explicit on this score:

> If the readers of our reports are the persons who populate our houses, schools, governments, and industries; and if we are to help them understand social problems and social programs, we must perceive and communicate . . . in a way that accommodates their present understandings. Those people have arrived at their understandings mostly through direct and vicarious experience. . . . one of the more effective means of adding to understandings for all readers will be by approximating through the words and illustrations of our reports, the natural experience acquired in ordinary personal involvement.

What we have said about person-oriented research (about studying the meanings and intentions of readers rather than reading skills) implies another methodological decision of consequence. Such research is optimally carried out in settings where the constructs and qualities that mediate children's learning are considered instructionally relevant and are accessible to observation and documentation. The classrooms we have selected for the study fit this description. Collaborating teachers provide room and reason for choice on the child's part and use information about children's choices as a basis for instructional decisions. Observation is therefore not an academic or research exercise for these teachers; it lies at the heart of their professional practice.

A final set of inferences constitutes our rationale for deciding on a collaborative mode of work. Individual-oriented research requires not only study over time but study over contexts in order for patterns and continuities to emerge. As the person who is in contact with children regularly, over developmentally significant periods of time, and across a variety of classroom and school contexts, the teacher clearly has the best opportunity to discern the meanings and intentions which children in the interactive dialogue of learning impose on an instructional environment.

Moreover, the relationship that obtains between teacher and children in a classroom is of a special order, akin to a tacit social contract in which certain expectations and privileges are implicitly understood and acknowledged by all parties (child, teacher, parents, school officials, and community at large). This special relationship allows the teacher to participate in children's learning and to come to understand their constructs in a manner barred to most other adults. For these reasons we see the teacher's perspective as categorically different from that of the external observer, who (no matter how astute or effective in building rapport) necessarily remains an "outsider" without full access to the participatory relationship with children or the contextually embedded meanings of classroom life.

The outsider, of course, brings other strengths that must be capitalized on if research is to yield a balanced perspective. The very nature of the teacher's participatory relationship can close off other views of the child that must be tapped for a multidimensional portrait. In addition, we need to consider the relatively direct and unfiltered statements of meaning that are reflected in the child's work—in drawing, writing, painting, oral reading, work sheets, and the like. These, too, need to be considered from many perspectives.

The assertions we have just made rest, in turn, on the proposition that the best "instrument" for *registering* human meaning and intent is an "instrument" that can *recognize* meaning and intent: namely, another human being. Similarly, we posit that the best way to correct for the error and fallibility of any one person is to include several viewpoints in research. Such inferences recommend a method of team collaboration in the study of children's classroom learning. Our study has used both the case history approach and this kind of collaborative methodology.

The ETS Collaborative Research Project on Reading

The collaborative study was officially launched in the summer of 1975 when we met with a group of practitioners (classroom teachers and advisors affiliated with teacher centers) for a two-week planning conference. The purpose of this meeting was to review the rationale of the project and to draft procedures for data collection and analysis. One major outcome of the conference was a plan for data collection organized around a team of three persons: a classroom teacher, an advisor who filled the role of an outside observer, and an ETS researcher. During the ensuing eighteen months, each team was to follow and document the learning progress of one or two children in the teacher's classroom.

A second major outcome of the meeting was the construction of guidelines for an interviewing process that was to become the principal means for obtaining the teacher's observations of each child in the study. We wanted to tap the kind of information that teachers acquire in the normal course of everyday classroom life, but we needed a method that would not be burdensome or interfere with ordinary instruction. We needed a systematic but unintrusive procedure. The solution resulting from the conference was a particular form of interview, something like a debriefing process, that we labeled a "Descriptive Interview." The meeting also produced a set of tentative guidelines for other major forms of data collection that are described below.

Data collection per se started in September 1975 and extended through January of 1977, covering approximately one-and-a-half school years. The majority of children were in the first or second grade when the study began and in second or third grade when data collection was suspended. To ensure continuity in this process, either teachers who participated in Year 1 of the study had combination classes (that is, 1-2, 2-3) and thus retained the children for two years; or teachers from a given school taught adjoining grades, so that the children passed from the classroom of one collaborator to another.

The majority of teachers and children were from schools located in large cities (New York City, Philadelphia) and serving neighborhoods of mixed (low and middle) income families. The remaining teachers and children were from communities in Paterson, New Jersey; Hartsdale, New York; New Rochelle, New York; and Bennington, Vermont. The study began with 37 teachers, 18 field-based observers (advisers), and 58 children. Due to staff and funding limitations, however, we continued really intensive work with approximately half that number as time progressed.

From March 1977 to the present, collaborators in the study have been working primarily on data analysis and integration.[2] At this point in time, then, both the data collection and the data analysis/integration procedures described below have been thoroughly field-tested and refined.

The Descriptive Interview. At regular intervals throughout the year, the research member of the team interviewed the teacher in order to gain access to the teacher's observations of a child over the preceding weeks. Guidelines for the interview helped both teacher and researcher organize these observations. Specifically, the guidelines draw attention to six general areas of the child's functioning (physical presence, relationship to others, emotional style, interests/themes, involvement, progress in school-related work other than reading) and to qualities that are more specifically related to language use and reading (listening patterns; general reading patterns; differential use of language in different settings; play with sounds or words; use of language as expression of self; relationship between drawing, writing, and story-telling; strategies of word identification; strategies for identifying meaning in context). Preparation for the interview on the teacher's part included reviewing the guidelines, organizing anecdotal notes or other forms of records that had been made, and identifying work samples that were particularly illustrative or revealing of the child.

Each interview began in an open-ended manner, with a request for information and/or impressions that were uppermost in the teacher's mind—things that seemed the most important or salient about the child at that moment. The interview then moved to other content in accordance with the guidelines. Since a single interview did not cover all topics in the guidelines, successive interviews built cumulatively. The role of the interviewer was to keep the guidelines in focus and to elicit (when necessary) specific descriptions, examples, and other low-inference information supportive of the teacher's observations and judgments. On the whole, however, teachers were fairly faithful in adhering to the overarching guidelines of making their observations as specific and descriptive as possible. The interviewer was also responsible for preparing a written report on each interview that became part of the child's documentary record. The interviews were tape-recorded and lasted approximately sixty minutes per child.

Observer's Narrative Records. Systematic observations of each child were also made by the observer member of the team. For the most part, these observations followed the form of "specimen descriptions" (Wright, 1960) and resulted in a narrative record of the child's activities over a ten to twenty minute period. In some cases, however, the observations took the form of a tape-recorded conversation with the child about some focused topic (for example, a book the child had read). Because we were primarily experimenting with the nature and form of this type of data collection, the frequency of observations varied from a minimum of two to a maximum of ten. The experience we have now gained suggests an optimal pattern of four classroom visits a year, with the observer making two to four observations per visit.

Work Samples. Samples or copies of work that were judged to be typical or particularly illustrative of the child's functioning were collected by teachers throughout the study. These were primarily examples of writing, drawing, painting, and worksheets, but also included photographs of three-dimensional constructions when these were a prominent part of the child's activity and interest. Teachers provided information about the context of the work, when and how it was undertaken, and the extent to which it was assigned or self-initiated. Although we sampled across all modes of work, a more extensive cumulative record was obtained for any medium (for example, writing or drawing) that was clearly preferred by the child.

Oral Reading Samples. Tape-recorded samples of the child reading aloud were obtained by teachers (and, on some occasions, by observers) at periodic intervals. In accordance with guidelines, teachers selected texts that varied in difficulty and in degree of familiarity to the child. Certain linguistic or phonic texts—with their highly constrained vocabulary and syntax—were included to contrast with conventional basal readers and typical children's story books; and some samples included a selection that was chosen by the child (for example, a story he or she had written or some favorite type of book or comic). Teachers added their own comments to the tape regarding the background of the material as well as their analysis of the child's approach to it. In addition, the research staff undertook miscue (error) analyses on a subset of the taped selections.

Assessment Tasks. Although oral reading served as the primary source of evidence regarding the child's progress, tasks of a more test-like nature were also administered by the research member of the team. These procedures were designed to tap specific understandings that are generally regarded to be supporting skills to the total process of reading such as word identification strategies and linguistic understanding.

Data Analysis and Integration. Although the various kinds of data mentioned above were periodically summarized for each child during the course of data collection, they needed systematic integration. Data analysis in this research, then, has really meant the integration of large amounts of descriptive information in an attempt to embed reading in the context of a particular person who is reading. It has meant highlighting the essential coherence of child-as-reader and child-as-intender. Our methods for achieving this are based on a process developed by Pat Carini (1975) and staff of The Prospect School in Bennington,Vermont. Since this process was initially developed for purposes of helping teachers and has been used extensively in that manner, it is intelligible and makes intuitive sense to most practitioners. At present, we are in the midst of adapting and articulating the process for general research purposes. Although space constraints prohibit a full discussion of the underlying rationale of the methodology, we can point to a few distinctive characteristics of the process.

First, the maintenance of original documentation records is critical to the methodology because all inferences are explicitly grounded in data. This is a cardinal rule of the procedure. A second rule specifies that interpretive statements be descriptive of the child's functioning (that is, manner of work, patterns of interest) rather than causal explanations of behavior. Since the purpose of data integration is to place reading in the context of a particular reader, it seeks to identify major continuities (thematic qualities) that inhere in the data across time, settings, and expressive media. The analysis also attends to evidence of counter-balancing themes and contrasting qualities. A third rule of restraint follows from these premises and cautions against the premature interpretation of any single characteristic as either a "strength" or "weakness." (The quality of quickness, for example, is not automatically assumed to be positive and strengthening nor the quality of dependency to be altogether limiting.) A particular characteristic gains meaning only when viewed within the full context of descriptive information.

By definition this type of analytic procedure cannot employ category systems that serve to circumscribe certain data and exclude others. To the contrary, data are classified and reclassified a number of times under different organizers or headings, with the specific proviso that a single datum be placed under as many headings as are appropriate. Such an organizing scheme entails the deliberate and systematic shifting of perspectives on data and implies the philosophical assumption that phenomena are knowable in infinite ways. From a practical standpoint, the process leads to the accruement of related elements within headings and of identical elements across headings. Thus, it builds patterns that reveal the interlocking themes which integrate the data.

Logistically, data analysis is accomplished by small groups of collaborators at an extended meeting of two or three days. The group is comprised of five to seven people and includes the three-person team (teacher-observer-ETS staff member) that originally collected the data in question. Materials are sent to all participants for thorough review in advance of the meeting. These materials include: (a) a complete report of all Descriptive Interviews and narrative observations; (b) a composite oral-reading tape (forty-five minutes in length) with portions of selections from each oral reading session; (c) a selection of work samples (xeroxed writing and drawing, color slides of paintings, and pictures of three-dimensional constructions if these figure prominently in the child's activities); and (d) quantitative results together with protocols or reports from the assessment tasks. The full range of original documentary records is available for examination at the meeting.

The group work proceeds in "rounds" that alternate between analysis of observational data (statements about the child) and analysis of work samples and assessment tasks (direct statements by the child). Meetings are conducted by a chairperson who ensures adherence to the specified rules and periodically summarizes the group's conclusions. Once the data are analyzed and major integrating themes identified, a detailed case history or a briefer portrayal of the child is written.

Part Two: Results of the Methodology

Only two of many results emanating from the collaborative research project will be discussed here: outcomes of the data integration process and the implications of collaboration for practitioners.

Outcomes of Data Integration

Presentation of a fully documented case history is beyond the scope and purpose of this paper. The audience for such detail would be educators and researchers specifically concerned with the teaching and/or theory of reading. In lieu of this, condensed write-ups will serve to illustrate the essential nature of this outcome. The first child we have chosen for presentation is relatively "simple" to follow to the extent that her overriding preoccupations in first grade were with reading and writing. The connections between these two realms, on the other hand, were anything but simple. We have added a few comments at the end of the write-up to point up some specific questions and issues that Jenny's case history brings to light.

JENNY

Jenny was the youngest child of the entering first-grade class, with her sixth birthday falling late in September. Her social immaturity relative to the other children was partially masked during the year by her serious, determined manner (which her teacher initially equated with independence) and by her rapid development of reading ability. Although a reserved child in many respects, Jenny was desirous of adult attention and showed a pronounced interest in reading and writing at the very beginning of the year. Throughout the fall months, these interests were expressed in much quasi-reading and quasi-writing. The teacher chose Jenny for the study because she so clearly exemplified this "as if" approach to reading displayed by many children.

Jenny often elected to read during a "choice" period in the afternoon, after her academic work was finished. She would completely memorize a book or else would fill in part of the story line from pictures and then "read" it to the teacher, refusing any help with words and insisting that she could actually read. One impromptu oral reading sample of this nature attests to her persistence despite noise and interruptions from other children. As the teacher reported it in October:

> She almost gets "insulted" when I tell her a word she can't read. She'll say "I know"—even when she's just misread it and I've just corrected it. She really thinks she can read . . . is very determined about this.

The earliest books she memorized were books from home. Later, in November, she began to memorize books at the Listening Center by following the text as she listened to the tape. When reading these books to the teacher, she would imitate the tape exactly—even to the point of pausing to hum for the music! In all of this "reading," however, Jenny could never recognize a word in isolation (when the teacher wrote it down) or pick out a particular word on the page. An especially striking instance of her memorized, "quasi-reading" ability and general approach to books is contained in the following observation.

> When she sits down with a new book, she only looks at pictures and doesn't try to explore the text. She looks at these books from

back to front. But in the books she has memorized and "reads," she never looks at text from back to front. Also, she doesn't point to words when she "reads."

Recently, she brought in a very complex book (*The Magic Wallpaper*) that had been read to her at home; it's a book about animals in wallpaper that talk. There were almost 200 words on the first page and she had it all memorized—complex words and structures like:

> and Jimmy asked, "May I see the wallpaper now before you unroll it?" Father said, "No you may not because the only way to see it properly is up on the wall."

She had this down exactly! She got bogged down in the middle of the book, but got almost 99% of the words at the beginning—just missed a few—and knew where one page ended and the next started. But she couldn't point to any word that I asked about—like, "Which word is giraffe?" When I later read the book to the class (because I thought it was a good story), she mouthed the words along with me.

By mid-November, Jenny could recognize two book titles in isolation: *The Gingerbread Boy* and *Three Billy Goats Gruff*.

Although Jenny never approached math in a "quasi" fashion, her writing showed the same tendency. She would experiment with it endlessly, with much erasing and rewriting so that the end result always looked extremely messy. In the teacher's words (from the Descriptive Interviews):

October	Jenny is interested in collecting words. She often just writes lists of words in a random pattern and doesn't put them in sentences.
October	Her handwriting and copying are fairly immature and hard to recognize. She has little sense of copying letters in order, but *she* can read back what it says.
November	Lots and lots of writing letters. Her drawings are getting more and more covered with letters. They're random for the most part, but sometimes *MOM* or *POP* will appear. She did a lot at the beginning of the year, but does even more now.
November	Handwriting is still poor . . . doesn't have a sense of individual words. She will leave no spaces between words, and then at times leave gigantic spaces between letters.
November	Doesn't have the sense of what a sentence is in diary writing. She'll write *POP POP* and call it a sentence.

When I ask her if she wants to write something more (approximating a sentence), she'll usually dictate something and I'll write it down. Then she copies it.

November   Also copies words from her dictionary into her diary, unattached to anything else.

November   Jenny is very disorganized about paper work in general. It ends up looking a mess. Lots of scribbles, erasures, writing all over the paper so you can barely see what's there. Her diary is typical of this . . . it's a disaster area!

Jenny's writing also showed signs of a potential problem reader: many letter and number reversals, mirror writing, right-to-left writing, and writing from the back to the front of her diary. Although her teacher never expressed concern about these signs, the fact that Jenny is left-handed added the last ingredient to an almost "textbook case." To illustrate this quality of her writing, the sentence below was written on a crayoned design that Jenny handed to the teacher. When asked what it said, Jenny replied, "Samantha is my favorite friend."

$$N a i Y T e \vee F i$$
$$M \ zi \ at \ h \ a M a 2 \quad (\leftarrow\text{begin here})$$

Along with these mechanical writing problems, Jenny also experimented with invented spellings. Most children invent some spellings in their beginning years of writing, but Jenny was preoccupied with the construction of a spelling system. The study team became increasingly interested as her inventions began to include many features discussed by Charles Read (1971) in his investigation of the subject.

In addition to reading and writing, other dominant themes that characterized Jenny in the fall and throughout the year were her love of the classroom animals (she would fondle them, talk to them in imaginary ·play, even read to them) and her intense interest in "messing about" with wax, paint, and weaving. She rarely tried to produce realistic or representational products in these media, but would experiment with various processes the media offered—color mixing, design, and the changing of shapes and textures. As with her writing, the end result of this experimentation looked messy and slip-shod and failed to reflect the resolve with which she undertook these efforts.

Because of the difficulties in letter and word orientation, the teacher did not begin formal reading instruction with Jenny in the fall. In December, she said she would continue to forgo formal instruction for a while to see how the writing and invented spelling progressed. By mid-January, however, Jenny had learned to read the first six word-lists in the beginning basal reader on her own, and she asked to start instruction.

By the end of January, Jenny knew all of the words in the first basal reader and had gone through two-thirds of the accompanying workbook. Unlike other, more deliberate children, Jenny's early reading was marked by much guessing, an exaggerated sounding-out strategy, and the production of ungrammatical errors (*his, hats* for *has*; *bag* for *dig*) as well as non-word errors (*nout, noup* for *not*; *diz, daz* for *dad's*). It is interesting that she only made such errors in the linguistic texts. When reading other stories, her errors were usually gramatically constrained and made sense. Jenny also concentrated so much on the words themselves (attempting to self-correct almost every mistake) that she sometimes did not know the meaning of what she read.

After Jenny finished the Level B SRA book, the teacher had planned to start her in another basal series to abate the pronounced sounding-out. At the end of February, however, Jenny suddenly became quieter, she stopped drawing altogether for a period of time, and her confidence seemed temporarily shaken. The teacher then offered her a choice between the Level C SRA, a Bank Street book, and an easier book in the Cambridge series. Jenny chose to stay with the SRA; and since the teacher judged that she was not "trapped" in the peculiar syntax and pattern words of the linguistic readers, she decided not to force a change at that time.

By early May, Jenny had gone through Level D of the SRA series and had exhausted much of the fiction in the room. By June she was able to read from the *Little House on the Prairie* series and to understand what she read, though the books themselves were too long for her to read in their entirety. The exaggerated phonic strategy had faded and she made few nonsensical mistakes. But her decoding skill was still ahead of her ability to demonstrate comprehension in workbook exercises. In June, the teacher reported the following example: The two alternatives given to the statement "I have the———: we need it to fish" were *wait* and *bait*. Jenny circled *wait* in the workbook, although she knew in discussing the sentence that *bait* was the appropriate word. The teacher attributed her difficulty to the fact that she was still young and somewhat "scattered."

> I don't think she's zeroed in yet on work involving pencil and paper. Everything on paper is still very messy.
> She's verging on being an independent reader, but I think she still needs a lot of support. Emotional support as well as corrective support . . . like when she is *sure* she knows a word and it's wrong.
> Also not very independent in the sense that she can finish a

piece of work and go on to the next thing. She constantly needs a lot of feedback and checking with me.

Interestingly, Jenny's invented spellings and inconsistent reversals continued throughout the year, even as she made rapid progress in reading. The following entries from her March diary illustrate this:

I LIKE TO ƇUPROP
(I like to jump rope)

JORDAN THIW HIS ERREƆ DAWN THE SWR
(Jordon threw his orange down the sewer)

I LIK TO ƬA
(I like to draw)

During the second grade, Jenny's progress in reading continued and she began to show a much firmer grasp of what she had read. In dealing with difficult text, she would either make sensible substitutions or simply gloss over it to retain meaning. And, like adult readers, she became more discriminating in her self-corrections. Whereas in the first grade she corrected most mistakes, she graduallly began to correct only those errors that eventually violated meaning. Also, Jenny seemed as if she were tuning out on herself and no longer listening to her own reading. Thus, pronouncing a nonword no longer served as a cue that she had made a mistake, as saying *nout* for *not* once had. In one oral reading session taped early in the second grade, for example, Jenny read the sentence "James *ussed* to be my friend." When the teacher interrupted to ask if that made sense, Jenny seemed not to understand the question until the teacher explicitly pointed out that she had said "*ussed* to be my friend" rather than "*used* to be my friend." Similarly, in her last taped oral reading, made in March of the second grade, she read a section from *Stuart Little* with considerable expression; but in a descriptive passage contained in the text she mispronounced two or three words and "swallowed" some others (like "sarsaparilla") without its ever interfering with the general flow or intelligibility of her reading. In fact, while Jenny sounded very much like a proficient reader on her last tape, strict adherence to the criterion that every single word must be accurate would make it appear as if she had regressed.

One final observation about Jenny. For all her reading progress, her writing remained much the same, with only minimal accommodations to convention. By the end of the study, her teacher had tried just about every corrective support she could think of with little success and was literally at an impasse. For Jenny, at least, reading and writing appear to be separate systems—both differentiated, to be sure, but differentiated according to unrelated rule systems.

Jenny's case speaks to theoretical issues in some obvious places—her motor difficulties in writing (that may, in another school, have classified her as a learning disability); her invented spelling; her switching of strategies with different kinds of text (linguistic or regular); her changing configuration of errors as she became a proficient reader. Other aspects of her reading behavior are largely unaddressed in the literature—her intent and determination in quasi-reading, for example.

The same could be said for most of the children in the study. Some of their behaviors could be related to a variety of theoretical issues and some could not. Of the many behaviors unrelated to existing literature, one pattern stands out as central to us—both because it was a finding that held for most of the children and because of the significance we attach to it. It was a general consistency between a child's early forays into reading—the style that characterized the approach—and his or her entry into other learning areas within the classroom. In Jenny's case this style was one of process orientation and a "let's pretend" attitude. In wax, painting, and weaving—as in writing—Jenny would experiment for long periods of time, never making representational products in these media but "messing about" with various processes the media offered (color mixing, design, and the changing of shapes and textures). Similarly, her "let's pretend" proclivity was as evident in her many imaginary conversations with the guinea pigs as it was in her quasi-reading. Usually, an elaborated case history would be written to highlight these interconnecting patterns of style and meaning within the learner that the data integration process uncovers.

Another purpose of the histories (and one that can reasonably be served by condensed write-ups) is to underscore the fact that substantial differences exist between children in their approach to reading. The following thumbnail sketch of Josh, another first-grade child, is therefore included as a contrast to Jenny.

JOSH

Josh's early writing and drawing attempts resembled those of a much younger child, and they suggested immature motor development. His drawings of people, in particular, were no more advanced than squiggly lines and tentative oval shapes, with little if any detail. This immaturity was coupled with some babyishness of behavior—but both characteristics were in marked contrast to his general verbal facility. Not only did Josh talk a lot (occasionally "too much"), he was capable of expressing sophisticated thoughts in precise language. And when precise language eluded him, he would create metaphors ("distance heat" for thermometer), would coin a phrase ("super uncalm"), or else would explicitly point out that he didn't know how to say what was on his mind.

During the fall months, Josh became more mature in his general behavior, but he made no ostensible progress in reading and very little progress with his writing. The teacher did not push reading with him during these early months, and he showed absolutely no desire to start learning how to read. His only formal classroom exposure to written language, therefore, was the writing that all children were required to do each day. Since the mechanics of this were very difficult for Josh, he wrote only the minimum amount of one or two sentences. Informally, he may also have encountered some text while looking at picture books during Sustained Silent Reading time, and he was indirectly exposed to many words that the teacher wrote on the board. These might be words from a class discussion, words the children wanted to know how to spell for their writing, or rhyming words that the children thought up as a game (an activity that Josh enjoyed very much).

Early in December, Josh surprised both his parents and his teacher by reading *Put Me in the Zoo,* a rhyming book in which he apparently had been practicing. According to his parents' report to the teacher, he said he had taught himself to read and had been "keeping it a secret." The teacher immediately taped an interview with Josh in which he read from his book and discussed the story with understanding. From this first oral reading sample, it was evident that Josh had an extensive vocabulary and a lot of information to bring to stories.

Although Josh started to make progress in the Dr. Seuss books, he soon reached a plateau where he stayed for the rest of the year, and he never demonstrated any particular enthusiasm for reading. The only exception to this was his excitement over a book of homonyms that the teacher read with him—an excitement reflecting his general interest and facility in oral language. The various assessment procedures administered in the spring rounded out a consistent picture. Josh did extremely well on the measures of linguistic knowledge and awareness, showing more advanced development than many of the older children in the study. On tasks requiring the reconstruction of scrambled sentences from a story text and the construction of original sentences, however, he experienced a great deal of difficulty.

The dominant theme for Josh throughout his first-grade year was an interest in imitative, dramatic play and in engaging in projects to make props for such play (for example, making badges and holsters for policemen, skis and ski poles for a "skiing expedition"). Both his teacher and the observer described him as a "person with ideas" who was bent on putting them into production. Unlike some children, however, Josh had great tolerance for what his end products actually looked like. Things did not have to look real, just so long as they had a functional utility and he could use them for his own purposes. He appeared to work out an idea in his head (a scenario so to speak) and then to make any reasonable set of props that would allow him to enact it with his friends.

At the beginning of second grade, Josh was still on the same plateau with reading and was experiencing considerable difficulty. In an oral reading taped in September of the second grade, he continually diverted from the act of reading to make comments about the pictures and about different contexts in which certain words could be used. At one point, he launched into an elaborate explanation of the plot as he had reconstructed it from the pictures. At another point, he explicitly stated, "I really don't read many words . . . the pictures are just about as good." Not until mid-year did he make a move, and then it was an extremely rapid one. His last oral reading sample (recorded in March of the second grade) documents the ground he had covered. This sample included selections from stories with difficult vocabulary and complex syntax, such as *How Perseus and His Mother Came to Seriphos*.[3] The second grade also saw Josh become increasingly interested in putting his unusual language capacity into written form (although the mechanical act of writing remained burdensome for him). For example, he constructed one book of pictures with humorous captions entitled *The Dingbat Series*. Three of his captions appear below:

This is an American green-blooded Dingbat.

This is a Dingbat called Oddface, because he looks very odd, don't you think so?

This is an ordinary Dingbat. (There has to be an ordinary one sometimes.)

Both Josh and Jenny challenge some of the "easy" generalizations one often hears about reading and reading readiness—Josh with his precocious language and slow reading progress; Jenny with her mirror writing and rapid reading progress. More to the point, they illustrate two children with very different styles and interests (imitative play and constructing functional products vs. imaginary play and experimenting with process) who also chose to explore different faces of language. Assuming, as many linguists do, that the deep structure of language has two surface representations (speech and writing), Josh appeared to be a "student" of spoken surface structure and Jenny a "student" of the written surface representation. Although they both became competent readers, they came along unique paths of style, interest, and language preference that must have entailed different cognitive evolutions along the way.

Professional Development

As stated at the beginning of this article, the rationale for collaboration in this project was derived from an analysis of methodological issues in educational research and from the nature of the particular research goals we had in mind. While the relevance of the study for teachers was a prime concern from the outset, the project was not designed as a program of teacher development per se nor was it intended to evaluate how research processes can promote professional development. Nevertheless, at an early stage of the study, it became evident that the sustained involvement of the teachers in the research, as manifested by their interest in the project and the quality of their contribution to it, was not so much contingent upon their investment in the ultimate research goals as upon the fact that the study's general orientation and methodology provided support for professional activity that was valued for its personal, practical, and theoretical consequences. In short, the procedures for sustained observation and inquiry into children's learning made it possible for teachers to examine classroom phenomena in such a way that their own experience became more accessible to reflection and analysis. The data the teachers worked with were data they had reported and collected, or that colleagues had recorded in their classrooms. It was the sort of information that is ordinarily encountered and stored intuitively, but that through the methods of the study is lifted out of the immediately experienced context and made available for review.

The ability and opportunity to profit from one's own experiences is seen by many to be at the heart of professional development, both for the individual teacher and for the knowledge base of the profession. At the same time, many factors in teaching mitigate against this, ranging from the press of institutional constraints and expectations to prevailing notions of teacher education that do not readily allow for a concept of continuing growth. Indeed, a central purpose of a number of recent advisory and teacher center programs, along with other curricular projects, has been to create in-service conditions that enable teachers to capitalize upon experience and to use observation in their own setting as an integral part of decision making. Without such capacity, teaching becomes routine and automatic; the phenomena in each year's transactions with children go unrecorded. As Thelen (1973) has pointed out, there is after all a distinction between twenty years of experience and one year repeated twenty times.

To the extent that this present project has fostered such opportunity, it seems important to look at its unique mechanism and procedures. One way to do this is to assess the methodology along lines that are closer to the vantage point expressed by teachers in evaluation and planning meetings and in more formal interview situations (Chittenden, Charney, and Kanevsky, 1977).

Classroom-Based Information. First, the study placed emphasis upon collection and analysis of descriptive, observational data of the kind that is available to teachers in the everyday functioning of the school and classroom. The study in effect asked teachers to be observers and through the mechanism of the Descriptive Interview offered support of that activity, with the result that teachers' observations became sharper over the course of the year. Moreover, teachers were not asked to change their instructional practices, nor did they need to step outside of their teaching duties. Instead, the work samples they collected—the paintings, the writings, the oral reading sessions—were taken from the ongoing program. Similarly, the observations they offered stemmed from their interactions with children in the course of normal classroom routine. These naturalistic qualities to data collection meant that the data, being tied to everyday occurrences and accessible on a continuing basis, were "ordinary," realistic, and recognizable to other teachers as well.

Individual Patterns. Secondly, the study was built around case material of one or two children in each classroom. If the data were "ordinary" in the above sense, the "unordinary" aspect was the opportunity to put information together and to review a record describing a child over time. The data integration process brought out patterns in the child's functioning and classroom behavior that are not usually visible. While such patterns may be sensed, teachers ordinarily do not have the chance to describe or ground them in the records of the child's work and behavior. The generalization value of the case approach was evident in the teachers' use of the material. As one expressed it, "In the long run you learn more about children in general by looking closely at individuals than you do by talking about children in general." Another teacher found the evidence of the mismatch between a certain type of instructional material (that is, linguistic texts) and the styles and strategies of a particular child to be both compelling and comprehensible. As a consequence she reassessed the generalizable value of this particular reading series.

Research Focus. From the teachers' accounts, their understanding of the research guidelines and procedures helped them maintain attention to the basic questions posed by the study at the same time that they were also dealing with the pressing everyday problems that are inevitably a part of teaching. Moreover, although the procedures of the study are open-ended in many respects, the bringing together of multiple perspectives and the requirement for substantiated observations and judgments, gave a certain discipline and organization to the teachers' efforts. These conditions, in turn, encouraged reflective participation on the teachers' part, which they felt provided an important balance to the more immediate, intuitive nature of instructional decision making.

Traditionally, the relationship of research to practice has been cast in a production-consumption mode, with the teacher depicted as a user of, but not a contributor to knowledge. In contrast, collaborative research of the kind reported here aspires to create a two-way flow between researcher and practitioner. This departure from the established pattern calls for certain minimal conditions that are not invariably present in all school settings. Since a main benefit of participation for teachers is the opportunity to consider, in a focused and disciplined way, aspects of their students' and their own classroom experience, the teachers must have sufficient professional autonomy to incorporate the results of their observations and reflections into their practice. In institutional settings where teachers are not viewed as instructional decision makers, but rather are expected to implement preordained curricula, a process designed to enrich the teachers' knowledge base for decision making may seem an academic exercise.

Participating in research also requires an "open door" policy on the teachers' part, with the willingness to give others access to their classrooms and practice. At the very least, an environment that has some tradition of collegial relationships, where teaching is considered the pursuit of common professional goals, is necessary. This is seldom possible in a school setting where the policy of the closed classroom door prevails.

In conclusion, a pattern of collaborative work requires several conditions to keep it going over a period of time, not the least of which is a certain amount of good will and the establishment of some common ground rules. But these, while necessary, are hardly sufficient. More importantly, there needs to be an essential congruity between the researchers' agenda (purposes and methods of work) and the teachers' agenda (instructional goals and needs). Such an intersection of priorities can provide reciprocal benefits without blurring the distinctive responsibilities of either role.

Princeton, New Jersey
June 1978

NOTES

[1]Some parent-scientists have provided accounts of the preschool acquisition of reading by their own children (Soderbergh, 1971; Steinberg and Steinberg, 1973).

[2]A descriptive report on the data integration process is in preparation.

[3]So that you may judge the difficulty for yourself, this story begins: "Once upon a time there were two princes who were twins. Their names were Acrisius and Proetus, and they lived in the pleasant vale of Argos, far away in Hellas."

REFERENCES

Amarel, M., Bussis, A., and Chittenden, E. An approach to the study of beginning reading: Longitudinal case studies. In S. Ball (Chair), *Conceptual and research problems in reading.* Symposium presented at the meeting of the National Reading Conference, New Orleans, December, 1977.

Bloom, L. Commentary of everyday preschool interpersonal speech usage: Methodological, developmental, and sociolinguistic studies by F. Schachter, K. Kirschner, B. Klips, M. Friedricks, K. Sanders. *Monographs of the Society for Research in Child Development,* 1974, *39,* 82-88 (3, Serial No. 156).

Bussis, A., Chittenden, E., and Amarel, M. *Beyond surface curriculum: An interview study of teachers' understandings.* Boulder, Colorado: Westview Press, 1978.

Carini, P. F. *Observation and description: An alternative methodology for the investigation of human phenomena.* (Monograph in the North Dakota Study Group on Evaluation series.) Grand Forks, North Dakota: University of North Dakota, 1975.

Chittenden, E., Charney, G., and Kanevsky, R. *Teacher response to in-service curriculum development and classroom research.* Paper presented at the meeting of the Association of Teacher Educators, Atlanta, February 1977.

Doyle, W. Learning the classroom environment: An ecological analysis. *Journal of Teacher Education,* 1977, *28,* 51-55. (a)

Doyle, W. The uses of nonverbal behaviors: Toward an ecological model of classrooms. *Merrill-Palmer Quarterly,* 1977, *23,* 179-192. (b)

Erickson, F. Some approaches to inquiry in school-community ethnography. *Anthropology and Education Quarterly,* 1977, *8,* 58-69.

Florio, S., and Walsh, M. The teacher as colleague in classroom research. In H. Mehan (Chair), *Studies of the social organization of the classroom.* Symposium presented at the meeting of the American Educational Research Association, San Francisco, April 1976.

Garfinkel, H. *Studies in ethnomethodology.* Englewood Cliffs, New Jersey: Prentice-Hall, 1967.

Hawkins, D. Learning the unteachable. In L. Shulman and E. Keislar (Eds.), *Learning by discovery: A critical appraisal.* Chicago: Rand McNally, 1966.

Kennedy, C. *Teachers and researchers: Toward a proper division of labor.* (Occasional Paper No. 2.) East Lansing: Michigan State University, The Institute for Research on Teaching, 1977.

Labov, W., and Fanshel, D. *Therapeutic discourse.* New York: Academic Press, 1977.

Lortie, D. C. *Schoolteacher: A sociological study.* Chicago: University of Chicago Press, 1975.

Mehan, H. Accomplishing classroom lessons. In A. V. Cisoural, et al. (Eds.), *Language use and school performance.* New York: Academic Press, 1974.

Read, C. Pre-school children's knowledge of English phonology. *Harvard Educational Review,* 1971, 41(1), 1-34.

Shulman, L. S. (Chair). *Clinical studies in the Institute for Research on Teaching: Some preliminary results.* Symposium presented at the meeting of the American Educational Research Association, New York City, 1977.

Soderbergh, R. *Reading in early childhood: A linguistic study of a Swedish preschool child's gradual acquisition of reading ability.* Stockholm: Almqvist and Wiksell, 1971.

Stake, R. E. The case study method in social inquiry. *Educational Researcher,* 1978, *1,* 5-8.

Steinberg, D., and Steinberg, M. *Reading in the crib: A program and case study.* Unpublished manuscript, Honolulu: University of Hawaii, 1973.

Thelen, H. Profession anyone? In D. McCarty (Ed.), *New perspectives on teacher education.* San Francisco: Jossey-Bass, 1973.

Tikunoff, W. J., Ward, B. A., and Stacy, F. D. *Toward ecologically-based curriculum: A model for professional growth through participatory research and development.* Paper presented at the meeting of the Association of Teacher Educators, Atlanta, February 1977.

Willems, E. P. and Raush, H. L. (Eds.). *Naturalistic viewpoints in psychological research.* New York: Holt, Rinehart and Winston, 1969.

Wright, H. F. Observational child study. In P. H. Mussen (Ed.), *Handbook of research methods in child development.* New York: Wiley, 1960.

Barak Rosenshine / *A Response*
to Bussis, Chittenden, and Amarel

Describers and Improvers

The descriptive part of the paper by Bussis, Chittenden, and Amarel of the Educational Testing Service (ETS) is extremely valuable. It illuminates classroom practice and progress in "open" or "integrated curriculum" classrooms with a richness I have not seen before. This illumination occurs because information is presented on *longitudinal* practice and longitudinal progress and because the report was written by very talented and experienced researchers. The descriptions of Jenny and Josh are treasures. I would hope that investigators of other instructional approaches (for example, traditional, direct instruction) and investigators in other subject areas could provide similar types of descriptions.

In using this paper as a springboard to discuss research in aesthetic education, I have attempted to cover two areas. The first includes descriptive research in general, the ETS report in particular, and suggestions for descriptive research in aesthetic education. The second part contains an awkward attempt to describe two groups in educational research—"describers" and "improvers"—some criticisms of the common practices in each camp, and an illustration of some research which utilizes the best of each camp.

Descriptive Research in Education

Not all descriptive research is necessarily valuable and illuminating, and those who are about to engage in descriptive research in the arts might profit from a short review of descriptive research in general instructional areas.

Descriptive research using category instruments (that is, counts of specific behaviors or "sign" approaches which count whether an event occurred in a short period such as five minutes) began to flourish about 1965, reached a peak of activity around 1970, and waned during the next

BARAK ROSENSHINE *is Professor of Educational Psychology at the University of Illinois.*

five years. Following the pioneering work of Flanders and of Medley, different researchers developed over a hundred different instruments to "describe classroom practice." These instruments were collected and published in the fourteen volumes of *Mirrors for Behavior* (Simon and Boyer, 1967 and 1970).

The problem with such descriptive research was that the investigators did not use any criteria against which to test their results. That is, they seldom related their descriptions to outcomes such as student achievement gain, student attitudes, or time on task. As a result, the investigators used their own judgment in deciding which teacher behaviors were positive or negative. Thus, we had investigators reporting their descriptive data and then saying that teachers talk "too much," that there is too little "student-initiated talk" and that teachers did not ask enough "high cognitive level" questions. (As it turned out, few of these "teachers should" statements were significantly related to student achievement gain.)

The lesson to be learned from the era of category instruments, then, is that the mere development of a variety of category instruments did not in itself constitute very productive research. Simply developing tens of instruments and then declaring that teachers should use more or less of a list of behaviors has not led to the improvement of the quality of teaching or student learning.

While the era of category instruments was waning, the era of ethnographic studies was waxing. These are also descriptive studies or case studies cloaked in a more scientific sounding name. To date, however, ethnographic studies have not concluded with lists of behaviors that teachers "should" or "should not" do. The investigators are to be commended for this restraint, and at the same time, we should be watchful that this does not occur.

A promising sign in ethnographic studies is that the investigators have been using criteria against which to test their results. For example: Tikunoff, Berliner, and Rist (1975) used student achievement gain as a way of testing the potency of the variables they developed. Kounin and Gump (1974) and Kounin and Doyle (1975) used student attention or engagement as a criterion for testing their hypotheses. In the ethnographic papers presented at this conference, Tikunoff and Ward obtained data on student attention and on student achievement gain, and Bussis, Chittenden, and Amarel have continual, longitudinal data on student achievement. Such efforts are to be strongly commended because they provide us and the investigators with criteria against which to test their findings.

Another example of criterion-based descriptive research is using a "known sample"; that is, a sample that clearly differs on a specified criterion. Tikunoff, Berliner, and Rist (1975), for example, used achievement gain data to divide their teachers into high achievers and low achievers and then searched their ethnographic records to find variables differentiating the two groups. Carolyn Evertson (1979) and her associates at the University of Texas have classified teachers as effective and ineffective managers on the basis of observed student engagement, and are now studying the behaviors that differentiate the two groups. There is a clear difference between taking a general sample of teachers (without criterion data) and describing practice, and taking a known sample and describing practice. Although there is a need for both types of research, the first technique has led to more unwarranted inferences than the second technique of first selecting a known sample.

There is a need for insightful, descriptive research on teaching in the arts, and one would hope that such research—whether it use category instruments or ethnographic techniques—will also include student outcomes (for example, achievement or engagement or attitudes) as part of the research.

The Value of Colleagial Research

When investigators are exploring a relatively unknown area, as in the report by Bussis, Chittenden, and Amarel, there is a value in working with like-minded colleagues as teachers. In this case, the investigators and the teachers shared the same general philosophy as to the value of an integrated approach to teaching coupled with quality and no-nonsense instruction. Similarly, in my own work, I find it easier and more insightful to work with teachers who share my orientation toward "direct instruction."

There is no evidence as to whether the science of studying teaching advances more by working with like-minded colleagues or with colleagues with a different orientation, and arguments have been made for either case. Despite the fears, my experience and that of the ETS researchers has been that even when like-minded colleagues work together there are numerous points of difference which enlighten and sharpen our insights.

The Value of Talent

In reading this study, I am impressed with the talent of the investigators. In contrast, many descriptive and ethnographic studies so overwhelm me with detail and prose that I conclude my reading with more confusion and no better insight than when I began. Labeling a study "ethnographic" or "descriptive" does not insure quality of content.

The advice, then, for research in teaching of the arts would be to reward talent when it is found but not to expect that every investigator will be talented.

The Problem of Generalizability

One problem in this type of research is representativeness or generalizability. That is, one is not sure the extent to which we can generalize certain practices to all teachers or the extent to which the outcomes of certain children are representative of all children.

The problem is well illustrated in the ETS study. Take the case of Jenny. Here we have a strongly motivated girl who was unable to read in the fall. Yet, she was so motivated, and so bright, that she memorized half a book with two hundred words on each page. It was not until mid-January that she began to receive instruction in sounding out words. The story does have a happy ending—by June she was able to read fluently and by the end of the second year, she was able to read quite well.

Despite the happy ending, I worry over the fact that this highly motivated girl went through four months of "let's pretend" before her reading instruction began when, using a structured phonics approach, it would have been possible to teach her fluent decoding skills in twelve to fourteen weeks. Thus, the months of September, October, and November could have been spent teaching her to decode instead of allowing the, apparently, frustrating and difficult time she had.

The question of representativeness of the teachers emerges at this point. I do not know if this postponing of instruction for a motivated child is typical of most open classroom teachers. I trust this practice is not typical.

One answer to the problem of the representativeness of the teachers is to work with a "known sample." In the ETS study, for example, one could have divided the teachers and/or the students into those who made greater progress than expected and those who made lesser progress than expected and *then* have presented the descriptive data on this known sample.

The representativeness of the children is also a question, but a less difficult one because we have prior categories for classifying children. Jenny appears to be a bright and motivated child, and Josh appears to be a very bright and independent child. In future case studies of this type, I would hope we could read descriptions of the activities and progress of average and below-average children.

Describers and Improvers

The ETS investigators give as one of their aims the collection of "descriptive data that capture the full complexity of learning phenomena as faithfully as possible." This desire to capture the complexity has motivated much of the descriptive research in education, be it category instruments, case studies, or ethnography.

But in descriptive research, what does one do with the complexity after it is captured? Usually, the investigators continue to capture and document more complexity. This description and documentation seldom becomes an "empirical base" from which one moves to experimental studies and the improvement of student outcomes. Those conducting descriptive studies seldom attempt to refine and validate their insights against criteria such as student achievement gain, and seldom move to experimental studies in which they attempt to improve classroom practice.

On the other hand, in the history of education, many of those who set out to "improve classroom practice" (or "provide something for the teachers on the firing line") seldom have an empirical base for their innovation and seldom collect empirical data on the effect of their improvements. Those improvers who gave us "inquiry training" and "creativity training" in the 1960s, and "student-centered instruction," "competency-based teacher education," and "values clarification" in the 1970s began their programs more from their imaginations than from an empirical base. The new curriculum programs, and the new textbook series which appear every year, are seldom derived from an empirical base, and the developers are seldom knowledgeable of the descriptive and basic research in their area. (Or else, they take two or three studies, oversimplify them, and then magnify these into a curriculum program.) Many of the skills which appeared in the teacher training programs in the early seventies were developed by teacher educators who sat around a table and brainstormed ideas.

Many of these improvers argued, with justification, that their strategy was first to get these new programs operating in the schools, and then to follow this with research on the effect of these programs upon students. In practice, this second step seldom occurred, and having completed one "development," the personnel simply moved on to new developments.

Even when empirical research emerges, the "improvers" find ways to discount it if it goes against their initial expectations. Although the research on "higher order questions" or "open classrooms" has consistently yielded nonsignificant or negative outcomes, the improvers have usually found ways to discount these findings. When all else fails, one can rely on The Educators' Creed:

> There are things that tests can't measure.
> These are the most important of all
> And our students did best in these.

In many ways, as Katz (1975) has noted, we are victims of our ideologies. In education, where there is little empirical data, she noted that we are forced to develop ideologies which enable us to make sense of what we see. But once having developed the ideologies, they become rigid filters that determine which empirical data we shall admit and which we shall discard and our energies are directed toward maintaining our ideologies rather than refining them.

Thus, we have describers who continue to capture complexity but seldom move to the improvement of practice, and improvers who swamp us with innovations that are seldom tested, or who manage to discount negative findings.

A Possible Alternative

Thus far, the descriptor model (or the "understanding the complexity model") has been criticized for not leading to attempts to improve student outcomes; the improver model has been criticized for lacking a research base before development and for ignoring or avoiding research after development. Is there no alternative?

As an alternative, I should like to discuss the work of Jere Brophy and Tom Good. These two became a team around 1968, developed the Brophy-Good Dyadic Observation Instrument, and rapidly became involved in descriptive studies. They did not collect student achievement data at that time. As others were doing at that time, they presented their decriptive results accompanied by lists of "teachers should" but did not have an empirical base (for example, student outcome data) against which to test their assertions.

After a few years of this, they changed. Brophy at Texas, and Good at Missouri, independently conducted studies in which they correlated their large number of descriptive teacher and student behaviors with measures of student achievement and attitudinal gain (Good, in press). They, and their associates, then moved to *experimental* studies in the grades and subject areas they had been studying. Their objective in the experimental studies was to take the more promising results from their correlational studies, add to these results the best hunches which emerged from the hundreds of hours they had spent observing, and package these variables in a list of promising teacher behaviors they believed would improve practice and student outcomes. One group of teachers was trained in these behaviors, a control group was not, and the experiments were conducted for six months to a year in regular classrooms. In both studies, the results favored the experimental group.

Each of these teams went one step further. During the experimental study they collected observational data in both the experimental and control classrooms, and they used this data to reanalyze their original experimental behaviors to determine which of these behaviors were important and which were not.

These investigators performed what Norma Furst and I (1973) once called a "descriptive-correlational-experimental loop." That is, they began with description, moved to a correlational study with student outcomes, used the best findings and hunches to develop an experimental study, and then looped back to a correlational study to refine their experimental results. These refined packages are now available for use by teachers. As a result of this process, one has more faith that their findings, if implemented, will lead to improvement of student learning and attitudes.

Such studies are extremely rare. In the last five years the only other investigator I could find who has done another such study is Jane Stallings (1979). Even more rare was to hear Tom Good report that when his results did not fit his ideology, he revised his ideology.

Summary

It seems part of the human condition that we continue to work in areas where we are most comfortable. Thus, laboratory researchers continue with laboratory studies, describers continue to describe, improvers continue to offer innovations, and synthesizers like me continue to synthesize. People such as Brophy, Good, and Stallings are welcome exceptions and may point the way for the rest of us. I am impressed with the richness of description and insight which the ETS study provides, and I hope that they, or their colleagues, can use their best findings and hunches in experimental studies aimed at improving student learning and attitudes.

There is clearly a need for descriptive studies of all types in aesthetic education, and the work of the ETS group or of Tikunoff and Ward provide models which can well be emulated. At the same time, I hope that researchers in education in the arts can avoid the pitfalls which we went through in descriptive research and can use the findings of such studies—and their best hunches—in experimental studies aimed at improving teaching practice and student outcomes.

Eugene, Oregon
August 1978

REFERENCES

Anderson, L. M., Evertson, C. M., and Brophy, J. E. An experimental study of effective teaching in first-grade reading groups. *Elementary School Journal,* in press.

Evertson, C., and Anderson, L. *Management techniques of successful teachers.* Paper presented to the annual meeting of the American Educational Research Association, San Francisco, 1979.

Good, T. L., et al., Experimental study of mathematics instruction in elementary schools. *Journal of Educational Psychology,* in press.

Katz, L. G. Early childhood programs and ideological disputes. *The Educational Forum,* 1975, *18,* 267-271.

Kounin, J. S., and Doyle, P. H. Degree of continuity of a lesson's signal system and task involvement of children. *Journal of Educational Psychology,* 1975, *67,* 159-164.

Kounin, J. S., and Gump, P. F. Signal systems of lesson settings and the task-related behavior of preschool children. *Journal of Educational Psychology,* 1974, *66,* 554-562.

Rosenshine, B. V., and Furst, N. F. The use of direct observation to study teaching. In R. Travers (Ed.), *Second handbook of research on teaching.* Chicago: Rand McNally, 1973.

Simon, A., and Boyer, E. G. (Eds.). Mirrors for behavior: An anthology of classroom observation instruments (Vols. 1-6). Philadelphia: Research for Better Schools, 1967.

Simon, A., and Boyer, E. G. (Eds.). Mirrors for behavior: An anthology of classroom observation instruments (Vols 7-14). Philadelphia: Research for Better Schools, 1970.

Stallings, J., Needles, M., and Stayrook, N. *The teaching of basic reading skills in secondary schools, Phase II.* Menlo Park, California: SRI International, 1979.

Tikunoff, W., Berliner, D. C., and Rist, R. C. *An ethnographic study of the forty classrooms of the Beginning Teacher Evaluation Study known sample.* Technical Report No. 75-10-5. San Francisco: Far West Laboratory for Educational Research and Development, October 1975.

William J. Tikunoff and Beatrice A. Ward

How the Teaching Process Affects Change in the School[1]

The title of this paper poses two challenges. On the one hand, it assumes that changes occur in what goes on in schools—a matter that has been questioned by several astute observers of the educational process. On the other, it suggests that teaching can influence and shape those changes—a condition that is likewise subject to question. In other words, the paper challenges us not only to suggest how teaching and change might be related, but also to indicate under what circumstances and through what research and development procedures change involving teachers and learners might be accomplished.

Given this state of affairs, we have chosen to approach the problem from four dimensions. First, we will review briefly the observations of several persons regarding school-based change, paying particular attention to changes that are relevant to the teaching-learning group; that is, the teacher, the students assigned to work with that teacher, and any non-teachers who may be available for use by the teacher. Building upon this information and adding insights from our own research on teaching, we then will propose a possible explanation for why change has been difficult to achieve. Next, we will present one way of analyzing the teaching-learning process as embedded in the entire classroom instructional-social system and apply it to bringing about change in aesthetic education. Finally, a research and development procedure will be described that has a high potential for utilizing the teaching process to affect change, given the concerns and viewpoints presented in earlier portions of the paper.

Observations Regarding School-Based Educational Change

As noted by Mann (1976):

WILLIAM J. TIKUNOFF is Director of Programs on Schooling, and BEATRICE A. WARD is Deputy Laboratory Director at the Far West Laboratory.

Most educators realize that the amount and pace of change has fallen far short of expectations. The problem is more profound than simply pointing at the unrealistic impatience of the sixties. Programs were planned, curriculum was developed, teaching/ learning units were packaged, teachers were trained, and the results were frustrating, uneven, unexpected and temporary. (p. 313)

Goodlad (1977) presents much the same viewpoint:

Such evidence as we now have about what goes on in schools suggests that a very great deal of what was intended in the proposed reforms of the Schooling Decade, 1957-1967, was either empty rhetoric or was effectively assimilated without redirecting the character of school life. (p. 4)

Inasmuch as these statements resulted from extensive studies of educational innovation—Mann[2] was reporting secondary analyses of data obtained from 293 school sites that were part of a study of programs supporting educational change, and Goodlad[3] was reporting a study of 158 classrooms in 67 schools—it appears that few changes in schools have been observed and that the teaching process may be preventing rather than facilitating change.

Jackson (1977, p. 25) provides two perspectives that, in our opinion, speak to this issue. He notes that while a search for the new is part of teaching, several ideas and concepts have been around long enough to become persistent. These include expressions such as "the whole child," "meeting the needs of children," and "individualizing instruction." Teachers use these sorts of phrases to describe what they do, with one teacher's interpretation of a particular phrase being very different from another's. Thus, what occurs in one classroom as compared to another may differ depending upon similarities and differences in the respective teacher's interpretations of such concepts. At the same time, Jackson (p. 41) points out that "the swiftness and unpredictability of classroom phenomena help justify the teacher's dependence on intuition in guiding him over pedagogical rough spots." We suggest that such intuitive behavior often builds upon and is consistent with the teacher's persistent concepts regarding instruction. The combined influence of these factors may result in the lack of change in schools and may explain why the teacher and teaching are fundamental elements for bringing about the change that does occur.

To illustrate: Consider the following statements from three fourth-grade teachers who worked with us in a study (Tikunoff and Ward, 1978) of the socialization of students into the instructional process at the beginning of the school year. In discussing the instructional systems they planned to install, the following statements were made:

Teacher J: It is my desire (and I hope it will be the desire of the children also) to function in a relaxed and pleasant atmosphere.

Hopefully, the children will adjust and feel free to be themselves in such a way that they can appreciate what they are as individuals and appreciate what others are. . . . Each student should establish a better self-esteem and self-image and be able to relate with those with whom he shares the whole year, including the teacher. . . . It's important for [students] to learn to verbalize, to be articulate, and speak out, not to be threatened. Children have to realize that they can voice opinions and they can hear other people voice opinions and still they have to have a certain amount of respect for that person although the opinion may contradict what they think or feel.

Teacher K: I would like to have as much going back and forth with the student as possible. I don't want the student feeling afraid to talk to me, to ask questions. I want a place that is not a fearful place, one where communication is free.

Teacher L: I like the room to be quiet most of the time. I expect the students to listen when I'm talking and I expect them to listen to each other and just talk one at a time . . . if students must have a conversation, they may step outside the door.

These viewpoints exemplify the persistent ideas that underscored teaching and learning in the classrooms. As such, they might be expected to influence the teaching and learning processes that occurred. Pre-planned curriculum, instructional activities, organizational patterns—all most likely would be selected and designed to encourage the types of interaction and communication desired by each teacher. Intuitive decisions and actions might be expected to support behavior that was consistent with their expectations. As a result, each teaching-learning group could be expected to function differently.

In fact, we did observe such differences, the dimensions of which will be discussed later in this paper. Teacher L's teaching-learning process differed markedly from that of Teacher J or Teacher K, and Teacher J's and Teacher K's differed in some respects from each other's but more in regard to degree than to totally different forms of interaction and patterns of communication. The types of instructional systems that were installed appeared to have been influenced by and to be consistent with each teacher's "philosophical" viewpoints. In this instance, teaching (teachers) did affect what occurred.

Given that few educational innovations have been implemented as planned and that those that have been implemented have not persisted, the statements of these three teachers illustrate how teachers and teaching may have contributed to this situation. If Teachers J, K, and L were to participate in the same *new* arts and aesthetics education program, the *form* of that program undoubtedly would differ in each classroom. What is more, for the *desired* change(s) to occur, these differences would need to be identified and accommodated or modified as the program was implemented.

Successful school-based change recognizes and attends to such requirements. For instance, using data from the study of 239 sites, McLaughlin (1976) notes:

> Without changes in the structure of the institutional setting, or the culture of the school, new practices are simply "more of the same" and are unlikely to lead to much significant change in what happens to students. . . . Where implementation was successful, and where significant change in participant attitudes, skills, and behavior occurred, implementation was characterized by a process of *mutual adaptation* [emphasis inserted by authors] in which project goals and methods were modified to suit the needs and interests of participants and in which participants changed to meet the requirements of the project. This finding was true even for highly technological and initially well specified projects; unless adaptations were made in the original plans or technologies, implementation tended to be superficial or symbolic and significant change in participants did not occur. (pp. 339, 341)

House (1975, p. 7) further indicates that "educational programs in the fullest sense must be grown rather than replicated—even when they look like the one next door." Goodlad (1977, p. 4) states that:

> We now know that neither a curriculum plan . . . nor a new scheme of school organization. . .is in itself sufficient for successful implementation. Each must be coupled with a strategy for change built on knowledge of schools and in collaboration with them.

Building upon the insights gained from the beginning-of-school socialization study mentioned earlier, we would add to the above statements that successful school-based change must attend to, adapt to, and accommodate not only the instructional aspects of the teaching-learning group but the social requirements as well. The teacher statements presented earlier contain both instructional and social goals and expectations. As will be demonstrated in the next section of this paper, these instructional and social goals, expectations, and behaviors interact in such a way that each influences and shapes the others and is shaped by them. As a result, an *instructional-social system* is established. For change to occur and persist, both dimensions of this sytem must change. If one facet is left unchanged, it will in time reshape and/or absorb the other. The eventual result is that the *changed system* will once again resemble the original instructional-social system, thereby confirming the *no-change* contentions observed by Mann and Goodlad.

To date, the preponderance of educational innovations—even those in aesthetic education—have emphasized change in only the instructional facet of the instructional-social system. What is needed is to give equal or more attention to the social facet. To understand and capitalize upon the entire system as it affects change in aesthetic education, it is necessary to delineate what is meant by an instructional-social system and to apply this knowledge to the analysis of a possible innovation.

The Instructional-Social System

Thus far, we have suggested that the instructional processes and social processes in a teaching-learning group are interconnected in ways that mandate a change in both in order to change either. Therefore, to study how teaching processes affect school-based change, it is necessary to study not just teaching itself, but the *instructional-social system* as it operates in a given classroom. Such a view builds from the perspectives of sociology in which:

> "Socialization" denotes all of those processes through which persons acquire the evaluative and normative orientations, the commitments, the cognitive and motor skills, and the knowledge that help to fit or unfit them for life in a society. . . . "Schooling" denotes that subset of explicit socialization processes that occur in schools. (Bidwell, 1972, p. 1)

It also incorporates our own experience with and insights gained from the study of the socialization process at the beginning of the school year; as Schlechty (1976) notes, it is a time

> when the behavior that occurs in the classroom is the behavior of a collectivity of individuals . . . [who] begin to function in ways that suggest the development of group life. (pp. 62-64)

Schlechty goes on to point out that "the degree to which the behavior of the participants is built into a system of interlocking roles, expectations, and rewards" may define the most important variables in classroom life.

As defined by Bidwell (1972, p. 1), schooling has two principal aspects:

- *technical socialization*—"developing intellectual and motor skills and learning items of information and systems of thought that organize them" (from our perspective, the instructional facet of the instructional-social system), and
- *moral socialization*—acquiring "values and goals for conduct," learning and becoming "responsive to moral rules" (norms), and gaining "a view of the social world as a moral order" (the social foci of the instructional-social system).

The interconnection of the technical (that is, instructional) and moral (that is, social) aspects of group life is confirmed in our observation of how the three teachers mentioned previously socialized their students into their instructional systems over the first seven weeks of school. Each teacher described in detail the instructional portion of his or her system—how it would look once it was operational, what variations would be used for particular curricula, how students would function appropriately within that system. All three also stated that they did not know what rules they would initiate in order to get the group started.

The findings, however, provide a different picture. Each teacher seemed to have in mind precisely how a student needed to behave (conduct himself or herself) in accordance with the way the *system* was to operate. Beginning with Day 1, all three teachers began using rules and sanctions to shape students to fit these respective images. While many of the rules were socially oriented (that is, established values and goals for conduct), their intended purpose was to facilitate operationalization of instructional processes. Although the teachers talked about their instructional systems separately from the requirements for their social systems, these two facets of classroom life when observed in operation were so interwoven that, as we have already indicated, they should be viewed as a single system with both instructional and social properties.

Data from Teachers J and L illustrate this point.[4] In considering these excerpts, place yourself in the role of a student in each classroom and reflect upon what your socialization experience and outcomes would be given that you spent 180 or so days in such a teaching-learning group.

In an open-ended self-report regarding her instructional system, Teacher J stated:

> I think one of the most important things to try and anticipate is the fact that the children will gain an appreciation of themselves and of their talents and will be able to contribute to the development of the total classroom environment. Academics, of course, are important and I think they need to have priority but I do not think that to be effective means to disregard being in a relaxed atmosphere. I would like to anticipate that we could have a happy and effective classroom situation and not necessarily stress structure, rules, and regulations. . . . My past experiences have indicated that children will react more positively if they have some say and some voice in establishing their own behaviors and their own guidelines . . . this year I hope to work out activities that will be more on a cooperative rather than a competitive basis.

In a discussion with the authors, Teacher J noted several additional dimensions:

> What I have in mind this year is not to separate. I'm not going to teach nouns or pronouns or something for thirty minutes. It will be integrated into, say, creative writing or a reading session. . . . I will try to develop units which incorporate the different skills.
>
> I would like to see these students pretty independent as far as being able to follow through and accept their own responsibility for getting certain tasks done.
>
> At the beginning you have to have it understood that everybody has to participate, to contribute. We expect everyone to be in a group. . . . They have to negotiate [group membership]. It wouldn't

be you're going in here and you're going there. They'll have to talk it over and settle it until they agree who is in the group.

I think [students] have to sense a certain amount of respect for each other and respect for what we aim to do as individuals and as a group.... They'd have to recognize what respect means; sharing and caring for someone else's rights. If they can recognize that they have certain rights and the person sitting next to them has certain rights and they shouldn't infringe on them, we would have a good feeling in the class. A lot of this is going to depend on the maturity of the [students]. It may be a learning process that takes nine months.

At the conclusion of an interview that took place before school began, one of the observers noted that Teacher J had eight basic expectations for the class:

1. She wanted students to have good feelings about themselves, to accept themselves.
2. She wanted students to have a sense of accomplishment at the end of the year.
3. She wanted students to be able to use learning tools independently.
4. She wanted students to know how to do research rather than memorize things.
5. She wanted more creativity in the classroom.
6. She wanted more experiences with self-expression for students.
7. She wanted less competition and more cooperation among students.
8. She wanted to develop a consideration of the rights of others and a tolerance of differences.

The interweaving of the technical (instructional) and moral (social) purposes of schooling is evident in Teacher J's preactive statements. The rule system that was placed into operation in her teaching-learning group further illustrates how the instructional-social system functioned as a single force. Teacher J established a total of 42 rules over the seven-week period of observation. These included 9 procedural rules, 12 academic rules, 3 talking and noise rules, 2 mobility rules, 4 ethical rules, 3 miscellaneous rules, and 9 school-imposed rules. Examples of procedural rules are:

Desks must be cleared and the classroom cleaned up before students can be dismissed for recess, lunch, to go home, or when starting a new activity.

Playground balls must be shared at recess.

Students who work as library aides are to keep track of their own schedules.

Academic rules included, among others:

Students may ask the teacher or other students for help with their work.

Reading group procedures in which they worked in twos, threes, or fours: One person is to serve as secretary to record what takes place and write down the answers that the group agrees upon. If members of the group have problems with reading the material, they are to help each other.

The talking/noise rules included:

Students must not talk and should pay attention when the teacher is giving directions.

Students may talk during work time as long as they do not disturb others and as long as talk is work-related.

Students may not talk during listening exercises.

Mobility rules allowed students to choose their seating assignments and go to a mattress in a corner of the room to work. Ethical rules stressed consideration for others, sharing, and solving problems through group meetings.

In contrast to Teacher J, setting up procedures and a routine for operation were important to Teacher L. She relied heavily on sequenced, commercially produced curriculum materials that approached knowledge and skills in a step-by-step developmental fashion. In order to achieve her instructional goals, she indicated that she probably would rely on the previous year's experiences, when:

Basically my approach was to schedule the classes so that I had as few [students] in the room as possible during instructional time for the skill subjects. I was able to do that because we have a reading center where the [students] go and I scheduled 10 [students] for each hour. I hope to do that again this year. [Then] I will have only two hours with the whole class.

She also made the following comments regarding the system she intended to operate:

I try to reduce to a routine as much as I can in order to free myself to do other things. I like little boxes and security.

What I try to do is take the [students] where they are and move them as fast as they can go. I try to get as much done in nine months as I can.

I'll probably structure one thing at a time. For instance, I'll take spelling and get them placed. I might spend all day testing for spelling. Then I might take math. I want to get into the regular routine as soon as possible.

I often group by things other than academic skills; for instance, work skills or sometimes I put [students] who need a lot of physical activity in one group.

I don't know if groups will be so flexible in math this year because one problem with that form of individualized work is that it is not always efficient for getting group instruction done.

If I have a, let's say, pink group who are capable of working on their own, I might be able to take, let's say, an orange group for instruction. If not, I'll have to instruct an orange-pink group all at one time.

I want to do more group instruction where I'm actually sitting down and saying, "Okay, this is the subject area I want to cover at this time."

Mostly, it turns out that it's teacher with children, rather than children with children, in a circle situation. I have tried to get the children to interact with each other . . . but I dropped it. It was going to take too long to get them [that] independent. I felt it was wasting too much time for what I wanted to do. . . . I [teach] usually in a circle situation. I'll teach from a chair and [students] are in a circle on the floor. . . . I get their attention better if they are sitting in a closed circle so I get that focus. I tend to do a lot of teacher-to-student and student-to-teacher kind of teaching . . . to be sure they're tuned in.

At one time I thought it was going to ruin their self-images if they knew that they were on a certain grade level. Now I make a point to say book B rather than book 2 but they know where they are anyway. . . . In the real world they are going to have to face the reality of where they are in relationship to others.

I think it is a healthy attitude to instill in a [student] that I'm competing with my prior performance rather than I'm competing against this curriculum.

Teacher L's rule system supported her desire to have a structured, routinized classroom. By the end of the seventh week of school, she had established 135 rules. These included 50 procedural rules, 52 academic rules, 8 talking and noise rules, 7 mobility rules, 6 ethical rules, 4 miscellaneous rules, and 8 school-imposed rules. Examples of the procedural rules included:

Check with the teacher before leaving the classroom.

When lights are turned off, students must stop what they are doing and "freeze" except before dismissals when they are to return and clear their desks.

Students may use the orange and green flag to ask permission to sharpen pencils when the whole class is not in the room.

Keep hands down while others are speaking.

Students whose names are on the board must see the teacher at the next break to determine disciplinary action.

Academic rules included such requirements as:

Students are expected to work alone.

The signal for assigned "correctors" to come to a student's desk is to have the test open on the corner of the desk.

Assigned correctors should work silently.

Work may be turned in only during the allotted time.

Partner work (which was allowed in social studies) should always be done outside.

Use orange flag if you need help.

Teacher has signals for question-answer response.

Teaching and noise rules included:

If students need to talk, they ask permission from the teacher.

If students need to talk, they can use the red flag to go outside for one minute of "time out."

Mobility rules restricted students' movement about the classroom. For example:

Students must stay seated unless the teacher gives them permission to move.

Students may not change their seating arrangements.

The ethical rules focused on:

Students should show consideration for others.

Students must not violate others' space or territory.

No cheating.

Obviously, the social facets of Teacher L's system corresponded to the step-by-step, teacher-directed process she planned to employ in instruction. Although this form of instruction need not necessarily incorporate the social expectations and norms for conduct that Teacher L installed, given her expectations and goals, the system took on those dimensions.

Our purpose in presenting this brief insight into two instructional-social systems as they were described prior to initiation and were observed in operation is to emphasize the need to consider both the instructional and social facets of the teaching and learning process when considering changes in school. Teacher L's instructional-social system would *consume* an aesthetic education innovation stressing open-ended creative expression on the part of students. Teacher J's system would *adopt* and possibly *expand* such an innovation. The next section of this paper explores how change in aesthetic education can be approached given the need to change an instructional-social system.

Innovation That Attends to the Instructional-Social System

As indicated above, understanding and explaining classroom teaching and learning in terms of the instructional-social system suggests a dramatic departure from the underlying premises of current educational R&D practices. For whatever reasons, the field has tended to rely predominantly on the methodology of educational psychology, and this has resulted in studies and evaluations based on the belief that differences in student outcomes are attributable to differences in teacher performance. Our own dissatisfaction with using the quasi-experimental approach based on this assumption has led us to the theories and research paradigms of disciplines and fields somewhat outside mainstream educational inquiry.[5] As we have applied these to our own work, it has become clear that in order to understand the teaching-learning process, one must attend to more than just the dyadic interactions of teacher and student(s) or the search to establish a cause-and-effect relationship between teacher performance and student outcomes.

Instead, we believe that a holistic approach to viewing what goes on in classrooms is essential, and that only by studying the multiple elements of a classroom instructional-social system and their interrelationships as they act upon, and are acted upon by, each other can we begin to understand classroom teaching and learning. Thus, in effect, we are suggesting that it is necessary to study the *total ecology of the classroom instructional-social system in order to understand any of its component pieces.*[6]

While this paper is not the appropriate forum for expounding on the value and meaning of utilizing an ecological perspective for studying classroom life, it is important to introduce some of that perspective's basic tenets so that a productive way of looking at change for aesthetic education can be proposed. However, a caveat is in order. The notion of applying an ecological perspective to studying classroom instructional-social systems is an emerging idea. Therefore, both its use and the discussion of its component facets must be approached in light of its seminal nature.[7]

Central to the ecological perspective as used for our purposes in this paper are two important facets. First, the focus of such a perspective is on how human interactions shape and are shaped by the physical, social, and psychological contexts of people and their environs. For the study of instructional-social systems, the ecological unit is the teacher-student learning group, defined in terms of both the shared activity of teaching-learning within the group and the actors involved.

A second facet important to this discussion is implied in the paradigm suggested. Viewing the total ecology of an instructional-social system implies a multiple-perspectives approach. Thus, the constructs and perspectives of different disciplines are incorporated to allow for and encourage diverse interpretations and explanations. By their very nature, differing disciplines will focus on different aspects of an instructional-social system in operation, and by attending to and understanding each we can better approach understanding the whole.

Therefore, the ecological perspective taken here suggests (1) that in order to understand classroom instructional-social systems one needs to inquire into and understand the social and physical elements as well as the psychological elements that comprise such a system and how they interrelate; and (2) that a fruitful path to such understanding is to employ the methods of inquiry found in disciplines not usually utilized in educational research. Such an approach implies careful, rigorous attention to the possibility that new understandings may augment and/or change previously held beliefs about classroom teaching and learning—indeed, about the schooling process itself—and that infusion into educational inquiry of the methods of social sciences other than educational psychology may produce fresh insights. Earlier, we illustrated how this approach in our own work led us to understand both educational change and the teaching-learning process as embedded within the instructional-social system of the classroom. It seems appropriate to apply what we are learning about the ecology of classroom instructional-social systems to the topic under discusssion here—bringing about change in the classroom, particularly change as it relates to aesthetic education.

One promising procedure for analyzing classroom instructional-social systems is that proposed by sociologists, and in particular by that group of sociologists interested in studying the nature of, and human interaction within social organizations. As its underlying principle, this perspective accepts that schools are complex social organizations; that "the organizational characteristics of schools have implications for what occurs in classrooms" (Schlechty, 1976, p. 43), and that classrooms themselves can be perceived as complex social organizations. Thus, a student matriculating through school learns far more than merely the curriculum prescribed.

For instance: Dreeben (1967) points out that schooling is in itself a process of socialization, providing the linkage between what a child learns at home and what he or she will need to learn for a successful adulthood. Socialization is accomplished by imbuing students with social norms, or principles of conduct; and "schooling contributes to pupils' learning what the norms are, accepting them, and acting according to them" (Dreeben, 1967, p. 27). In keeping with Bidwell's (1972) notion, which we discussed earlier, that schooling has as its major goals both technical and moral socialization, Dreeben further suggests that these are accomplished through the introduction in school of four norms which are not a part of those learned at home. These are independence, achievement, universalism, and specificity. He states that in relation to these

> individuals accept the obligations, respectively: to act by themselves (unless collaborative effort is called for) and accept personal responsibility and accountability for their conduct and its consequences (independence); to perform tasks actively and master the

environment according to standards of excellence (achievement); and to acknowledge the right of others to treat them as members of categories often based on a few discrete characteristics rather than on the full constellation of them representing the whole person (universalism and specificity). (Dreeben, 1967, p. 28)

Each of these four norms can be observed in the emerging socialization of young children as they enter school and can be contrasted with home learning. Whereas the child learns to call upon others for help at home, school tasks require that one must learn to work independently, to be self-reliant, to accept responsibility for one's own behavior and the consequences thereof, and to differentiate between when it is all right to work with and help others and when it is wrong to do so. Achievement in completing school tasks means competing against some standards of excellence and often puts the child in competition with others, while at home the child is motivated to achieve home tasks primarily through nurturance. Universalism and specificity—wherein one learns to accept being categorized by others as well as to "confine one's interest to a narrow range of characteristics and concerns, or to extend them to include a broad range" (Dreeben, 1967, p. 41)—are often in conflict with home learning which emphasizes the individuality of identity. In fact, teachers and parents alike perceive this norm to be dehumanizing although they operationally exhibit its use in their own sanctioning behavior with children.

It is relatively easy to predict how the learning of such norms as these is operationalized in one's adult life. All four are relevant principles of conduct for achieving success as an adult, and the degree with which an individual understands and acts upon each probably contributes greatly to that success. Conversely, the idealized state of an aesthetically educated adult might not be achieved through the emphasis in schooling upon norms such as these. In fact, this premise is one which we shall argue for later in this paper in light of Dreeben's own admonition that schools ought to provide activities which offer alternative routes to achievement and success; for example, music and dramatics which provide arenas for experiencing success and recognition without "the persistent, systematic and potentially corrosive evaluation typical of the [academic] classroom" (Dreeben, 1967, p. 39).

One might well ask how such norms are learned given that they appear nowhere in the official, prescribed curriculum of the school. After all, school is for acquiring knowledge and knowledge resides in the content of the curriculum. However, if we recall John Dewey's belief that "we learn what we do" and expand this by adding the admonition of Marshall McLuhan that "the medium is the message," we approach one possible answer.

Reflecting on both Dewey's and McLuhan's statements, Postman and Weingartner (1969) state that

> A classroom is a learning environment and . . . the way it is organized carries the burden of what people will learn from it. . . . *the critical content of any learning experience is the method or process through which the learning occurs.* (pp. 18-19)

This position seems to agree with that taken by Dreeben (1967, 1968), Bidwell (1972), and Bossert (1978). As Bossert states:

> what students are exposed to should affect what they learn. Yet, the structure and methods used to transmit the content of the curriculum and to facilitate the development of required skills also are important determinants of learning. (p. 13)

The unit of analysis in which such learning can best be identified and described is referred to by Bidwell (1972) in discussing Dreeben's (1967) work as the *activity structure,* and it is based on these assumptions:

> (1) Tasks, constraints, and opportunities available within social settings vary with the structural properties of those settings; (2) individuals who participate in those tasks, constraints, and opportunities derive principles of conduct (norms) based on their experiences in coping with them; and (3) the content of the principles varies with the setting. (Dreeben, 1967, p. 44)

Dreeben's assumptions regarding specific learning within activity structures grow out of the work of Breer and Locke (1965) who investigated how social experiences help to form ideas:

> It is our thesis that in working on a task an individual develops certain beliefs, values, and preferences specific to the task itself which over time are generalized to other areas of life. (p. 22)

Repetition of certain patterns of behavior enbedded in tasks which continue to be reinforced by recognized achievement and success results in generalizing such patterns to other task situations. As Bossert (1978) points out in discussing Breer and Locke's work:

> the form of the task, not its content, affects behavioral orientation. . . . certain actions are more instrumental than others for doing a particular task, and the successful completion of the task reinforces the behavior pattern. Through its use in similar, recurrent task situations, this pattern becomes a task-specific norm. (p. 29)

According to Bossert (1978, pp. 11-12), the elements of activity structures include the following criteria:

1. the modes of behavior which constitute the activity itself;
2. the reward structure embodied in the activity;
3. the sequencing of rewards or punishments in relation to behavior;
4. the collective character of the activity, for example, number of people involved, internal division of labor, choice of behavioral options; and

5. the nature of social relations in an activity.

To illustrate, we draw on three activity structures identified in Bossert's (1977) own investigations. These are *recitation, class tasks,* and *multitask.* Each will be presented drawing on Bossert's (1978) discussion and the above criteria, which will be referred to by number.

Recitation is a familiar activity structure in most classrooms. In recitation, questions are directed by the teacher, and students sit listening, raise their hands when they want to be called upon, and give answers to the questions publicly (Criterion 1, above). Because a student's answer is public, everyone in the class knows whether the question is answered correctly or incorrectly regardless of whether a teacher uses a formal system of rewarding correct answers (Criterion 2). Repeated successes with correct responses, or repeated failure with incorrect responses, and the reaction both of the teacher and other classmates, will determine to a great degree the responses of a student to the activity (Criterion 3). Recitation is by and large a whole-class activity, but students are expected to speak only when called upon (Criterion 4). Finally, there is little opportunity for interaction among students in the activity, and since repetition of similar recitations for a given subject reveals who knows the answers and who does not, all performances can be compared by the teacher and students, and such judgments can affect subsequent social interaction (Criterion 5).

Class tasks include assignments to the entire class which students are expected to accomplish at their seats independently, although some teachers may allow students to work together (Criteria 1 and 4). Performance is less public, and depending on how the teacher structures the assessment of assignments and the monitoring of students' work, a student's achievement is likely to remain private (Criteria 2 and 3). If students are asked to work independently, there is little opportunity for social interaction; if they are allowed to work in groups, social relations are apt to result (Criterion 5).

Multitask as an activity structure differs from class tasks primarily in the degree of freedom of choice allowed to students (Criteria 4 and 5). Thus in a multitask activity structure, a variety of possible activities would be simultaneously provided to the students, and they would have the option of choice. They might choose to work independently or with others (Criteria 1 and 4), and their performance is made public only to the degree that they choose to make it so (Criteria 2 and 3). Interactions among students may take place (Criterion 5), and the teacher must devise a system for assessing and monitoring student progress (Criterion 3).

These three activity structures—recitation, class task, and multitask—are easily recognizable in most elementary school classrooms. Their significance becomes most apparent, however, when examined in light of the instructional-social system of a classroom, as Bossert (1978) reminds us:

an activity molds the way in which individuals experience their environment, others, and themselves. Social experience is embodied in the meanings that phenomena have for the actor. Since an activity entails a temporal ordering of and relationship among phenomena, it structures the meaning of acts and objects by placing them in context with other acts and objects. The acquisition of shared meanings is fundamental to the process of socialization [and] the socialization outcomes of any social organization arise from its structuring activities. (pp. 2-3)

A dramatic contrast of experiences for a student can be illustrated by looking at how each of Bossert's three activity structures and their distinguishing criteria were manifested in the classrooms of the two teachers whose instructional-social systems we discussed earlier in this paper. Teacher J's instructional-social system did not include recitation as an activity structure. Instead, students worked in groups on some assignments and independently on others while she moved about the classroom, monitoring their progress and instructing informally. While some instruction was accomplished by presentation to the whole class, Teacher J used direct instruction after which the students grouped themselves to work together so they could help each other. Emphasis was placed upon students learning to work in such an open environment by assuming responsibility for their own behavior and not infringing upon the rights of others. Often, there were multitask activities where students could opt for an activity, choose to work with a group to complete it, or choose to work independently. Assessment of student progress was privately carried out between teacher and student, and was accomplished through monitoring and informal instruction.

In contrast, Teacher L's instructional-social system was based on recitation within small groups. She taught only in small-group settings, and devised her schedule to allow one-third of the class to receive instruction outside the classroom in the reading lab while she worked with a second group in a recitative mode. A third group did seatwork independently, completing worksheets. To accommodate such a system, students had to work quietly and independently. Within groups, recitation made public her assessment of student progress. No opportunities existed for multitask activities, since students were all diagnosed into a precise curriculum and moved through it sequentially.

Obviously, the meaning a given student might derive from Teacher J's and Teacher L's instructional-social systems is quite different. Behaviorally, students in Teacher J's classroom learned that it is all right to work with others in accomplishing tasks, that freedom of mobility is permissible, that talking is permitted, that the teacher is available to help or other students may help—all, however, within the boundaries of acceptable limits which Teacher J described as "common sense" and with the prescribed belief that students would learn to be responsible for their own behavior. In Teacher L's classroom, students learned that the classroom is a work place, that each person is expected to work independently and quietly, that mobility is limited and directed by the teacher, and that the "good student" is one who can accomplish assignments with a minimum of interaction with the teacher and no interaction with other students. The reward structure and sequencing of rewards/punishments were also obviously different. Teacher J's system of rewards and punishments was primarily private, while Teacher L's was public during recitation in small groups, through assignment to these groups by ability level as determined through diagnostic testing, and through her sanctions for off-task student behavior.

The collective character of activities within the two classrooms differed as well. In Teacher J's classroom, students learned to select from options which activities they wanted to be involved in, and they could work in groups. In Teacher L's classroom, students learned to work independently on the same class-assigned task. Thus, the opportunities to develop social relations in Teacher J's classroom were plentiful, while in Teacher L's classroom they were few.

As discussed earlier, the introduction of innovations into classroom instructional-social systems demands that *both* components of the system allow for and accommodate such change. Given the two instructional-social systems described above in relation to the three activity structures identified by Bossert, it is readily apparent that—given the nature of the innovation—major changes in the instructional-social system may have to occur before any innovation can be accommodated. Further, depending on the innovation and its fit, some instructional-social systems are more readily open to changes than others. As we have pointed out, Teacher J's instructional-social system was flexible, while Teacher L's was much more formal and structured. Although no opportunity for observing implementation of an innovation presented itself during the beginning-of-the-year study, it is our opinion that the more flexible system will accommodate change more readily.

In the case of bringing about change in aesthetic education in schools, this is a particularly important point. While little empirical evidence has been gathered to support this point, probably more classrooms across the nation than we might like to believe are utilizing activity structures like recitation and class tasks which are tied primarily to academic content. In addition, these classrooms are likely to feature formal, structured instructional-social systems insensitive to change. This is perhaps not surprising given the current national emphasis on raising student achievement in the so-called basic skills areas.

With these conditions in mind, we suggest that one educational innovation that might be inserted into classrooms is an activity structure we label *performing*. Performing is particularly suited to aesthetic education, especially if we are interested—as Bidwell (1972) says we ought to be—in one of the five major societal goals for schooling: "shaping students' creative and appreciative impulses in the major areas of intellectual and aesthetic culture" (p. 4). Given the underlying premise presented in this section of the paper, students learn the structure and methods used to transmit content as much as they learn the content itself. Bossert (1978) reminds us, "To the extent that these activity experiences differ, so too should the technical and moral outcomes derived from schooling" (p. 50). We maintain that the predominant activity structures in schools today do not foster the development in students of those "creative and appreciative impulses" which will educate them aesthetically.

In fact, if we believe what Postman and Weingartner (1969) maintain "is communicated by the structure of the classroom itself," what we might find students learning is:

Passive acceptance is a more desirable response to ideas than active criticism.

Discovering knowledge is beyond the power of students and is, in any case, none of their business.

Recall is the highest form of intellectual achievement, and the collection of unrelated "facts" is the goal of education.

The voice of authority is to be trusted and valued more than independent judgment.

One's own ideas and those of one's classmates are inconsequential.

Feelings are irrelevant in education.

There is always a single, unambiguous Right Answer to a question.

English is not History and History is not Science and Science is not Art and Art is not Music, and Art and Music are minor subjects and English, History and Science major subjects, and a subject is something you "take" and, when you have taken it, you have "had" it, and if you have "had" it, you are immune and need not take it again. (pp. 20-21)

What do we mean by performing?

As an activity structure that may be used to communicate any content of the curriculum and to communicate, at the very least, an appreciation of aesthetics, performing is defined by several properties. First and foremost, the end goal is performing itself—for others as well as being performed for. The form of performing can vary, but its essential purpose is to communicate something: an idea, an emotion, a concept, a narrative story, facts, or information. Teachers, for instance, perform when introducing a new concept, and often use every trick in the book to illustrate and embed the concept in their students' minds. Why not students?

A second property of performing is deciding what to perform. For students, decisions such as the following become necessary: What is the idea I want to get across? Who is my audience? What form of performance shall I use? How can I shape my idea to communicate it to my audience? Shall I perform publicly (before an audience) or privately (through media)? Which is most appropriate and most effective for getting my idea across?

Third, preparing for performing is an important property. Preparing demands that students decide: Shall I perform alone or with others? If I perform with others, who will do what (division of labor)? What skills does each member of the group possess, and how can we best use them? How shall we budget our time to allow for preparation?

Rehearsing is the fourth property of performing. Rehearsing suggests that students will have to confront: Who will take what role in the performing? When will we rehearse? Who is "directing" the performing? How do we know when we have honed what we are performing until it is "just right"?

The fifth property of performing is evaluating. When one performs or is performed for, judgments are made. Here, we are not seeking answers to questions such as, Was it good or bad? but rather: Did I like what I saw (heard, read, experienced, tasted)? What was it about the performance that I liked best? Liked least? Why? How might I have done differently what I saw (heard, read, experienced, tasted)? Within this property of evaluation we are seeking to build the concepts of personal taste and selectivity, and also the tolerance for deviance—the knowing that, while one may not like particularly what one saw (heard, read, experienced, tasted), others obviously enjoyed it, so it must have some value. We are not seeking criticism in the sense of evaluating "good" and "bad," although others may argue that this is the end goal of evaluating. Evaluation *by* the performers might include: Did I accomplish what I set out to perform; that is, was my idea communicated? Was the audience response what I expected? What did the audience response tell me?

Performing as an activity structure, then, allows for these five properties: deciding what to perform, preparing it, rehearsing it, performing it, and evaluating it. As we have looked into classrooms across the nation and across time, we have seen some of these properties utilized but seldom have we seen them used with the intent presented here. In addition, it is reasonable to suggest that as one moves upward in the grades from Kindergarten through Grade Twelve, one finds increasingly less attention paid to the type of performing we are suggesting here and, conversely, more attention to more familiar modes of instruction. Performing is an activity structure with possiblities for *all content curricula* and not just for play, free time, or "aesthetic appreciation." It is a way to transmit content (curriculum) through a form of aesthetic experience (performing) and demands significant changes in the way instruction—and therefore instructional-social systems—are organized.

Recognizing how difficult it is to bring about change in classroom instructional-social systems, inserting performing as an activity structure will be no small task. A mechanism for accomplishing such complex, multi-faceted changes is presented in the concluding section.

The Need for Interactive Research and Development

The previous sections of this paper have discussed the need to consider and change all relevant aspects of the instructional-social system in order to change what goes on in schools, more specifically what occurs in teaching-learning groups. The need to view teaching and learning from a multifaceted (ecological) and multidisciplinary perspective has also been discussed. Activity structures have been proposed as one way for analyzing and approaching school-based change given the above requirements, and performing has been suggested as a viable innovation for aesthetic education. Throughout, the power of the teacher in this process has been discussed and illustrated.

Given these conditions, one might ask whether change can be accomplished or whether the current state of affairs, whatever it might be within a particular teaching-learning group, will prevail. Inasmuch as the field of aesthetic education appears to be unwilling to accept a "no change" situation, proposing alternate change strategies appears to be a necessary next step. This last section of the paper, therefore, presents one change strategy that we have developed and have been testing for some eighteen months. This is Interactive Research and Development on Teaching (Tikunoff and Ward, 1977; Ward and Tikunoff, 1976). Prior to describing the strategy, however, the requirements for successful change, as we see them, need to be reviewed.

Three requirements of any change process involving the teaching-learning group are obvious based on the points raised in the earlier sections of this paper. First, the *teacher* must be involved. Second, change is more likely to occur if the teacher agrees that the new procedures, processes, materials, organization, and so on meet a *critical need* that he or she has identified, solve a problem that is of concern to him or her, or answer questions that are pertinent to him or her. Third, in order to bring about change, a teacher needs *resources*. Each requirement is discussed below.

Teacher involvement in change has never been an issue in education. What has been and, in our opinion, continues to be the issue is how and when and what kind of involvement. To date, teacher involvement has taken two major forms: The "Let us *help* you put into operation the change we've already identified as being needed" approach and the "We want to undertake the development of a new curriculum, teaching strategy, and so on—Who would be interested in working with us?" approach. We submit that while these approaches lead to changes in some teaching-learning groups, they are inadequate for initiating and undertaking change that calls for modification in the entire instructional-social system; for example, introducing a performing activity structure in Teacher L's teaching-learning group. What is needed is a change strategy in which the teacher has an opportunity to identify questions and problems that he or she deems to be critical; to participate in investigating these questions or problems; to help identify, develop, and test any *changes* that appear to be necessary; and to develop a systematic means for observing and tracking the *change* for purposes of affirming that it is still operating and/or for monitoring whether it is *changing* what the teacher set out to change or changing other parts of the instructional-social system unintentionally.

Enactment of such an approach is carried out best when a *team* of people is involved. The team may assume a variety of configurations. Based on our experience with Interactive Research and Development on Teaching (IR&DT), a team that includes teacher(s), a researcher, and a developer appears to be highly desirable for purposes of resolving critical educational problems. Within this framework, teachers tell researchers and developers where their R&D efforts should focus. Researchers and developers cooperate with the teachers to create and implement the desired change(s).

Based on our observations of IR&DT, we know that teachers—given an opportunity and the resources and support to do so—will identify problems, set priorities among various problems, and participate in identifying realistic procedures for inquiring into and resolving these problems. The more sophisticated a teacher's understanding of the complexity of what goes on in the classroom, the more readily such responsibilities are assumed. Less sophisticated teachers turn more frequently to a researcher or a developer to assist in refining and shaping their questions and problems but even they have no difficulty suggesting problem areas.

From our perspective, change that begins with teacher-identified problems has several advantages over change that begins with researcher or developer concerns. Since the problems emerge from actual instructional-social system(s), changes that result from the effort should answer questions that are actually being asked and provide improvements in teaching and learning that are considered to be worthwhile by teachers as well as by researchers and developers. Changes should also be in a form that is workable within existing instructional-social systems or that involves realistic and feasible modifications of the system. Commitment to change should also exist.

To accomplish change in this manner, teachers need resources. They need information about existing research and development outcomes. They need procedures for inquiring into what to change in order to resolve particular problems. They need procedures for observing and documenting change as it occurs and for deciding whether the change has, in fact, accomplished what they wanted to accomplish (that is, resolved the problem). Help of this sort might be provided by a researcher and/or a developer. In addition, they need assistance in maintaining the change once it is operable, a role that the developer and/or another teacher might assume.

From an aesthetic education perspective such a team might include teachers, a researcher who has been involved in studies related to aesthetic education (especially research that has been conducted in classrooms), and a developer who has been concerned with both aesthetic education curriculum materials development and with designing and testing teaching and learning processes and procedures emphasizing activity structures that provide aesthetic experiences for students.

As part of our study of IR&DT, we have hypothesized and are studying the implementation of the roles the members of such a team might assume (for example, see Griffin, 1977 and 1978). Generally, the roles reflect the processes that have been outlined above.

In recommending that an interactive approach has a potential for encouraging *teaching* to *produce* as well as to *affect* change, we are building upon the advice of Goodlad (1977), and Jackson and Kiesler (1977).

Goodlad summarizes what he learned regarding change:

> First, it became strikingly clear that, to make any difference to what happens in the school-based learning of students, all the projects, research, work of specialists in state or local offices of education, and so on, ultimately must come to roost within the finite dimensions of a school day, week or year. Second, most of what goes on outside of and in the name of schools has little to do with their functioning and never comes to roost there. Third, a good deal that does come to roost there is so irrelevant or inappropriate that it does more to impede than to aid school functioning. Fourth, with help and guidance from an informed, caring outside resource, school staffs can become extraordinarily aware of what is required to improve and discriminately selective in what they reach out for and bring into the school. Fifth, most inner-oriented change is directed to doing better what is assumed to be required of the school and, consequently, is well suited to refinement of practices. Sixth, the incentive to make fundamental changes seems to require awareness of pronounced discrepancies between existing programs and rather clear alternatives. Seventh, seriously attempting to do something about such discrepancies requires legitimization by a supportive surrounding infrastructure. (p. 5)

Jackson and Kiesler (1977) propose that practitioners (for our purposes, teachers) have special perspectives. These include:

> (1) a view of reality, (2) a vision of the achievable, (3) know-how, and (4) a commitment to act. (p. 14)

Interactive R&D capitalizes upon these perspectives. As a result, it provides one mechanism for increasing the possibility that teaching will support and implement desired changes in the instructional-social systems in the school in the area of arts and aesthetic education and in numerous other areas.

San Francisco, California
June 1978

NOTES

[1]The authors wish to acknowledge the support of the National Institute of Education, Department of Health, Education, and Welfare. Many of the thoughts that underlie this discussion are the result of work under NIE Contract NE-C-3-108 and NIE Grant OB-NIE-C-78-0103 to Far West Laboratory for Educational Research and Development, San Francisco, California. The opinions expressed here do not necessarily reflect the position or policy of the Institute and no official endorsement should be inferred.

[2]For further information regarding the original study see among five reports: P. Berman and M.W. McLaughlin. *Federal programs supporting educational change, Vol. IV: The findings in review.* Santa Monica, California: Rand Corporation, R-1589/4-HEW, April, 1975.

[3]For further information regarding the original study see J.I. Goodlad, M. Francis Klein, and Associates. *Looking behind the classroom door.* Worthington, Ohio: Charles A. Jones, 1974.

[4]Teachers' descriptions of their instructional systems were obtained in three ways: (1) each teacher prepared an audio-tape recording in which he or she discussed the system in an open-ended manner; (2) the teacher was interviewed by the two observers who were to be in the classroom for the seven weeks and these observers audio-recorded their respective interpretations of the interview; and (3) the teacher met with one or both of the authors to add any information that may have been omitted in the previous two data sources. This latter discussion also was audio-recorded. Typed manuscripts were prepared of the audio-recordings resulting from each of the above data-gathering efforts. The information reported here is taken from these transcripts and from the case study of rule-setting that was developed for each classroom.

[5]The general dissatisfaction in the field with methodologies based primarily on nomothetic psychological theory has led to much discussion about the need for alternative strategies. See: N.H. Azrin. A strategy for applied research: Learning based but outcome oriented. *American Psychologist,* 1977, *32*(2), 140-149; D.T. Campbell. *Qualitative knowing in action research.* Paper presented at the annual meeting of the American Psychological Association, New Orleans, September 1975; L.J. Cronbach. Beyond the two disciplines of scientific psychology. *American Psychologist,* 1975, *30*(2), 116-127; R.C. Rist. On the relations among educational research paradigms: From design to detente. In W.J. Tikunoff and B.A. Ward (Eds., Special Issue), *Anthropology and Education Quarterly,* 1977, *8* (2), 42-49; and P.C. Schlechty. *Teaching and social behavior: Toward an organizational theory of instruction.* Boston: Allyn and Bacon, 1976.

[6]The notion of applying the ecological perspective to studying classroom life is relatively new to educational research. R. G. Barker and his group at the University of Kansas applied the perspective to psychology: (see both his *Wanted: An eco-behavioral science.* In E. P. Willems and H. L. Raush (Eds.). *Naturalistic viewpoints in psychological research.* New York: Holt, Rinehart &

Winston, 1968; and *Ecological psychology: Concepts and methods for studying the environments of human behavior.* Stanford, California: Stanford University Press, 1968.) More recently, the writing of Urie Bronfenbrenner: (see, for instance, Toward an experimental ecology of human development. *American Psychologist,* 1977, *32*(7), 513-321; and with S.F. Hamilton. *School effectiveness in ecological perspective.* Paper presented at the National Institute of Education's National Invitational Conference on School Organization and Effects, San Diego, January 1978). And Walter Doyle (see *Learning the classroom environment: An ecological analysis of induction into teaching.* Paper presented at the annual meeting of the American Educational Research Association, New York, April 1977; and Paradigms for teacher effectiveness research. In L. Shulman (Ed.), *Review of research in education,* Itasca, Ill.: F.E. Peacock, 1977). And our own work, especially Toward ecology based curriculum: A model for professional growth through participatory research and development. In R. Edelfeldt and E. Brooks Smith (Eds.). *Integrating curriculum development and inservice education: Multidimensional approaches.* Washington, D.C.: Association for Teacher Educators, 1978; and *Conducting naturalistic research on teaching: Some procedural considerations.* Paper presented at the symposium of the American Educational Research Association, Toronto, March 1978.

[7]As indicated above, several approaches to applying an ecological perspective to educational research are underway. While they agree in principle, each is proceeding in unique fashion toward developing this perspective. Under the auspices of funding from the National Institute of Education, the authors are engaged in a proposed five-year effort to develop an ecological theory of teaching. Based on the premise that teaching is as much a sociological activity as it is psychological, the program of research and development proposes (1) to develop a theory that utilizes the multiple perspectives of such diverse social sciences as human ecology, human ethology, anthropology, sociology, environmental psychology, and sociology; (2) to identify and/or develop appropriate research methodology for studying both the elements of the theory and their interrelationships in the naturalistic classroom setting; and (3) to develop appropriate strategies for training teachers, students, and relevant others in applying the theory. The project will culminate with a test of the theory in the nature of a restructuring experiment.

REFERENCES

Bidwell, C.E. Schooling and socialization for moral commitment. *Interchange,* 1972, *3*(4), 1-27.

Bossert, S.A. Tasks, group management and teacher control behavior: A study of classroom organization and teacher style. *School Review,* August 1977, *85* (4), 552-565.

Bossert, S.A. *Activity structures and student outcomes.* Paper presented at National Institute of Education Conference on School Organization and Effects, San Diego, California, January 1978.

Breer, P.E., and Locke, E.A. *Task experience as a source of attitudes.* Homewood, Illinois: The Dorsey Press, 1965.

Dreeben, R. The contribution of schooling to the learning of norms. *Harvard Educational Review,* Spring 1967, *37*(2), 211-237.

Dreeben, R. *On what is learned in school.* Reading, Massachusetts: Addison-Wesley Publishing Co., 1968.

Goodlad, J.I. What goes on in our schools. *Educational Researcher*, March 1977, 6(3), 3-6.

Griffin, G.A., Tikunoff, W.J., and Ward, B.A. *Interactive research and development on teaching: Evaluation design Part I*. San Francisco: Far West Laboratory for Educational Research and Development, 1977.

Griffin, G.A. *Interim report: Degree and nature of interaction of two IR&DT teams during formulation of research designs*. San Francisco: Far West Laboratory for Educational Research and Development, 1978.

House, E.R. *Transferability and equity in innovation policy*. Paper presented at National Conference in Innovation and Change, Detroit, Michigan, September 1975.

Jackson, P.W. The way teachers think. In J.C. Glidewell (Ed.), *The social context of learning and development*. New York: Gardner Press, Inc., 1977, pp. 19-49.

Jackson, P. and Kiesler, S.A., Fundamental research and education. *Educational Researcher*, 1977, 6(8), 13-18.

Mann, D. Making change happen? *Teachers College Record*, February 1976, 77(3), 323-338.

McLaughlin, M.W. Implementation as mutual adaptation: Change in classroom organization. *Teachers College Record*, February 1976, 77(3), 339-351.

Postman, N. and Weingartner, C., *Teaching as a subversive activity*. New York: Delacorte Press, 1969.

Schlechty, P.C. *Teaching and social behavior: Toward an organizational theory of instruction*. Boston: Allyn and Bacon, Inc., 1976.

Tikunoff, W.J., and Ward, B.A. *A naturalistic study of the initiation of students into three classroom social systems*. Paper presented at the annual meeting of the American Educational Research Association, Toronto, Canada, March 1978.

Tikunoff, W.J., and Ward, B.A. *Research and development: A resource in the resolution of conflict*. Paper presented at the National Education Association Accountability Conference, Washington, D.C., March 1977.

Ward, B.A., and Tikunoff, W.J. *An interactive model of research and development on teaching*. San Francisco: Far West Laboratory for Educational Research and Development, 1976.

Richard Lewis / *A Response to Tikunoff and Ward*

Possibilities for Artist-Teachers

My response to this absorbing and thorough paper is conditioned by what I understand to be its possibilities—particularly for artist-teachers working in the schools, such as myself. At this point I would mention a problem which has been of concern to me throughout this conference—namely, the collision of languages when the artist attempts to describe certain internal and intuitive processes, and the social scientist, utilizing a specific vocabulary and observational techniques, attempts to describe similar processes. What emerges from this difference of description is perhaps a misunderstanding of the motives of each discipline and the habitual widening of the gap between the scientist and the artist. I don't think this necessarily has to be the case—and for the purposes of this conference, I don't think it would benefit us to perpetuate the gap.

With this in mind I would like to respond to this paper as a teacher of the arts based on my own experience in working with teachers of all kinds over an extended period of time within schools. For example, when the authors say, "to be successful, school-based change must attend to, adapt to, and accommodate not only the instructional aspects of the teaching-learning group but the social requirements as well," I interpret "social requirements" as the way a teacher perceives (or is made to perceive) the use, nature, and function of the arts, both personally and socially. There is, of course, a wide spectrum of opinions that teachers have toward the arts, and any change in the way the arts are used in schools must ultimately change a teacher's *personal* sense of the arts. This personal sense can be affected when teachers are in turn engaged in seeking some kind of artistic expression that influences their own ability to create through different expressive mediums.

The authors speak of the necessity of studying "the total ecology of

RICHARD LEWIS *is Director of The Touchstone Center for Children in New York City.*

the classroom instructional-social system in order to understand any of its component pieces." Extending that idea, I believe we need to study what I would call the ecology of the human imagination, and the degree to which the imagining capacity of both the teacher and the child, the inner world of each, affects the outer world, in this case the classroom. What I am suggesting is a kind of collaborative insight obtained when both the artist and the social scientist pool their observations of the interactions taking place between the inner and outer needs in the social-instructional framework manifest throughout the classroom setting.

Later when they say, "Given the nature of the innovation, major changes in the instructional-social system may have to occur before any innovation can be accommodated," I question how we can change a system without first making the "innovation" a need realized by individual teachers. Obviously we agree that systems don't change—people do. In terms of the arts then, the question is, How do we get teachers involved in the arts so that they use them personally and with children, thus enabling change to come from within rather than from the outside? This is a complex question and a problem we have given our attention to over a number of years. What we have realized in this connection is the importance of "innovating" change slowly—and the necessity of engaging people in a long-term process in which they are able to re-learn their personal connectiveness to the varieties of human expression.

What interested me most about the paper was the idea of "performing." By performing I suspect you meant more than just "creative drama"—and I interpreted your ideas here as implying the degree to which the "dramatic" and the actualizing of it is a process by which any kind of knowing and learning is ultimately made possible.

The last point in the paper concerning teacher involvement is, of course, very important. I am in complete agreement that long-term, substantial changes come about when the need to change is initiated by the teacher, and are realized by and through a teacher's involvement throughout the change process. Again I would add the importance within this process of teachers confronting their own values and perceptions of ideas and events beyond the immediate problem or situation to be changed. Classrooms are no more or less then reflections of our personal understanding of children, knowledge, and learning. It is these understandings which so often take time to articulate—and to ultimately look at differently.

By and large your paper has made me think about how words such as *environment, ecology,* and *performing* can be keys to bringing the arts into greater relevance in the schools. With this in mind I would like to share some thoughts with you that the paper, and the conference, have brought into the arena of my own concerns. Given the many issues discussed, I would like to make a very strong plea that we not pigeonhole certain functions of the arts, qualities of the arts that continually resist categorization. Good teaching, in any discipline, does not come about because we can absolutely define it—if anything, it is those very aspects of *inspired* teaching that often defy definition, that allow the artist in the teacher to be his or her own best judge of why and how the chemistry of inspiration is at work. We would do well to leave certain secrets of this inspiration untouched, and undefined.

If we are to respect the ecology of the artistic and imaginative vision, we should make sure we do not tip the ecological scale by weighting down, with our analytic powers, the special powers of intuition, spontaneity, playfulness, and improvisation in ourselves.

We would do well, it seems to me, to investigate and record the *new* possibilities of the teacher in the arts: the emerging capacity of such teachers to integrate, through the arts and other disciplines, what we are now learning about the integrative abilities of young children to think, feel, and express themselves without making unnatural separations, divisions, and fragmentations—indeed to respect the comfortableness of the child to extend metaphorically and imagistically into the commonalities of different experiences and forms of knowing.

We have at our disposal exciting new information, which is being applied on a practical level in schools and other institutions, on how the teaching of the arts can become an important catalytic agent in the revision of how we approach and perceive knowledge, and subsequently teach, experience, and learn such knowledge. These should be encouraged and documented and brought to the attention of a wider public.

We should carefully examine the implications of the use of the eclectic and generalist arts teacher and the ways such teachers might broaden the base sustaining the arts within the complexities and economics of present-day schools. By rethinking our ideas about specialists we do not necessarily forfeit quality, but instead bring qualitative concerns into wider accessibility.

We are on the verge of introducing to the practice of education the means by which the long traditions of the imaginative and artistic impulses common to all human beings can become sources of personal engagement and participation.

I, for one, hope that such possibilities will not be frittered away by pettiness and misunderstanding. What is important is *why* the following poem about singing by a ten-year-old child is able to communicate to us so many basic elements that too often in the past were rejected as part of the learning process—and *why* such expressions and experiences are needed in the course of our lives.

Singing
The children are singing,
their mouths open like sleepy fish.

Our teacher conducting the class
waves her arms
like a rhyme in water.
The girls sing high:
our ears ring for the sweetness.
Listeners stand in dazzling amazement.*

New York, New York
July 1978

---

*Poem by Peter Shelton in R. Lewis (Ed.), *Miracles: Poems by children of the English-speaking world*. New York: Bantam, 1977.

Roy A. Edelfelt

Staff Development and Teaching in the Arts

I was asked to give a general overview of methods and trends in staff development that "may affect the teaching process in general and specifically the teaching of the arts," and "to describe the effect of the role of the teacher and of the teachers' organization on teaching, and their effect on change in the school."

From staff development to impact on teaching is a great leap. I will deal more often with the possible effect of staff development on teachers, assuming that influencing teachers affects teaching. I will also comment on the role of the teacher and the teachers' organization in teaching, and their effect on change in the school.

Space limits the degree to which I can address my charge. I have developed my ideas with reference to both the teacher in the arts and all other teachers who influence teaching in the arts. I begin with a section identifying the strong similarities between attitudes and approaches in staff development, and attitudes and approaches in education in the arts. In the second section I discuss some of my persuasions about learning in relation to both staff development and teaching K-12 students. Following that section is one on aesthetic understanding and appreciation.[1] Finally there is a section on staff development and the role of teachers and teacher organizations.

Had there been more space I would have included a section on adult learning with comments on how the circumstances of adult learning make the learning situation different. I would also have tried to make more distinctions between the staff development of teachers in the arts and the staff development of other teachers. Such distinctions are probably not necessary: learning and teaching are essentially the same phenomena in any area. But it would be interesting to probe differences and similarities between arts and non-arts teachers.

ROY A. EDELFELT *is Professional Associate, National Education Association.*

Parallels Between Staff Development and the Arts and Aesthetics

In the United States education in the arts and aesthetics has been the privilege of the few. Worse yet, the arts until recently have been so narrowly defined by the tastes of the middle or upper-middle class that the majority of people have not been included as participants or contributors. Concert halls and art galleries, opera houses and ballet theatres are populated by comparatively wealthy people. There are not many nonwhite or poor people in the Kennedy Center and Lincoln Center audiences or at the Metropolitan Museum of Art and the National Gallery. The arts and aesthetics, the so-called finer things, have been the private preserve of a very small segment of the American population.

There are at least two reasons why access to the arts and aesthetics is limited. One is that the system is undemocratic and unfair. A second is that the arts are too restricted to so-called serious works. The two notions are related.

In education there is no equal opportunity for access to the arts in the usual definition of the term, and art idioms not qualified as good by middle-class standards are not recognized as art.

As a result of limiting the arts to serious works, art that is "of the people" has not been supported or legitimized, particularly in education. For example, a junior-high general music class is seldom encouraged to study jazz, to sing pop songs, or to participate in country music. The curriculum in music is more often an introduction to classical, romantic, and modern (not too modern) composers, and the singing is most often the well-accepted folk song or traditional school song. Creating or composing that grows out of situations teenagers themselves experience seldom happens. If any part of training approaches learning notation, the written language of music, it usually involves memorizing all the major and minor key signatures and other nomenclature. Too often, the emphasis is on becoming literate in music, and too seldom on helping aesthetic sensibilities grow or learning technicalities in support of aesthetic experience.

Imposing "the good" in the arts on students creates a kind of snobbishness that is antithetical to the whole notion of art. It is not just a matter of separating out the good from the bad; there are increasingly higher levels of selection as one becomes more "sophisticated." One quickly learns to hide a love for Tchaikovsky and to display an interest in Bach or Mozart; Peter Ilyitch's music is too schmaltzy to be serious.

In-service education in general warrants similar criticism. Teachers are seldom more than recipients of in-service education. Some higher authority usually decides what is good for teachers. A common standard of quality and a designated amount of quantity are usually required of all teachers. And teachers seldom have the freedom to attend the conferences and work sessions at which major decisions about education are made.

Furthermore, the serious works in in-service education often exclude the real world of teaching and learning in schools, and dwell on esoteric themes. Too little emphasis is put on what the teacher can create, on what grows out of real encounters with students, on what the experience of schooling is (as opposed to what the products are), and on how to enhance the quality of life in schools.

I think that students remember schools and teachers more for the kinds of experiences they had than for the actual content they learned. Human experiences and the quality of life *are* aesthetic and artistic dimensions of schooling. Every teacher has opportunities to make artistic and aesthetic experience and learning a part of his or her particular area of study. The arts and aesthetics, therefore, should permeate the curriculum. They are more basic than the so-called basics.

Finally, satisfying experiences—whether in learning or in the arts—are what people want to return to, or recapture, or find in another experience. The goal, then, in both learning in general and aesthetic experience in particular should be to whet appetites, to entice individuals to come back for more.

A Foundation for Staff Development

Teaching should be considered a science as well as an art. This section is concerned mainly with the scientific aspect of teaching—with what research tells us about behavior and the implications of this information for instructional processes.

The teacher involved in any type of instruction, including staff development, should have some foundation for teaching, in addition to having competence in the content to be taught. By "foundation" I mean a base on which instructional behavior can be built. Ideally a foundation consists of notions about psychology, tempered by one's own philosophy of education. Such a foundation should be defensible, reasonable, consistent, based on solid thinking, and flexible. It should provide direction in all teaching situations. It should be clear enough to provide positive direction and yet not be restricted by a narrow interpretation that might dictate stereotyped thinking or teaching. My own view of staff development can be best stated as an assumption, which I will not attempt to prove valid because I hope educators involved in staff development will be challenged by the strength of my arguments to test it themselves. The assumption is that educators offering staff development activities should operate on principles of teaching and learning based on the best evidence available from the psychology of learning and human growth and development.

Psychological studies of learning are usually organized into two categories: the psychology of learning (that is, information on how learning takes place); and human growth and development (that is, information about the biological, social, and physical growth of the learner). In this paper I deal only with the psychology of learning.

American culture is my implicit frame of reference.

The following statements about and discussion of my own notions about learning are based on modern psychological thought (cf. Hilgard and Bower, 1975; Hulse, Deese, and Egeth, 1975) and a philosophical view primarily drawn from Dewey (1934). Among the nine notions there are both overlaps and interrelationships. A notion can be misinterpreted if the qualifications introduced by other notions are not considered. The interrelationships and overlaps suggest that this view of learning be considered in its entirety and that judgments about its adequacy be withheld until all of the notions have been presented.

Notions About Learning

1. *When learners find that their previously acquired ways of behaving are inadequate to reach a desired goal, they are ready for new learning. There must be sufficient physical, emotional, and intellectual maturity for learning to take place. Part of achieving such maturity is recognition of a goal.*

It is always difficult for teachers to recognize that learning that has been exciting, interesting, and stimulating for them may not necessarily be so for their students. The teaching strategy implied here is to guide students to realize that there are better and greater goals to be achieved, and to recognize that their present ways of behaving may not be adequate to reach the goal they have identified as desirable.

2. *Individuals vary in physical, intellectual, and emotional characteristics. Each learner has different abilities, aptitudes, interests, talents, ambitions, needs, and capacities. Learning is improved when the uniqueness of the individual is considered.*

Providing for the uniqueness of the individual in the learning process involves at least two steps. First, the teacher must discover, on the basis of good evidence, the individual differences of students. Seeking out significant evidence on each student is time-consuming, and yet it must not be superficial. Second, the teacher must take action in terms of the information gained. The quality of action depends initially on the thoroughness and objectivity of the first step.

Discovering and assessing individual differences is a continuing process. Rediscovering or reassessing the student's unique qualities might be considered a third step. It is similar to the first step although the method for gathering information may be modified and the comprehensiveness of investigation may never approach that of the initial search.

3. *Learning is aided and reinforced by success, approval, and satisfaction. A feeling of adequacy is inherent in emotional stability. Group learning provides social reinforcement; and, if cooperatively arrived at, it provides a feeling of adequacy. Reward should be intrinsic as well as extrinsic. Punishment is of little if any value in learning.*

Approbation is usually given in terms of the mores of the culture. For this reason, success, approval, or satisfaction is most often realized either directly through the acclaim of other individuals or indirectly through students' own perception of what is good, desirable, or beautiful, or what is achievement or accomplishment, in their culture. Teachers wield special power by dint of their status, a power that should be used wisely to ensure for students a balance between a recognition of inadequacy, as suggested in the first notion, and a feeling of adequacy. Establishing the appropriate balance between success and failure may well be at the discretion of the teacher, and it should be determined in consonance with the notion of individual differences.

4. *Retention is increased when learning results in conceptualization or generalization. Learning that results in generalization has the greatest chance of being useful in other situations. Frequent use of generalization, association, or learning fosters retention. Isolated, incongruous, and unrelated learning is easily forgotten.*

Efficiency in learning is a matter of conserving energy as well as minimizing time. Learning that has relevance in many situations and that is applicable in various circumstances is often learning that has been brought to the level of generalization. Such learning contributes to efficiency and also tends to be remembered longer.

Another aspect of this notion is whole-part learning and the degree of retention it promises. Material is remembered best when it is seen in all its interrelatedness and when it is learned and used as a part of an organized body of material. This statement is a positive way of saying what the last sentence of the fourth notion draws attention to—the short life of isolated, incongruous, or unrelated learning.

The fourth notion also mentions the frequent use of learned material. Frequent use should be intentional for the learning that the teacher considers essential, and such use should foster variety. This notion is closely related to repeated trial, stated in notion five.

5. *Repetition should be repeated trial but not changeless trial. Trial-and-error learning, or learning by approximation, is the way in which much learning takes place. In its most perfect form it becomes learning by insight.*

A key phrase in most modern discussions of repetition is "not changeless trial." The meaning of "repetition" for the psychologist is not the dictionary definition of "repeated action." The method of learning is not changeless repetition. One does not think or do over and over again exactly what one thought or did when first confronted by a learning task. Rather, relationships are sought in successive trials, and responses undergo reorganization as mastery is approached. Some psychologists use the expressions "approximation and correction" and "analysis of relations" as better terms for conveying the meaning of deliberate and desirable trial and error. This concept of trying or testing in order to learn, places a considerably different emphasis on the way in which skills are acquired. The shift to an experimental notion of learning is evidence that teachers who have imposed memorization tasks for the development of all skills need to reexamine the nature of the goals they wish students to achieve and to determine whether they have overorganized their systems for gaining command of skills. Students should not be allowed to stumble in confusion, but neither should the teacher always teach or emphasize a particular scheme of organization. Students should get the necessary guidance in experimentation.

The students' need for such guidance provides the teacher with the opportunity to help students select a goal toward which they can make progress as they develop the desired skill.

6. *All cognitive learning involves association, which in turn makes transfer of learning possible. New learning is in part a transfer of former learning. The degree to which transfer is possible depends on the learner's ability to see relationships between new and old experiences. New learning tasks that have marked similarities and yet are basically quite different should not be presented in succession; transfer is confused by such experience. The best learning has maximum transfer value.*

To justify the existence of the school or college in our society, we must assume that transfer of learning is possible and probable. Too often, unfortunately, transfer is taken for granted. There is no overwhelming evidence that what is taught in the classroom has great transfer value; it is not common practice to test the amount of transfer that takes place from courses of study to on-the-job or private-life behavior. One reason for the lack of such evidence is, no doubt, the difficulty of measuring transfer of learning. One kind of transfer, however, should be testable: the extent to which students are able to transfer skills in learning from one task to another.

To increase the possibility of transfer, the teacher must be able to test when it takes place. Such discovery is related to determining when generalization is possible (notions four and five). The most important single factor in determining the amount of transfer possible, and the one about which the teacher can do something, is the learner's awareness that what is being learned can be transferred. The teacher, then, can play a very important part in facilitating the probability of transfer. Planning should affect both the selection of material to be taught and the way in which it is taught.

Perhaps one of the greatest needs for staff developers or graduate school faculties is to know more about the generally accepted facts relating to transfer of learning. What should also be recognized and appreciated is the interdependence of a philosophy of education and a theory of transfer.

7. *We learn only by doing. Either overt or implicit involvement of the learner is essential for learning to take place.*

This notion may appear to be the most simple one. Its simplicity and brevity are misleading.

Involvement cannot be passive. Doing is not merely going through the motions of an activity. Doing means learners interacting with their environment; they are not quiescent. Learning is an individual matter. So is involvement. The kind, quality, and degree of involvement will depend on individual capacity, ability, and background, and the nature of the learning task. The quality of learning is of vital concern to teachers; therefore, they need to give attention to the quality of doing. The quality of involvement may be directly related to the strength of motivation.

8. *Learning is stimulated by wants, needs, interests, or motives. It may be necessary to influence motivation. However, motivation is best when it is intrinsic.*

The relationship of motivation to the foregoing notions is well illustrated by its relation to the notion that we learn only by doing.

The skillful teacher must be adept at influencing motivation when necessary. Adeptness involves recognizing readiness for a particular task, providing for individual differences, maintaining an appropriate balance between approval and criticism, helping students to make associations and to generalize, and using students' own motives. Influencing motivation is manipulation in its most ethical sense.

In attempting to influence motivation, teachers must remember that their own personality may be their most important asset or liability. The type of person providing an incentive may be more important than the nature of the incentive. What is learned and how it is learned is greatly influenced by the emotional response of the student to the teacher.

When the mere performance of an activity produces satisfaction, motivation is intrinsic. For example: If a student is working on the skill of perspective in sketching, it is possible to practice that skill while deriving genuine pleasure from the activity of sketching. Such a relation is desirable. However, it should be remembered that when developed effectively, all relations of satisfactions to activity become to some extent intrinsic. Tasks that are motivated by the teacher primarily through artificial or arbitrary means usually are not learned as well or as easily as those for which the learner has personal incentives or motives. I am not suggesting that the teacher must base whatever is learned on static incentives for and motives of the learner, for motivation is not static—nor are motives, incentives, or goals. The job of the teacher is to capitalize on the motivational potential at hand.

9. *In many instances concomitant learnings are more important than the learning at which effort may have been directed; for example, attitudes about a subject or a teacher may have far more influence on the learner than experiences in an area with a teacher. Although teachers may have rather specific goals in mind, they have little assurance that*

the goals will become the central focus of the student. For this reason goals or tasks that are cooperatively identified by the teacher and student are more apt to become the student's focus as well as the teacher's. Even in such instances the relative importance of specific learnings cannot be predicted for the individual student.

Wise teachers encourage concomitant learnings, which as far as possible should not be fortuitous. If teachers hope to foster and teach understandings, appreciations, attitudes, and values of quality in addition to information and skills, and all within the framework of the psychological notions set forth above, they certainly have no other choice.

The foregoing notions and the implied philosophy of education apply to any level of education. The fact that they do is especially significant for the teacher educator, for students tend to teach as they were taught. Therefore, teachers of teachers should make every class an educative experience for the personal growth of the student as well as an opportunity to observe good teaching in practice.

Developing Aesthetic Understanding and Appreciation— A Major Teaching Task

A major teaching objective in any of the arts is to develop aesthetic understanding and appreciation, including a basic understanding of the interrelationship of the fine arts. Words such as "interrelationship," "association," and "transfer," which I used in a prior section, point up the importance of connecting learning with something already known. Making a connection is particularly important in instruction that is directed at aesthetic understanding and appreciation. In my view such instruction should be related to everyday life.

This objective is an example of the whole-part concept that was discussed in the section on notions of learning. Aesthetic enjoyment is the whole, the primary and ultimate purpose of artistic experience. Aesthetic enjoyment involves conceiving the whole, the totality, of artistic expression. There are good reasons artistically for setting the development of aesthetic understanding and appreciation as a primary objective of teaching in the arts. If art has meaning, it is through aesthetic experience that such meaning is communicated. Dewey (1934) stated about as clearly as anyone the nature of communication in art: "The work of art tells something to those who enjoy it about the nature of their own experience of the world ... it presents the world in a new experience which they undergo" (p. 83).

Unfortunately, for the lay person—and among school teachers there are a good many lay persons—the aesthetic as far as the arts are concerned seems to connote something that is removed from everyday, ordinary experience. Many think of the aesthetic as lofty, contemplative, and esoteric in nature. Such a connotation makes study directed at aesthetic understanding and appreciation both forbidding and baffling to the novice. Such a connotation is fallacious. Aesthetic enjoyment is more closely akin to emotional sensitiveness than to intellectual erudition. The problem for teachers is to dispel notions about aesthetics that are too high-minded, and to teach in a way that will de-emphasize the complicated theories put forth by philosophers and artists. Neophytes need to begin to enjoy the arts at their own level of experience. There are reasonable assurances that aesthetic enjoyment is possible without a knowledge of theory. For example, music need not be fragmented in the teaching process. Students do not need to know about themes and development, key changes and signatures, or the history surrounding the writing of a great work to develop an aesthetic understanding and appreciation of music.

> Technique is certainly useful, not to say indispensable, to the composer or the performer; a knowledge of musical theory is certainly an advantage to the performer and practically inescapable for the composer. But theory, in the sense of generalization, is not of the least use to the listener; in practice it is a veritable encumbrance if he allows preoccupation with it to interfere with his contact with the music as such. He can derive both interest and help from whatever can be pointed out to him in connection with the specific content of a piece of music; but he will only be misled if he is persuaded to listen in an exploratory rather than a completely receptive spirit. (Sessions, 1950, p. 96)

Quoting George Santayana's remark that music "the most abstract of arts serves the dumbest emotions," Aaron Copland (1952) commented:

> Yes, I like this idea that we respond to music from a primal and almost brutish level—dumbly, as it were, for on that level we are firmly grounded. On that level, whatever the music may be, we experience basic reactions such as tension and release, density and transparency, a smooth or angry surface, the music's swelling and subsiding, its pushing forward or hanging back, its length, its speed, its thunders and whisperings—and a thousand other psychologically based reflections of our physical life of movement and gesture, and our inner, subconscious mental life. That is fundamentally the way we hear music—gifted and ungifted alike, and all the analytical, historical, textual material on or about the music heard, interesting though it may be, cannot—and I venture to say should not—alter that fundamental relationship. (pp. 14-15)

The Nature of Aesthetic Enjoyment

Aesthetic enjoyment or appreciation entails immediate emotional response. Although aesthetic enjoyment is enhanced by knowledge, unless such knowledge is so much a part of the appreciator that it is called into play unconsciously, it tends to hinder the receptiveness that aesthetic experience necessitates. Aesthetic enjoyment, therefore, does not involve understandings that are intellectual in the sense that they require the ability to explain or account for feeling; it is more a matter of establishing emotional contact.

Most people can recognize beauty or ugliness in objects of everyday life, and many can recall aesthetic experiences in nature, such as viewing a sunset or a particularly impressive landscape, but they often fail to recognize these experiences as aesthetic. More important, perhaps, they fail to recognize similar experiences in the arts.

The discontinuity between experiences in the arts and everyday experiences has been too great. Our schools place too much emphasis on memory, too little on creativity. Of course, our educational system is not completely to blame. The complexities of modern living—for example, the specialization in vocations and professions—have also contributed to this discontinuity. People without special interest, which must be developed, just do not take or have time to see the similarities and the relatedness of experiences in the arts and everyday experience. There is, too, the rough, tough pioneer spirit, which did not die with the conquering of new territory, that frowns on emotional expression, the notion being that those who cannot suppress their feelings are weak. It is still fairly common to look with suspicion on men and boys who give attention to the emotional aspects of living. Better understanding of mental health has helped to dispel this notion. When intolerance of sensitivity does occur, the arts teacher may well seek the help of the psychology teacher to get support for the notion that sensitivity to emotions and the expression of human feeling are normal and healthy.

Experience and Aesthetic Quality

Making an association between everyday life, which all people understand to some extent, and aesthetic experience provides an opportunity to use and capitalize on former learning. It also makes possible immediate involvement of the student. If everyday experience is considered as the raw material of the arts, the relationships and associations of aesthetic and everyday experience are more easily made clear.

Everyday experience needs to be defined. The word "experience" is especially ambiguous. Dewey (1934) has defined an experience:

> We have an experience when the material experienced runs its course to fulfillment. Then and then only is it integrated within and demarcated in the general stream of experience from other experiences. A piece of work is finished in a way that is satisfactory; a problem receives its solution; a game is played through; a situation, whether that of eating a meal, playing a game of chess, carrying on a conversation, writing a book, or taking part in a political campaign, is so rounded out that its close is a consummation and not a

cessation. Such an experience is a whole and carries with it its own individualizing quality and self-sufficiency. It is *an* experience. (p. 35)

In reflecting on everyday experience one can identify the factors—that is, design, shape, form, harmony of feelings, movement, proportion, wholeness, simplicity, and efficiency—that go to make up such experience. Everyday experience has aesthetic quality that gives it unity—"no experience of whatever sort is a unity unless it has esthetic quality" (Dewey, 1934, p. 40).

For the neophyte, aesthetic understanding and appreciation of experience may be most easily achieved by *reflecting* on everyday experience. Reflection provides time and space for understanding and appreciation of the factors that make an experience. For the novice to aesthetic considerations, the beginning, flow, rhythmic movement, pauses, unrepeated quality, plot, successive phrases, and close of an experience are not easily seen or appreciated at the moment of occurrence because the novice is preoccupied with the action of the event. An awareness of the aesthetic quality in everyday experience can be achieved first, and perhaps best, through reflection. Gaining an awareness of and a sensitiveness to the factors that are characteristic of experience by reflecting on past experience is progress toward an ability to recognize the aesthetic in everyday experience, as well as progress toward learning that can be related to artistic aesthetic experience.

Aimless, incomplete experience is not significant living. It provides little if any satisfaction, immediate or reflective. Perhaps aesthetic enjoyment can make a contribution to the teacher's way of life, as well as to his or her appreciation of life, by suggesting the value of design, organization, selectivity, clarity, and simplicity. "The esthetic is no intruder in experience from without, whether by way of idle luxury or transcendent ideality, but . . . is the clarified and intensified development of traits that belong to every normally complete experience" (Dewey, 1934, p. 46).

The twofold concept of doing and undergoing provides a helpful safeguard against limiting the idea of everyday experience to the superficial or purely enjoyable experiences in life. "A man does something. . . . In consequence he undergoes, suffers, something. . . . The properties thus undergone determine further doing. . . . The process continues until a mutual adaptation of the self and the object emerges and that particular experience comes to a close" (Dewey, 1934, p. 44).

"Experience is limited by all the causes which interfere with perception of the relations between undergoing and doing" (Dewey, 1934, p. 44). The speed of life in our industrial, mechanized society offers little opportunity for deep, complete experiences. Flitting from one thing to another with only superficial attention to living interferes with the balance of relations between doing and undergoing. Commercialism, glamorizing, smugness, and conceit help to confuse values and contribute little to encouraging genuine, full, real experiences. If everyday life is superficial, flighty, and incomplete, it is difficult to experience and understand, to cherish and appreciate the aesthetic, which is built on genuine and complete experience.

Everyday Experience and Aesthetic Experience in Art

In making an association between everyday experience and aesthetic experience there is real value in looking into the work of art as a production. Not only does such inspection enhance understanding of the artist's work; it also helps one understand the relationship between the act of producing a work of art and the act of perceiving, appreciating, and enjoying art. Understanding the work of art as a production also helps in comprehending re-creation as well as creation.

> Art, in its form, unites the very same relation of doing and undergoing, outgoing and incoming energy, that makes an experience to be an experience. Because of elimination of all that does not contribute to mutual organization of the factors of both action and reception into one another, and because of selection of just the aspects and traits that contribute to their interpenetration of each other, the product is a work of esthetic art. . . . The doing or making is artistic when the perceived result is of such a nature that *its* qualities *as perceived* have controlled the question of production. The act of producing that is directed by intent to produce something that is enjoyed in the immediate experience of perceiving has qualities that a spontaneous or uncontrolled activity does not have. The artist embodies in himself the attitude of the perceiver while he works. . . .

> The doing may be energetic, and the undergoing may be acute and intense. But unless they are related to each other to form a whole in perception, the thing done is not fully esthetic. (Dewey, 1934, pp. 48; 50)

The Creator and the Re-Creator of Aesthetic Experience

The student of the arts—whose primary role is that of the perceiver, the appreciator, the enjoyer—must be aware of the similarity between the experience of the creating artist and his or her own experience. "We are given to supposing that" the perceiver/appreciator "merely takes in what is there in finished form, instead of realizing that this taking in involves activities that are comparable to those of the creator" (Dewey, 1934, p. 52). The perceiver must be participating, doing. Involvement cannot be passive. Receptivity is "a process consisting of a series of responsive acts that accumulate toward objective fulfillment" (p. 52). Perception causes "an act of reconstructive doing, and consciousness becomes fresh and alive" (p. 53). We may recognize or undergo, but when we perceive, reaction continues through an "act of reconstructive doing."

In order to perceive aesthetically there should be continuous interaction between the object and the total organism. "The esthetic or undergoing phase of experience is receptive. It involves surrender. But adequate yielding of the self is possible only through a controlled activity that may well be intense" (p. 53). This controlled activity is, of course, participation, involvement, conscious doing. Aesthetic experience, therefore, "involves the cooperation of motor elements" and the senses "as well as cooperation of all funded ideas that may serve to complete the new picture that is forming" (p. 53). And, Dewey continues,

> To perceive, a beholder must *create* his own experience. And his creation must include relations comparable to those which the original producer underwent. They are not the same in any literal sense. But with the perceiver, as with the artist, there must be an ordering of the elements of the whole that is in form, although not in details, the same as the process of organization the creator of the work consciously experienced. Without an act of recreation the object is not perceived as a work of art. The artist selected, simplified, clarified, abridged and condensed according to his interest. The beholder must go through these operations according to his point of view and interest. In both, an act of abstraction, that is of extraction of what is significant, takes place. . . . There is work done on the part of the percipient as there is on the part of the artist. The one who is too lazy, idle, or indurated in convention to perform this work will not see or hear. His "appreciation" will be a mixture of scraps of learning with conformity to norms of conventional admiration and with a confused, even if genuine, emotional excitation. (p. 54)

I have dealt in some detail with the concept that aesthetic experience can be developed from and through everyday experience. It is important that the connection be made. First, making the connection indicates what is meant by beginning with learners where they are and with what they understand, by approaching the whole before investigating its parts, by *involving* learners in learning, and by considering the uniqueness of each individual. It is an extension of some notions about learning into the realm of teaching the arts. Second, making the connection goes beyond the cursory or esoteric attention advocates of teaching generally give to development of aesthetic understanding and appreciation. Finally, the concept affects the manner in which all skills and content areas in the arts are taught.

I have not attempted to prescribe how aesthetic appreciation *should* be taught because it cannot be taught by itself or in isolation. Rather, I am suggesting that teaching all aspects of the arts should be in accordance with the concept of developing aesthetic experience from and through everyday experience. It should serve as a frame of reference, a value system, within which the arts are taught. The same notion holds for staff development that is designed to help any teacher be more effective in helping students learn about the arts and aesthetic education.

Trends and Approaches in Staff Development

In-service education has been roundly criticized in the last several years as overly prescribed, "low-level, piecemeal, and patchwork" and yielding "too little in the improvement of teaching or school program":

> In school district programs, the focus is on introducing new curriculums, beefing up existing programs, or following new fads and trends, typically at the supervisor's discretion. In formal graduate work, study is largely divorced from the specifics of the teacher's job. (Edelfelt and Lawrence, 1975, p. 14)

Despite general condemnation of the present state of in-service education, there is quite the opposite opinion about the need for in-service education. Educators may not like what they get in in-service education, but they believe strongly that in-service education is needed. Surprisingly perhaps, teachers, school administrators, higher education faculty and administrators, and teacher organization representatives express quite similar views about dissatisfaction and need (Joyce, McNair, Diaz, McKibbin, Waterman and Baker, 1976).

Staff development has begun to get major attention, partly because of the widely expressed dissatisfaction, but also because attention to the initial preparation of teachers has diminished; the supply of teachers is greater than the demand. The public (and the profession itself) is pushing for staff development that will keep teachers and other personnel current and vital. The greater stability of school faculties has prompted administrators and school boards to assume that money spent on staff development will not be as easily dissipated as it was when teacher mobility was great.

The motivation and commitment to do more with staff development is evident. The question is what to do. Too many educators still see staff development as a didactic process—teachers gathering in courses to absorb knowledge or refine skills. Although teachers now have more influence in staff development, the few precedents for innovative programs (that involve teachers) provide very little guidance on alternatives to present practice.

We get some guidance from a comprehensive review of research in in-service education by Gordon Lawrence and some of his colleagues (see Edelfelt and Lawrence, 1975). A number of specific suggestions for approach, location, duration, decision making, and staffing of in-service education are included in the more important findings of this review:

1. School-based inservice programs concerned with complex teacher behaviors tend to have greater success in accomplishing

their objectives than do college-based programs dealing with complex behaviors.

2. Teacher attitudes are more likely to be influenced in school-based than in college-based inservice programs.

3. School-based programs in which teachers participate as helpers to each other and planners of inservice activities tend to have greater success in accomplishing their objectives than do programs which are conducted by college or other outside personnel without the assistance of teachers.

4. School-based inservice programs that emphasize self-instruction by teachers have a strong record of effectiveness. . . .

5. Inservice education programs that have differentiated training experiences for different teachers (that is, "individualized") are more likely to accomplish their objectives than are programs that have common activities for all participants.

6. Inservice education programs that place the teacher in [an] active role (constructing and generating materials, ideas and behavior) are more likely to accomplish their objectives than are programs that place the teacher in a receptive role (accepting ideas and behavior prescriptions not of his or her own making).

7. Inservice education programs that emphasize demonstrations, supervised trials and feedback are more likely to accomplish their goals than are programs in which the teachers are expected to store up ideas and behavior prescriptions for a future time.

8. Inservice education programs in which teachers share and provide mutual assistance to each other are more likely to accomplish their objectives than are programs in which each teacher does separate work.

9. Teachers are more likely to benefit from inservice education activities that are linked to a general effort of the school than they are from "single-shot" programs that are not part of a general staff development plan.

10. Teachers are more likely to benefit from inservice programs in which they can choose goals and activities for themselves, as contrasted with programs in which the goals and activities are preplanned.

11. Self-initiated and self-directed training activities are seldom used in inservice education programs, but this pattern is associated with successful accomplishment of program goals.

(Edelfelt and Lawrence, 1975, pp. 8-19)

In another study (Edelfelt, 1977) twenty-nine criteria for in-service education were enunciated. The criteria cover essentially the same content as suggested in the review above; they also encompass the relationship of in-service education to curriculum development, instructional improvement, teacher and student needs, research, teaching load, resources, financing, preservice preparation, and the individual growth patterns of teachers. As may be obvious, these criteria are helpful in suggesting not only how substance and process should be determined but also how activities should be paid for and related to the job of teaching.

Federal laws creating the Teacher Center Program and broadening the emphasis of Teacher Corps to include in-service education give additional momentum to the staff development movement. The new Teacher Center Program holds particular promise for some radical improvement in staff development—improvement, incidentally, that is consistent with the research findings of Lawrence and his colleagues. A more significant role for teachers in decision making, for example, may come about through the provision in the Teacher Center legislation that teachers constitute a majority on a center's policy board (provided, of course, that teachers do not get co-opted). The allowance in Teacher Center regulations for released time provides opportunities for teachers to work together developing curriculum and planning instruction as a regular part of their teaching load. Both provisions set new precedents for the definition of staff development; that is, teachers determining the content and process of staff development is new in in-service education, and learning on-site as a part of improving one's effectiveness is a mode of staff development very different from present practice.

American teacher centers could make another significant change in staff development by adoption of the advisory practice prominent in some British teacher centers. The advisory system provides supervisory personnel who have staff rather than line functions. The advisor is nonthreatening and supportive, a counselor and facilitator. The advisor works with teachers in the teacher center in learning new content and developing material for or approaches to instruction, and then helps provide the linkage to practice by going into the schools to assist the teachers in applying what has been learned or developed. The advisor also serves as an observer, a confidential critic, a mirror for teacher analysis of teaching performance. Some advisors also demonstrate. Others teach cooperatively with the teacher. The special functions of the advisor could provide the connection (and support) between theory and practice, between good talk about teaching and implementation, that has so long been lacking in teacher education.

Teacher use of teacher centers has been voluntary in most instances in this country, following the practice of teacher centers in Britain. If the use of teacher centers remains an option, there can develop a new spirit and attitude in staff development, and a more mature kind of professionalism; that is, the primary responsibility in continuing professional education would become that of the individual professional.

In all of these developments teachers and particularly teacher organizations have played an influential role. Collectively teachers have power, and they are beginning to exercise that power in the causes of professionalism. For example, the National Education Association (NEA) shaped and lobbied for the Teacher Center legislation. The regulations for the program were substantially influenced by teacher organizations, and NEA takes credit for the precedent set by the legislation of providing financial support for released time for in-service education. Avowed purposes and goals of NEA are that in-service education be

- perceived as an essential and continuous function of a career in teaching and an extension of preservice preparation.
- established largely on the basis of teacher needs as identified by teachers.
- planned, governed, and evaluated by teachers and others directly related to the schooling enterprise.
- integrated into each teacher's professional assignment through negotiated contracts.
- financed by public funds.

(Darland and Luke, 1976, pp. 143-144)

Teacher organizations will continue to champion the cause of teachers in their desire to become more professional and to ensure politically the fair and objective evaluation of professional practices and performance. The recent evaluation of Teacher Center proposals illustrates nicely how the political power of teacher organizations can be used to assure teacher dominance in the review process while maintaining objective application of evaluation criteria. At the insistence of teacher organizations, three of five reviewers were K-12 teachers, but the review (it has been reported) adhered to criteria, not political power.

Obviously teacher organizations are involved in changing schools. The illustration of teacher organization influence on staff development in relation to teacher centers is but one instance. Teacher organizations are concerned about a host of instructional matters. Their concerns can be easily documented by reviewing NEA or American Federation of Teachers resolutions. Most of the concerns deal with curriculum and instruction, teacher education, and standards of preparation and practice. Some matters of concern are resolved through bargaining. Others are lobbied in state and national legislatures. Still others are argued for and promoted with civil servants and other educators in the institutions and agencies involved in decisions affecting teachers and students.

Increasingly, teacher organizations are watching research in education. As I suggested earlier, there is concern about how research in learning or in the arts will be applied. Teacher organizations are pushing to get teachers involved in determining research agendas; you may be sure that all I have said in this paper either reflects the concerns of or will be considered by the organization for which I work.

There is reason and goodwill among teachers, but there is also commitment to assuring that the conditions under which teachers function will be improved, and that commitment includes provision for in-service education that is helpful and meaningful to teachers.

Inherent in the concern for the arts and aesthetic education is a recognition that something needs to be done about improving the quality of life. The parallel between staff development goals to improve the quality of life and the goals of advocates of the arts and aesthetic education to provide significant, fulfilling experience is clear. Both sets of goals encompass being thoughtful and reflective, being involved and being a participant. They require recognizing one's own experience and self as unique.

There is the possibility that staff development in the arts for all teachers can make living more complete and significant, provide more intrinsic rewards than most other experiences, and serve as an antidote to the commercialism, superficiality, and falseness that characterize so much of life. No experience requires more integrity than aesthetic experience.

Washington, D.C.
October 1978

NOTES

[1]Both of these sections reflect a long-term interest in and study of arts and aesthetics. I have drawn on and updated materials from Chapters 2 and 3 of my doctoral dissertation, *The improvement of instruction in music in teachers colleges preparing elementary school teachers* (Edelfelt, 1954).

REFERENCES

Copland, A. *Music and imagination.* Cambridge, Massachusetts: Harvard University Press, 1952.

Darland, D., and Luke, R. The NEA's views on in-service education. In *Creative authority and collaboration: A collection of position papers.* Inservice Teacher Education Concepts Project, Report No. 4. Palo Alto, California: Stanford Center for Research and Development in Teaching, 1976.

Dewey, J. *Art as experience.* New York: Minton, Balch & Co., 1934.

Edelfelt, R. A. *The improvement of instruction in music in teachers colleges preparing elementary school teachers.* Unpublished doctoral dissertation, Columbia University, Teachers College, 1954.

Edelfelt, R. A. Criteria for local in-service education programs. In R. A. Edelfelt (Ed.), *In-service education: Criteria for and examples of local programs.* Bellingham, Wash.: Western Washington State College, 1977.

Edelfelt, R. A., and Lawrence, G. In-service education: The state of the art. In R. A. Edelfelt and M. Johnson (Eds.), *Rethinking in-service education.* Washington, D.C.: National Education Association, 1975.

Hilgard, E. R., and Bower, G. H. *Theories of learning* (4th ed.). Englewood Cliffs, New Jersey: Prentice-Hall, 1975.

Hulse, S. H., Deese, J., and Egeth, H. *The psychology of learning* (3rd ed.). New York: McGraw-Hill, 1975.

Joyce, B. R., McNair, K. M., Diaz, R., McKibbin, M. D., Waterman, F. T., and Baker, M. G. *Interviews: Perceptions of professionals and policy makers.* Inservice Teacher Education Concepts Project, Report No. 2. Palo Alto, California: Stanford Center for Research and Development in Teaching, 1976.

Sessions, R. *The musical experience of composer, performer, listener.* Princeton, New Jersey: Princeton University Press, 1950.

J. Myron Atkin / *A Response to Edelfelt*

Issues in the Continuing Education of Teachers

I would have preferred to react to a paper about a topic I knew something about—but then there would have been a problem finding me an assignment.

Most of the paper by Roy Edelfelt centers on the psychological basis for effective programs of continuing education for teachers. I certainly am not qualified to talk about that subject, and will not. Then there is a considerable segment about arts and aesthetics, and although I am disquieted by the "peoples' art" approach in his paper, others here are in a better position to comment than I. So I will spend what little time has been assigned to me talking about certain issues in the continuing education of teachers.

Today there are strong pressures (and they are not new) in all the professions to make preservice as well as in-service programs highly practical. Classroom teachers, for example, face extraordinarily complex and difficult tasks. They expect, understandably, that a program of professional development will help them in meeting their classroom problems. Often they do not feel that they receive much of value in existing university-based programs in facing these every-day difficulties. Partly as a consequence (though by no means is it the only reason), as the organized teaching profession has developed greater power in matters of teacher certification and continuing education, they have tended to use that power to put more responsibility for training in the hands of current practitioners. Teacher leaders, particularly in the National Education Association (NEA), seem to believe that teachers learn best from other practitioners. They advocate an apprenticeship model, though they are reluctant to use the term.

This general policy may be desirable. Apprenticeship activities work well in many fields. Perhaps they would in teaching, too. I do not choose

J. MYRON ATKIN *is Dean of the College of Education at the University of Illinois at Urbana-Champaign.*

to argue that point here. Rather, the problem I wish to highlight is that some universities are finding it difficult to accept the move toward apprenticeship training in certain of the professions—particularly in social work, librarianship, and teaching. (In professions with high prestige, universities are accommodating to a greater role for practitioners more readily.) Furthermore, universities are becoming more sophisticated about assuring that various programs on a given campus hew to the values that are emphasized on that campus.

As economic constraints become stronger, many universities seem to be reaffirming their traditional values. On my own campus, for example, we have an elaborate, internal evaluation scheme—the Council on Program Evaluation. On a systematic basis, faculty selected from departments across the campus investigate a given unit and make comments about its condition and recommendations about its future. What happens? Our library school is ranked by librarians around the country and by faculty at other library schools as unquestionably one of the top three in the country. Practitioners assert that at Illinois they learn how to be good librarians. However, the Council on Program Evaluation raised fundamental questions about whether or not the library school should exist on campus because it was not honoring a research and scholarly tradition as that research and scholarly tradition has come to be understood at the University of Illinois at Urbana-Champaign.

The Council on Program Evaluation, in investigating the College that contains a journalism faculty that easily ranks among the top ten nationally, recommended that the College of Communications should be eliminated, partly because it operates too much in an apprenticeship mode. The staff was not giving sufficient attention to identifying the issues that should be capturing the field. It was not giving enough attention to its leadership role because it was preoccupied with training the most effective practitioners. In addition, there was not enough research.

One possibility over the next decade is that as the NEA enhances its influence in determining who will enter the teaching profession and what kind of training they will have, certain kinds of institutions more wedded than others to established scholarly traditions will choose to drop teacher preparation. The institutions that were created in the last century as normal schools to train teachers will be the ones that most readily adapt to the new requirements of the profession. Research-oriented universities may retreat from the kind of heavy involvement in teacher education that we have seen in recent decades if that training is insufficiently based on strong scholarship.

It may be salutary if leaders of the organized teaching profession would ask themselves whether this is a desirable turn of events (and, of course, whether or not it is even a plausible development). I must say, however, that I am not sure how long we will remain in teacher education at the University of Illinois. I am not sure how much we will want to remain in this field if teacher education moves along some of the paths that are in evidence today and that seem to be advanced by the NEA.

In discussing NEA's advocacy of moving preparation programs toward the "field," I am not questioning the rigor or quality of the kind of school-based research and inquiry we heard about this morning. Those of you who know anything about my work know that I have been engaged in research cooperatively with teachers for a long time. In fact, we need a scholarship in education that is rooted in practice in order to enhance our own studies at the university, even if there is no noticeable effect in the schools. Thus, I am not arguing at all about the need for professors to be more actively involved in classrooms, but it is hard to detect how much attention there will be to the kind of work Ted, Betty, and others have talked about at this conference—as against a brute apprenticeship—in staff development and teacher education. (See Bussis, Chittenden, and Amarel and Tikunoff and Ward, this volume.)

Teacher centers have been used as an example of an effective method of in-service education, and I would concur enthusiastically. In Britain certainly, there is no question' that a great deal of beneficial staff development goes on in these institutions. The question we need to ask ourselves is whether or not teacher centers reflect a university-level activity. It seems to me that it is necessary and desirable to do a great many things to help teachers improve. Some of these activities, however, have no relationship to earning a degree or to obtaining university credit. The point I am making is that certain universities will very likely not give credit for the kinds of activities that go on in the best teacher centers, such as many of those I have seen in Britain—which, by the way, tend to be units that exhibit more reflectiveness and thoughtfulness about the teaching task than those I have seen so far in the United States.

The major point of my few minutes this morning is to try to raise the question of how much we want accomplished at the University level in teacher education, recognizing that universities are not going to change easily. My guess about change in universities at the moment is that we in academia will retreat to what we are most familiar with, that is to traditional norms regarding scholarship and research. If there is any change at all, it is not clear that it will be "progressive" as defined by the conferees here. In order to advance a movement which I think this group at Aspen would like to see, we have to understand more about the canons of scholarship associated with work like that of Tikunoff and Ward, and Bussis, Chittenden, and Amarel. If we can satisfy ourselves about what constitutes rigor in this kind of work—what are or are not the demands for generalizability in Rosenshine's sense—then perhaps we will make progress. Barring that, I think there may be only two types of universities that focus on teacher education in the future—the former normal schools that have an historic commitment to teacher education and the self-confident graduate universities like those in the AAU who can take chances in fields like this because they are not putting as much at risk; they have excellent reputations.

My suggestion, in partial summary, is that we might improve the quality of our discussion if we did not start with the assumption that the university must be involved in either preservice teacher education or continuing education.

Urbana, Illinois
June 1978

Arthur Efland

Conceptions of Teaching in the Arts

Orientations in Aesthetics

The history of aesthetics is a history of beliefs about the nature of art. Many of these beliefs influence the ways the arts are taught in the present and have been taught in the past. Such beliefs are usually part of a system of wider beliefs although the connections between art and life, knowing and valuing are not always apparent to artists and their audiences nor to teachers and their students. For this reason, I begin my discussion of teaching in the arts not with a survey of recent trends but with a brief glimpse at the ideas of two venerable authorities from the ancient world, Plato and Aristotle. I do this first to show that their ideas about art and its value were derived from their ideas concerning the nature of knowledge and truth, which in turn influenced their beliefs about the teaching of the arts, but also to uncover four major theoretical elements that come into play in almost all discussions of aesthetics, this to provide a general framework for identifying and analyzing leading conceptions of teaching in the arts.

In *The Republic* (Jowett translation, Book X, 595a), Plato tells us that Socrates would ban the poets and painters from his ideal state. The reason for this is made clear in that oft quoted illustration of the three beds: the ideal form of the bed created by God which is most true; the actual bed made by the carpenter which is an imitation of the ideal; and finally the bed that appears in a picture painted by an artist which is termed an "imitation of an imitation." Since the picture is three removes from reality, it and by implication all works of art are less reliable sources of knowledge than either the ideal bed or the actual bed. The cognitive value of art is being questioned—a revolutionary step to take in a culture where poets, dramatists, sculptors, and architects are relied on to transmit the socially valued heritage. Elsewhere, Plato tells us (Schaper, 1968, p. 34) that Socrates questioned the reliability of artists because they often worked in a state of irrational abandon without a true knowledge of what

---

ARTHUR EFLAND *is Professor of Art Education at The Ohio State University.*

they were doing. If this were not enough reason to question the efficacy of the arts, Socrates also worried about the effects of "bad" art upon the young and impressionable minds of the future guardians of the Republic.

Plato regarded teaching of the arts as an important obligation of the state because art was too serious a matter to be left to the artist and because the arts could contribute to the health and order of society (Beardsley, 1966, p. 50). Aristotle had a more charitable view of the arts: they were endeavors of a *practical* nature in contradistinction to philosophy which was an endeavor of a *theoretical* nature. Though this may not have been his intention, Aristotle demonstrated that one could discuss art as an objective entity, solely in terms of its parts and of how these are fashioned to give the work form.

According to Abrams (1953, pp. 3-29), there are four elements in the total situation of a work of art that most theories of art discriminate and make salient:

1. the *work* of art itself
2. the *artist* as the work's creator
3. the *audience* to whom the work of art is addressed
4. the *universe* represented in the work; that is, what the work is about.

All reasonably adequate theories of art take some cognizance of all four elements, but almost all theories, Abrams claims, exhibit a discernible orientation toward one of the four elements. For example: A teacher will base his or her practice upon a conception of art weighted in favor of one of these elements.

In Abrams' discussion, art theories whose orientation lies toward the universe or nature are *mimetic* theories. In such views the main criterion for judging art is the degree to which it presents accurate representations of life. Art theories whose orientation lies in the direction of the audience are *pragmatic* in that the work is seen as an instrument that achieves certain effects on an audience and is judged by the degree to which it achieves an intended effect. An orientation toward the artist produces *expressive* theories. When Socrates described how artists behaved when they were inspired, he was voicing a version of expressive theory; and so did those in the nineteenth century who defined art as the spontaneous overflow of the artist's emotions. The degree to which works express the emotions of their makers are the criteria used to judge them. Finally, there are the *objective* theories where the work of art is regarded in isolation from all external points of reference, where it is analyzed as a self-sufficient entity constituted by its parts in their internal relations with judgment based solely upon criteria intrinsic to the work's own mode of being. The formalism of Clive Bell and Roger Fry are latter day versions of objective theories.

Although Abrams and other writers on the history of aesthetics create the impression that these four views occurred roughly in a historical sequence with mimetic and pragmatic theories evolving first, to be succeeded by expressive and objective theories, it would be wrong in my view to conclude that each new wave of theory swept away the traces of its predecessors. Older theories like the mimetic still influence the critical discussion of art today—especially the mass arts like cinema and television. When it is said that a particular film is sexually too explicit or that the violence on television is out of proportion to what one is likely to witness in daily life—that is, when the work was either too real or not real enough—mimetic criteria are involved in the judgment.

Pragmatic views of art abound in the writings of Marshall McLuhan where the medium is the "massage" as well as the message. Similarly, there are implied references to expressionist art theory in statements like, "Any artist who paints that way has to be crazy," or "The author must have suffered greatly to be capable of such profundity." Finally, we hear references to objectivist art theory in statements like, "The drapery colors work well with the dominant colors of the room," or "The musical score in the film was inappropriate for its action."

Orientations in Psychology

Why do these aesthetic orientations continue to influence our thoughts about the arts including our ideas about how they could or should be taught? One part of the answer is simply that we tend to talk about one thing at a time. It is difficult to talk about an artistic process, the qualities of an art product, the subject of a work, and the effects it has upon its perceivers—all this in one sentence. Another part of the answer is due to the fact that many of our ideas about artistic learning, perception, and creation are derived from psychological theory and research as well as from traditional or contemporary aesthetics. Like aesthetic theory, contemporary psychology also has several major orientations which bear some strong resemblances to those in traditional aesthetic theory.

Mimetic Aesthetics and Psychological Behaviorism

In this pairing, art is the imitation of nature and behaviorism asserts that learning is acquired by imitation. The child learns to draw by copying pictures made by others. He or she learns to imitate actions of actors by watching television and films, and learns the social conventions of audience behavior by imitating models like parents or teachers (Bandura and MacDonald, 1963).

Pragmatic Aesthetics and Cognitive Psychology

Here the aesthetic experience is the result of a transaction between the viewer or listener and the work of art. Correspondingly, the cognitive view of human behavior sees symbol making and using as processes resulting from interaction with the world. For example, when a child's audience understands what his or her drawing represents, then he or she is able to infer a rule for making that kind of representation successfully (Korzenik, 1972).

Expressive Aesthetics and Psychoanalytic Psychology

Expressive theory in aesthetics says that art is the expression of the artist's emotions, while psychoanalytic psychology views all human behavior as the product of unconscious needs and drives all elaborated, compromised and channeled into overt behavior by the ego (Kreitler and Kreitler, 1972, p. 67). Accordingly, the artist expresses subconscious desires in a sublimated symbolic form, and the perception of works of art affords vicarious fantasy gratification for unsatisfied wishes in a sublimated form. Therefore, when they make-believe, children express their wishes for satisfactions that their environments either make taboo or may not afford them.

Objective Aesthetics and Gestalt Psychology

Objective theory in aesthetics regards the work of art as a self-sufficient autonomous whole directly accessible to the viewer in perception. It corresponds with Gestalt psychology which states that in human behavior the whole is more than the sum of its parts. Researchers have attempted to show that the mutual relations among the elements of a work of art can be best understood through their role and position in the whole (Kreitler and Kreitler, 1972, p. 89).

While I am not claiming that these psychological theories are logically or causally bound to the aesthetic orientations just described, I do suggest that a person schooled in a given orientation will tend to view artistic phenomena from the purview most compatible with the preferred orientation. For example: A psychonanalyst will most probably view a work of art as an object that reveals something about its maker and will be generally disinclined to study it as a representation of nature. My object here is not to question the objectivity of psychology with respect to the arts but simply to point out that the traditional aesthetic orientations continue to influence our thought and actions with respect to the arts. Figure 1 represents the major alignments between the aesthetic and psychological theories discussed above.

Orientations in Teaching

Now, I would like to extend my analysis to include arts teaching by setting up four hypothetical questions:

1. If art is imitation and learning is by imitation, what then is teaching?
2. If art is viewed as a transaction between the viewer and the art object or, for that matter, between the artist and the object made, what then is teaching?

Figure 1

Alignments Between Aesthetic and Psychological Theory

Orientations in Aesthetic Theory

Mimetic Major Premise: Art is an imitation of nature. Works of art are understood when the objects and events being represented are understood by the viewer. The quality of the work is judged by its faithfulness to the model. Mimetic theory has not undergone any development for the last two centuries yet mimetic criteria are often cited in the criticism of the mass media; for example, the portrayal of sex is said to be too explicit.

Pragmatic Major Premise: Works of art can be known through the effects they have upon their audiences. A viewer's experience is determined by the transaction between the object of perception and the disposition of the viewer. Though artists may create works out of their imagination, certain assumptions about the nature of the audience may play a role in the creation and presentation of the work.

Expressive Major Premise: Art is the expression of the artist's emotions. Art is not an object legislated by rules but is a product that comes into being as a result of the artist's insight. The work of art is also seen as a revelation into the personality of the artist. Though the artistic genius began to be celebrated as a cultural hero in the Renaissance, it was in the early Romantic era of the nineteenth century that this view of the artist acquired the status of a cult.

Objectivist Major Premise: The work of art is a self-contained entity that can speak for itself. One does not have to know the intentions of the artist nor even much about the historical context out of which the work developed to understand the work in question. The work should be an organic whole, self-existing and self-sufficient in all its complexity and unity.

Orientations in Psychological Theory

Behaviorist Major Premise: Learning is by imitation of the behavior of others; for example, children learn to speak the language of their parents. When the model is imitated correctly and reinforced, the learning is made secure. In the arts children learn by copying the drawings, the sounds, and the movements made by others. Motivation for learning is provided by reinforcement.

Cognitive Major Premise: Behavior is mediated by the prior experience of the individual. These experiences affect the ways new events are perceived and understood, and these understandings enable individuals to adapt their behavior to the environment. Children represent what they know in their artistic expression. How they choose to make these representations will be affected by their knowledge of the intended audience, that is, what will please or evoke a response.

Psychoanalytic Major Premise: All behavior is in part expressive and is often motivated by unconscious motives such as repressed wishes. These become channeled by means of the process of sublimation into socially accepted forms of expression. Children's art is governed not by what they copy but rather by what they feel. Distortion is not an error but is essential to self-expression.

Gestalt Major Premise: The meaning of forms is accessible directly in their perception. Art forms are good gestalts that express their inherent nature in the clearest way by the most economical means. Perception is a lawful process governed by specific forms of organization such as closure, simplicity, similarity, figure-ground, and so on. Children's art develops according to certain innate laws moving from the simple to the complex by a process of differentiation.

3. If art is the self-expression of the artist and all behavior is motivated by subconscious drives, what then is teaching?
4. If art is an objective autonomous object with a formal structure capable of being understood directly in perception, and learning is a process involving the perception of wholes, what then is teaching?

Let me provide some quick, general answers to these questions.

Teaching in the Mimetic-Behavioral View

Teaching in this view would consist of providing models of performance and developing ways of cuing the student with knowledge of results. Knowing the rules of art and when these rules have been observed with success, the teacher would direct the learning experience and evaluate the results.

Teaching in the Pragmatic-Cognitive View

Teaching here would lead the students into situations where their expectations about art would undergo some kind of reality testing. The student making art would attempt to predict how viewers would respond, while the student as audience member would approach the aesthetic situation with certain expectancies or hypotheses to be either confirmed or denied. The teacher would be a person who creates problem-solving situations, usually ones involving the creation or the perception of art in a social situation like a classroom, auditorium, or the community as a whole.

Teaching in the Expressive-Psychoanalytical View

Teaching would be more involved with bringing the learner to a state of his or her own self-realization. No rules would be externally imposed either by the discipline or the teacher. Teaching would provide a therapeutic climate that would produce not only works of art but healthier students.

Teaching in the Objective-Gestalt View

Teaching would direct the student to perceive qualities in works of art that are objectively real. Such qualities are learned by discovery but teaching would be a way of helping the learner see beyond the obvious aspects of a work of art to those qualities that might escape detection on the first encounter. Teaching would also involve the setting up of situations where students can differentiate and integrate their responses to works of art. The rules for art would be discovered in creative experiences and a teacher would need to be aware that certain kinds of perceptual discriminations may not be available to the child until his or her perceptual apparatus has undergone sufficient development.

Figure 2 shows how the four orientations are aligned with teaching practices. What I now intend to show is how the four orientations live on as teaching traditions in the arts today.

Visual Arts

The Mimetic Tradition in Art Education

In the nineteenth century copying was an approved method of art instruction. Beginning students worked with the copybook exercises of teachers like Walter Smith (1872) while the more advanced copied "the masters." Copying as an approved method seems largely to have disappeared in formal art instruction but much of the art that is learned is often learned by copying. Wilson and Wilson (1977) have conducted a series of clinical studies with children and adolescents with a marked propensity for drawing and painting. They have found that in most cases these individuals have taught themselves to draw largely by processes involving copying.

In the last decade a number of approaches to art teaching and curriculum planning have appeared which make use of behaviorally based instructional objectives. In my view, these have an implied kinship with the mimetic tradition in aesthetics although explicit copy tasks need not necessarily be involved in the instruction at hand. For example, the following performance objective taken from the *Florida State Assessment Project in Art* (1972) does not involve copying per se:

> Given the definition of the art term contrast (that an art form achieves balance through contrast when opposite elements are included, e.g., bright, dull, hard edge, soft edge, curved, straight, etc.) and shown three different art forms chosen by the teacher because of their representative characteristics, the student will point out how "balance through contrast" exists in each of the three different art forms. (p. 31)

Notice, however, that such an objective requires a teacher to generate a situation where attainment of the concept is identified by a performance calling for a kind of matching process with a given model.

The Pragmatic Tradition in Art Education

When the Progressive Movement in education was ascendant, there was a gradual drift away from the teaching of art as a specific subject and toward the integration of art with other subjects. The integrated curriculum that was popular in the thirties was compatible with the Deweyan experimentalist position where experience is viewed as the product of transactions with the environment, and the values one finds in these experiences come about as a result of these same transactions. Examples of teaching imbued with this philosophy were documented in

Figure 2

Psychological Orientations

Aesthetic Orientations

Mimetic	Pragmatic	Expressive	Objective

Behaviorist

Art is an imitation of nature.
Learning is a change in behavior.
Behavior is acquired and modified by imitation.
Teaching provides students with models to imitate.

Cognitive

Art is an instrument that produces effects upon an audience.
Learning is the organization of experience by means of structures and symbols.
Behavior is mediated by previous learning.
Teaching provides students with problems to give structure to experience.

Psychoanalytic

Art is the expression of the artist's emotions.
Learning is social adaptation or sublimation, the finding of acceptable channels for needs and drives.
Behavior is motivated by needs and desires which are often hidden or repressed, and all observed behavior is a reflection of these.
Teaching provides a therapeutic environment, nurturing and sheltering the learner.

Gestalt

Art is a self-sufficient autonomous whole.
Learning is the discovery of structure, differentiation, and integration.
Behavior is holistic in which parts find their meanings in wholes.
Teaching provides preceptual training, pointing out what is there to be discovered.

Haggerty's *Art, A Way of Life* (1935), a report on the Owatonna Art Education Project, and in the 1943 issue of *Art Education, Today* subtitled *Art Education and the War* which described such activities as poster-making, the design of booths to sell war bonds and stamps, and the like. Art in these contexts is a resource with which to solve the problems of daily living.

In the post-war years the "integrated" approaches to teaching assumed a new form known as the "core program" or the "core curriculum." In this method, teaching was organized around a basic core of subjects consisting of English and history, or social studies and the language arts. The visual arts, music, and physical education were brought into the core as resources for use in solving problems.

In his book *A Foundation for Art Education*, Barkan (1955) made use of ideas derived from the transactionalism of Dewey and Mead. He recognized self-expression as a goal of art education and viewed art as communication, characterizing the self as something that develops in response to social experience and activity (Barkan, 1955, p. 156). Artistic communication from this standpoint has instrumental value in that it can help individuals come to know who they are.

By the late fifties a significantly different view of cognition was taking shape which was to have a major impact on both curriculum and instruction in the arts. Writers like Bruner (1956, 1966, 1973) began to describe human behavior as behavior that can only be explained relative to a knowledge base possessed by the learner. Bruner's theory of instruction is based on providing structure for the learner: "the merit of a structure depends upon its power for simplifying information, for generating new propositions, and for increasing the manipulability of a body of knowledge. Structure must always be related to the status and gifts of the learner" (1966, p. 41). Bruner's ideas about structure were especially influential because they responded to the social needs felt when Russian success in launching the first space satellite triggered a wave of criticism about the quality of education in American schools. While this resulted in a renewed emphasis upon mathematics and science and a lessening of commitment to the arts, the impact of Bruner's thought was instrumental in extending the scope of content in art education. Writers such as Eisner (1964) and Barkan (1962, 1964) began to describe the structure of content in terms of categories such as studio activities, art criticism, and art history, all to be furthered by appropriate and distinctive teaching strategies.

In the seventies the view of cognition posited by Bruner and others began to undergo changes that are reflected in the work of Project Zero which for the last decade has been devoted to the study of the development of symbol systems in language and the arts in early childhood (Perkins and Leondar, 1977). The teaching implications of this latter view of cognition are still to be felt and worked out, but certainly, the tendency to divide instruction into cognitive, affective, and psychomotor aspects in the manner suggested by Krathwohl, Bloom, and Masia's (1964) taxonomies would seem to be ill-advised.

The Expressive Tradition in Art Education

Free expression or creative self-expression as a method of art instruction appeared for the first time at the end of the nineteenth century in the Saturday morning art classes of Franz Cizek in Vienna, Austria. Artists were looking for new sources of inspiration including the art of so-called primitive peoples and also the art of the child. Cizek's methods involved "more freedom for the child to look at the world and to experiment in congenial ways of expressing himself in some artistic medium" (Munro, 1930, p. 311).

A generation later Viktor Lowenfeld was to draw upon Freudian insights in the preparation of his two books on art education, *The Nature of Creative Activity* (1939) and *Creative and Mental Growth* (1947). In Lowenfeld's view, the work of art could be read as an indicator of the psychological status of its maker and the making of art objects was a therapy that helped the individual integrate his or her inner drives with social reality (Efland, 1975).

Just as the psychological base for teaching was influenced by Freudian theory in Lowenfeld's writing, another view stimulated largely by Jungian ideas appeared in the writings of Herbert Read (1944). Teaching methods described by Read make use of play: "*to give coherence and direction to play is to convert it into art*" (p. 219, italics in original).

The expressive-psychoanalytic tradition had its greatest impact upon teaching in the visual arts in the period between the end of World War II and the late fifties, a time when there was a tremendous expansion of art in the schools. Consequently, the methods associated with this orientation are still widely espoused and practiced. The persistent stereotype of the art teacher is that of a person encouraging students to be creative by drawing upon their personal experiences and fantasies as sources of expression, a person who discourages copying of the work of others and who for the most part avoids directive methods of teaching. Though psychoanalytic theory is now generally less popular as a learning theory, the modern extension of this orientation continues in the third force psychologies; for example, Maslow (1971). Although they have not written specifically about art education, they view artistic pursuits as potential means for satisfying the individual's need to actualize his or her potential.

The Objective Tradition in Art Education

The development of the aesthetic theories of Bell and Fry and the appearance of Gestalt psychology were events occurring in roughly the same time frame. One of the results of these developments was the emergence of new ways to look at art. Now for the first time it became possible to view art as an independent entity apart from its cultural origins, the world of appearances, morals, or, for that matter, the intentions of the artist. Formalism was part of the intellectual climate. In the early decades of the twentieth century Arthur W. Dow established a method of teaching based upon a system of universal elements and principles. This was the first serious alternative to the copybook exercises still in use in schools and colleges.

Although the system was rationally coherent, it had some disadvantages which were noted by Munro (1930, pp. 329-337). One was the fact that it had little or nothing to do with art styles like post-Impressionism then being practiced by contemporary artists, and a second was that the rigid order of progress in the exercises was not addressed to the interests, needs, and developmental capacities of young children, factors that were increasingly recognized by educators.

A second major development having a strong impact on both twentieth century art and art teaching was to come from the Bauhaus, a radically new type of art school founded in Weimar, Germany in 1919. Gropius proposed a new form of art education which would attempt to bridge the gap between the fine arts and the crafts. Each student at the Bauhaus would be taught by two teachers, a master craftsman and an artist. Although the Nazi regime was responsible for closing the Bauhaus, the quality of industrial design, architecture, and crafts education was strongly influenced in places where individual members of the Bauhaus faculty resettled. The Bauhaus influence can be seen in textbooks like Pearson's *The New Art Education* (1941) which was used extensively as a text in the years following World War II. A number of exploratory activities such as paper sculpture and construction, photograms, and texture collages that have become commonplace in art teaching were a direct outgrowth of the Bauhaus preliminary course.

A third development within this tradition was the view of teaching derived from the writings of the Gestalt psychologists themselves, in particular Schaefer-Simmern (1948) and Arnheim (1954). According to Arnheim, individuals develop what he calls perceptual concepts which he defines as the overall structural properties of a given form grasped in vision. For example, the overall property of the human head would be its circularity. A young child might represent this experience by drawing a circle, but in such a case, the child would not be imitating the head as such but providing the viewer with a structural equivalent of it. Structural equivalents are determined both by the pervasive form of the object giving rise to the experience and by the medium itself. Thus a child representing the head with a pencil would draw a circle, but one working in clay might model a ball or an egg-like solid (Arnheim, 1954, p. 178).

In Arnheim's view, the wise teacher would neither impose adult ideas upon children, nor abandon the child to wallow in self-expression. The teacher would provide two basic forms of experience: (1) experiences of an exploratory nature to enable children to develop their powers of perception; and (2) experiences with art media to enable children to construct representational concepts that stand for and symbolize their experience. In this way the child could see the order and harmony underlying the world, in a word its Gestalt character.

A number of independent developments that have a strong affinity with Gestalt psychology began to make their appearance in the forties. In 1941 Nicoliades' *The Natural Way to Draw* presented a method for teaching drawing that relied very heavily upon attention to perception. Less well known but worthy of mention was the *Drawing by Seeing* (1947) method developed by Sherman at The Ohio State University. This method involved the perception of visual fields arranged in a successive order of complexity.

Broudy (1964) and R.A. Smith (1968) seem to approach instruction as a process entailing the discovery of objects, events, and qualities that are there to be discovered. Teaching in this view involves the pre-arrangement of teaching materials to attain a concept pre-ordained by the selection of the materials themselves. Hence specific "exemplars" known by the teacher to be important works are pre-selected and pre-arranged so that students might discover their good-making qualities themselves.

Music

The Mimetic Tradition in Music Education

Though ancient Greece prized her drama, poetry, architecture, and visual arts, none of these were treated as "proper" studies in the education of citizens. Music was an exception. Plato believed that it was important to expose children to those musical modes containing the "right" virtues. The presumed moral effects of music also served as one of the bases for its inclusion in education in the American colonies more than two thousand years after Plato.

American music education had its beginnings in Boston under the leadership of Lowell Mason who set forth a set of teaching principles derived from a somewhat mistaken interpretation of the principles of Pestalozzi, the noted European educator of the early nineteenth century (Leonhard and House, 1972, p. 41). Mason believed that learning should occur through the senses, through hearing, and did not introduce the reading of music until after the skills of listening and performing were learned. Music was introduced in the upper grades of the elementary school, and after a period of trial, it was introduced into the lower grades and also into the high schools which were then being formed.

In the first two decades of the twentieth century the prevailing learning theories were the behaviorism of J.B. Watson and the connectionism of Thorndike. Both of these strongly influenced methods of teaching music. Each of these theories stressed the importance of drill and practice as essential requisites to any kind of musical learning and reduced the emphasis upon the appreciation of music while tending to deny the importance of any intellectual understanding of the music.

In the period following World War II, numerous systems of music education began to gain popularity in this country; for example, the systems developed by Zoltan Kodaly in Hungary, Carl Orff in Germany, and the Suzuki method of violin instruction. Unlike the visual arts which have largely forsaken the teaching of art by methods involving copying and imitation, imitation is still in use in the teaching of music today; for example, the MENC National Commission on Instruction has produced a publication entitled *Instructional Objectives in Music* (Boyle, 1974). While such objectives are subtly biased in favor of a mimetic view of the arts, this does not seem to be quite as troublesome in the case of music and, to some extent, the other performing arts, since the artistry entailed in the practice of these arts involves the task of re-creating the art work from a written score.

The Pragmatic Tradition in Music Education

Plato discussed musical modes in terms of their desirable and undesirable moral effects upon the young. With the coming of Christianity the Church adopted an essentially Platonic conception of the pragmatic value of music. Music was a tool through which the mind and soul were prepared to receive spiritual truths. To this day there is much discussion in the music education literature concerning these so-called extra-musical effects and the role these might play in "selling" music education to philistines on local school boards (McMurray, 1958, pp. 30-61). Singing schools, an historical outgrowth of the medieval *schola cantorum*, were the first form of music education in colonial America and continued to serve the musical needs of the country well into the nineteenth century when public-school music began to appear.

In the early decades of the twentieth century the grip of the *art for arts sake* philosophy (see Beardsley, 1966, pp. 284-290) began to loosen under the impact of an increased concern for social responsibility. This shift in philosophy can be seen in the essays of the composer Edward MacDowell (Tellstrom, 1971, pp. 172-173). One of the first manifestations of this view in music education was the rise of group and community singing, which was also used to inspire patriotism and social cohesion. Another reflection of this tendency is the rise of a correlational approach to music. In this view music would be correlated with nature study, geography, history, and literature. Songs would coincide with the seasons in nature study, while history and geography would utilize the folk songs of the countries and music related to historical events being studied (Tellstrom, p. 180).

During the Progressive Era, especially during those years coinciding with the Great Depression, there was a drift away from the construction of precise and detailed courses of music instruction (in spite of the prevalence of graded music textbooks) toward the project method involving the integration and correlation of music with other subjects in the curriculum. The MENC Yearbooks of the period exemplify this; however, there were some cautionary voices in the music education field whose influence helped music to retain its identity in the school curriculum.

The Expressive Tradition in Music Education

The child-centered curriculum originated in the progressive education movement. The child's developmental, social, and emotional needs were bases for curriculum decisions, and these decisions were, if possible, to be made by the child. One of the manifestations of this child-centeredness was self-expression in the arts, but the movement did not have the impact on music that it had upon the other arts. Nevertheless, there were certain changes in approaches to the teaching of music that took place in this era.

There was a shift away from the focus upon music as a subject to concern for the well-being of the child as a psychological entity. To this end the development of musical interests as a part of the emotional life of the child became recognized as an important goal in music education supplanting what some writers have described as an unremitting concern for musical performance as the primary goal.

In order to understand the liberalizing trend in the teaching of music, it should be recalled that in the teens and twenties music teaching involved a combination of rote learning methods and methods for the teaching of music reading. Thorndike's connectionism with its prescriptions of drill and repetition was the learning theory in force in the schools. In the late thirties and early forties writers like James Mursell (1948) began to advocate a new set of goals. In his view the highest aim for music teaching was to develop an understanding and appreciation of music; the acquisition of skills should never be allowed to obscure musical values.

Mursell's teaching psychology came largely from a Gestalt orientation and in one sense his contributions to the teaching of music should be discussed in that context. My justification for discussing his influences here is that Mursell was one of the thinkers of the period who moved music education toward a child-centered approach to teaching (Tellstrom, p. 224). Mursell's child-centeredness thus shared much in common with those self-expression advocates in the other arts who said that artistic expression began with a felt need or a problem to be articulated by means of a process of personal investigation. Mursell's text *Education for Musical Growth* (1948) parallels in many remarkable aspects the Lowenfeld text in art education, *Creative and Mental Growth* (1947).

Though self-expression as a movement in music education seems not to have had the career that it had in the other arts, music educators did develop a related concept—"improvisation." At least three major systems of music education fostered improvisational learning in music: the Orff system, the Kodaly system, and, in this country, the Manhattanville Music Curriculum Program (MMCP).

Carl Orff's approach to music teaching begins with the premise that *feeling* precedes intellectual understanding (Wheeler and Raebeck, 1972, p. xix). According to Orff, the element of rhythm is the device through which the child can be led to explore music because rhythm is related to the child's own speech and movement. Music is built by beginning with the rhythmic pattern of a word, then two words, followed by phrases, and it is taught without notation.

The Kodaly approach differs from the Orff system in that it provides a sequential system of sight singing which leads children to an understanding of musical notation. Kodaly's basic aim was to teach children to read and write music through singing. Unlike the Orff system, the study of notation keeps pace with the singing.

The introduction of improvisational methods of music teaching like Orff and Kodaly was part of a revolt against an older type of instruction involving the singing of songs in music books by rote learning methods. These newer methods involved children with experiences that would enable them to make discoveries about musical sounds, how they are produced, and how they can be combined in various ways to create musical compositions. Such approaches to music education placed the child in situations where he or she could act out the roles of singer, instrumentalist, and composer, as well as interpreter and critic. One of the more powerful new thrusts in this direction was the federally funded Manhattanville Music Curriculum Project designed for children between the ages of three and eight (Nye and Nye, 1977). The program begins with the concepts that music is sound, that sounds are everywhere in the environment, and that such sounds can be described and classified by their various qualities. Thus, for example, children begin to discriminate between sounds that are high or low, soft or loud, long or short, steady or pulsating. They begin to develop an interpretive vocabulary to characterize the qualities in question. Following that, the children are then introduced to the concept that sounds have pitch. The children proceed through five stages of learning which culminate in compositions of their own music as notated in their own system.

The Objective Tradition in Music Education

In Roman times the teaching of music assumed the form of a mathematical discipline based upon the Pythagorean system of tonal intervals (Leonhard and House, p. 41). To the present day there is a conception of music as an individual discipline with its own structure and content.

In the seventeenth century when rationalism was the predominant philosophy, the model for all thought was mathematics, and musical structure was presumed to be based upon certain objective laws of harmony which have provided the basis for classical music as we know it. With the rise of Romanticism the laws of harmony were applied with less absolutism.

Hanslick's mid-nineteenth century view of the self-sufficiency of music required teaching that concentrated on those attributes that make music what is is — namely, rhythm, melody, tonal texture, and structure. It was not until the 1920s and later that music teaching developed approaches compatible with the formalism implied by his stand. These took the form of Gestalt learning theory which was critical of the rote methods of teaching commonly used. With the advent of Gestalt principles teachers began to help children grasp musical compositions as a whole. In such a view, the student would be involved not in the formulation or invention of a structure but in finding out what is there to be found out.

In music as in other arts Gestalt concepts were reworked during the Progressive Era. Then, the curriculum was conceived as the whole with each subject assuming the role of the parts. In a very real sense, Gestalt concepts had the effect of de-emphasizing the structure of music *as music* while allowing it to become the handmaiden of other subjects in the curriculum—although music retained more of its integrity in the classroom than did the other arts.

By the sixties a number of music educators felt it was necessary to redefine the nature of their field as a discipline in its own right. Using the model of the Woods Hole Conference which was devoted to the reform of mathematics and science instruction (Bruner, 1960), two major conferences were held at Yale University in 1963, and at Tanglewood in 1967. Both had the effect of asserting the view that an appropriate musical understanding "could only be achieved through a knowledge of the *structure* of music," and "fundamental to such training is the study of the elements to include melody, harmony, rhythm, and form" (Tellstrom, pp. 242-243).

Earlier I discussed the musical systems developed by Orff and Kodaly, and the MMCP as evidence of a tendency to provide children with opportunities to improvise in the playing of music and musical composition. We can also view these instructional approaches as ones providing specific structures for the teaching of music.

Contemporary views of music education seem to be shaped by the realization that neither the emphasis upon sight reading, drill, and practice, nor the approach to music as pure enjoyment is likely to be adequate as a basis for serious musical study. All such elements need to be incorporated into instruction if intellectual comprehension and emotional response are to be realized. A serious attempt to incorporate these elements is reflected in the instructional approach developed by Reimer (1970, 1973).

Dance

The Mimetic Tradition in Teaching

Within the Western tradition dance finds its earliest champion in Plato who treated gymnastics as a way to impose a harmony upon the body, akin to the harmony that music brings to the soul. In numerous non-Western traditions dance was and is an integral part of ritual observances of a social or religious nature.

In the history of teaching dance, it is important to recognize that the various forms of the dance had a specific social meaning, and as such each of these forms was treated in a somewhat different way. For example, the children of the European aristocracies were to be schooled in the social dances expected of members of their class and social station. In seventeenth century England, for example, dance was considered an important part of the education of gentlemen for it was thought to impart "manly thought and carriage," and it was to be taught not only with the correct step but with the proper "carriage and dignity, ease and grace" (Locke, 1690, quoted in Marks, 1976, p. 27). Such a view of dance instruction sounds like a mimetic approach to learning.

In eighteenth century America with the emergence of a wealthy class along the eastern seaboard, dance was incorporated into the curriculum of some private schools. Books such as Rameau's *The Dancing Master* published in 1725 (see Marks, 1976, p. 27) were not uncommon in private libraries. But by the beginning of the nineteenth century dance had found its way into the physical education programs of many private schools in the form of healthful gymnastic exercises which were a substitute for "playing and romping." At Mt. Holyoke College the exercises consisted of such dance-like steps as double springs, skipping steps, and the "five positions." The Deo Lewis system of "new gymnastics" and Sargent's "Aesthetic Calisthenics" were both systems of dance movements done by large groups in strict harmony with time and music. Along with these systematic approaches some social and folk dance was introduced into dance instruction at this time.

At the turn of the century, "aesthetic dance" under the influence of Isadora Duncan (Hoyt, 1951) became a more highly expressive art form. Drills using folk dance steps, solo couples, sets, and group forms took on movements from sport, work, and play. Concurrent with Duncan's efforts, Colby developed the concept of "natural" dance over the period 1914-1917. And at the same time, Bird Larson of Barnard College began to develop dance instructional technique based on the sciences of anatomy, kinesiology, and physics. These more or less scientific techniques were incorporated into natural dance to encourage students to develop themselves through dance. Margaret H'Doubler stressed that unformed movements and mere self-expression in movement did not constitute the art of dance. Dance was "nature given and man-molded" (quoted in Lippencott, 1960, p. 53). Though she stressed the biological basis of dance, the major thrust of her work was toward the expressive aspect.

Later Thompson (1933) stressed the importance of the student gaining control of "her" body and developing a sense of rhythm through specific exercises done to music. The instructor presented these in a variety of ways and combinations to form simple patterns and compositions. The student in this instructional scheme was not asked to create dance forms until "she" had acquired an instrument of expression, a trained and responsive body, and a vocabulary of movements. The use of simple movement patterns usually analyzed and taught from a highly scientific base typified the dance education of the twenties and thirties (Nadel, 1970, p. 331).

For the most part, twentieth century developments in dance took place on the college level. Dance was only occasionally introduced into elementary and secondary programs and here, too, it took the form of "imposed patterns involving only the response to a direction or command" (Murray, 1953, p. 17). By the early forties dance was introduced as a part of the physical fitness program in the schools. By the fifties there was a general increase in the number of teachers trained in choreographic skills. Students of such teachers generally learned through imitation to perform works of their teacher-choreographers.

In the sixties and seventies dance education can best be described as having adopted an eclectic approach to teaching. According to Ellfeldt (1976), "It is not uncommon today for two or more philosophies to exist in one school setting with opponents not even caring what happens outside their environs." The artists-in-the-schools program, for example, will use dancers as artists: some will teach by having students imitate or invent according to their own particular philosophy of dance and view of teaching, others will choreograph for a particular performance, and some, particularly at the elementary level, will introduce dance as a form of personal expression. The widespread knowledge and application of Laban notation in educational settings has further increased the potential for an imitative approach to dance technique and composition in such areas as jazz, folk, modern dance, and ballet insofar as the technique enables dance scholars and choreographers to preserve forms of dance from other times and places.

The Pragmatic Tradition in Dance Education
In discussing this tradition in dance, the following developments are grouped together: (1) those uses of dance to achieve extra-aesthetic ends such as religious observance, health, and moral training, where dance is justified not by what it is but by the kinds of effects it achieves either in the student dancer or upon the audience witnessing the dance; and (2) the development of a professionalist orientation in dance education where dance is taught for the purpose of creating an artistic event of high quality.

In the nineteenth century "aesthetic gymnastics" based on the

Delcorte system of dance instruction was described as a vehicle for the expression of various emotions. The system entailed the use of statue posing and tableau making in connection with the recitation of poems and the singing of songs usually of a moral or a sentimental nature (Marks, 1876, p. 98). Because dance, unlike art and music, did not occupy much of a place in the schools, there was no push to integrate it into the total curriculum, although it was not uncommon for folk dances to be taught to children who were studying a particular culture.

The development of a professionalist approach to instruction in dance can be traced to the Denishawn School (Todd, 1951) which trained many teachers in a freer, more theatrical form of dance. Denishawn's touring company spread the popularity of dance as an art form to many parts of the country. They taught a form of "direct pictorial dance drama" to many public school teachers who began to introduce it into their classrooms. Another indication that dance for performance had become a major educational goal was Margaret H'Doubler's formation of an "Orchesis Club" at the University of Wisconsin in 1926. In the 1930s the touring and concertizing of Denishawn, Ted Shawn's men's group, Martha Graham, Doris Humphrey, and Charles Weideman was to create a much greater interest in technical mastery, in expanding the range of dance movement, and in developing a recognition of dance as an art form rather than as a useful means of catharsis or self-expression. In 1934, the advent of summer schools in dance conducted by Graham, Humphrey, and Holm drew dance educators from many parts of the country and imparted to them advanced techniques, stagecraft, and choreography. The professional point of view with an emphasis on performance became a profound influence in dance circles (Kraus, 1969, p. 225), and this viewpoint continues as an important aspect of many programs to the present day. Murray's *Dance in Elementary Schools* (1953) recommended a twofold program of dance education: (1) making and performing dances and (2) practicing and exploring movement. Dance was to be taught through problem-solving activities and performance was for the "pleasure of self and others."

The Expressive Tradition in Dance Education

The nineteenth century Froebelian kindergarten movement introduced learning through play, song, gesture, and self-expression which included many dance-like activities (Marks, 1976, p. 92). Francis Wayland Parker, one of the forerunners of progressive education, based much of his work on the ideas of Froebel. He introduced a crude form of expressive dance toward the end of the nineteenth century but his efforts were greeted with much resistance (Marks, p. 93).

In the early decades of the twentieth century Isadora Duncan inspired a flowering of the expressive use of the dance. Dance for children in the classes of some pioneers in the dance education movement became free and unstructured and based on the child's interpretation of the essence of the music. Margaret H'Doubler regarded the dance primarily as a way to develop the student's personality though she also felt that a biological basis must be added to the student's intuitive movements if there were to be an art of the dance. Similarly the development of personality and creativity are recognized as goals in Thompson's 1933 text *Fundamentals of Rhythm and Dance.*

The earlier forms of children's dance involving imitation gave way by the mid-thirties to an emphasis on free unstructured movement, self-discovery, and spontaneous response to music. Directions from the teacher were held to a minimum and the teacher's task was to create the inspiration to move. The high-school approach to dance at this time was also extremely free and aimed at developing personality rather than professional dancers. Personal creativity and aesthetic expressiveness were deemed sufficient. In the elementary and secondary schools the concept that the body had to be trained as a tool or an instrument was minimized (Kraus, 1969, pp. 134-135).

A less extreme position was taken by H'Doubler in the 1940s who recommended that deep emotional tensions be transferred to the dance with a resulting increase in personal power. Techniques should be simple enough to afford the student sufficient mastery of the body as an instrument of expression and should provide a rhythmic scope broad enough to include the varying personal rhythms of students (H'Doubler, 1940, pp. 162-164).

The Objective Tradition in Dance Education

At the turn of the century Rudolph Von Laban had already begun the work that now profoundly influences the teaching of the dance. He began analyzing and teaching the physical laws governing dance movement: the planes, directions, dimensions, extensions, speed, force, and flow that are the objective components of dance. By mid-century there was a rise in what has been called "non-objective," "non-literal," "non-representational dance" (Turner, 1971). In all these forms of dance the subject matter of the dance was dance movement or "motion" as Nikolais called it. Criticism of this trend in educational institutions was based on the fact that dance requires the human being, the dancer, as the medium. "The personality, the person-ness is integral to the art act. One might . . . question whether this really is dance, or whether it is merely geometry with mechanized figures, who, except for the fact that they breathe, might well be automatons, for they are being presented as mechanical objects, as impersonal shapes, as non-objective elements." The author questions whether this feelingless approach to dance through its formal aspects is a new use of dance or a misuse of dance (Krevitsky, p. 14-16).

The 1960s saw a rise in the dissemination of the teachings of Von Laban which brought about a concentration on the elements of dance in experimentation, and an analysis of how each body part can possibly move, the efforts it can move with, the space shaped when the body moves, and the relation between dancers and objects in space. The lessons in this approach are centered in sixteen themes which include the elements of space, time, effort, and flow in various combinations and isolations. Experimentation and asking the proper question at the proper time "aids in the perception of the various elements of the dance" (Russell, 1965). Improvisations must be clarified so that the child can clearly show in his or her body an awareness of its shape (symmetrical or asymmetrical, angular, curved, and so on), its flow (easy or resistive), its pathway (twisted or straight), its effort (forceful or fine touch), and so on. Exploration of such dance elements leads to understanding, body mastery, and expressiveness (Russell, 1965). Laban's theories have had a profound influence on dance education from pre-school through university to the present day.

Exploring the materials of dance is the approach of Margery Turner who has written in physical education publications on the subject of nonliteral dance. Her basic premise is that "art may exist for its own sake" (Turner, 1971). She suggests that movement and motion are among the basic materials to be explored in the art form. In a similar vein, Maxine Sheets (1970) states that dance can be valued for what it is: "a vital human experience as both a formed and performed art to be experienced by both the dancer and audience in its immediacy." Through the lived experience the "structure" in the phenomenon will become apparent. In this latter approach to dance instruction, the analysis of dance structure, temporality, and spaciality are included in the education of the dance student.

Theatre

The Mimetic Tradition in Theatre Education

As with the other arts the historical roots of theatre education can be traced back to classical times. In The Republic, Plato (Jowett translation 401-402) distinguishes "play" as a basis for education from theatre which like the other arts is deemed an imitation of an imitation and hence without educative value. In one sense, his distinction between play and theatre is a forerunner of the debate that has divided theatre educators for much of the present century, one which only recently shows signs of resolution—namely, the conflict between the proponents of "children's theatre" and "creative dramatics." In the former the emphasis is upon the production of plays in a pre-designated manner in which the play as the work of art is reproduced in much the same manner as a written piece of music. The latter type of activity is an outgrowth of children's natural tendency to play or to "make believe." The work of art is improvised out of the materials developed by the interaction of children and teachers.

The practice of reproducing the classics was initiated during the Renaissance and has continued well into the twentieth century. Curtis (1914, p. 58) mentioned that the classical play as well as plays in foreign languages were presented at many universities in the early decades of the century as part of the activities of commencement week. Play giving was a favored activity "because of the student's gain through close acquaintance with the thought and purpose, the melodious and rhythmic phrasing, and concise statement of great writers." Curtis also described the types of plays and dramatic activities that were common in elementary schools. Many of these consisted of activities calling for the imitation of animal characteristics, industrial occupations, outdoor sports and pastimes, movement in nature, and so on. These activities showed a strong tendency to be teacher directed and Curtis goes on to describe the children's responses to them as "stereotyped and repressive" (pp. 95-96). Nevertheless their use in elementary schools was quite extensive as attested to by the fact that these teaching materials went through several printings. Thus, the kind of dramatic activity, like the copy book exercises in drawing classes, relied heavily upon imitation as a teaching method.

In more recent times Shaw (1968, 1970) exemplified a tendency to be concerned with the establishment of educational behavioral objectives for creative dramatics. According to Shaw the mastery of cognitive and affective goals is the basis for all education and thus it should be possible to give the student specific objectives to master. The particular objectives she listed were derived from the major texts in creative dramatics organized by the models provided in *Taxonomy of Behavioral Objectives: Handbooks I and II* (Krathwohl, Bloom, and Masia, 1964). Similarly in 1971 the California Department of Education published their *Drama/ Theatre Framework* which also lists specific behavioral objectives for students to master.

The Pragmatic Tradition in Theatre Education

As in the discussion of dance education, the discussion of the pragmatic tradition in theatre education groups together those uses of the art form to achieve extra-aesthetic ends, and those aimed at the development of a strong professionalist stance. This latter orientation is promoted by the proponents of children's theatre as opposed to creative dramatics. The use of theatre as education for moral purposes began in the Middle Ages and continued well into the twentieth century (Courtney, 1968, and Curtis, 1914). To this day the moral integrity of a play is an important consideration in its educational adoption.

The elementary grades have always used plays as teaching devices for all kinds of learning: There are health plays, safety-first plays, English, geography, history, and science plays. Commenting upon this role imposed upon the dramatic art form, Ward (1930) noted that dramatics was not recognized as an art form but was made "the slave of every other school subject," a complaint that is shared by numerous music and art teachers.

Pestalozzi devised a series of "object lessons" to develop students' sensory awareness and powers of oral expression. These lessons were used by Shelton in the Oswego, New York Schools and are considered the first use of creative drama in American classrooms (Landy, 1975, p. 49). Landy characterized these first efforts as a kind of "show and tell" and criticized them for the "parroting" they tend to impose upon the child. In the 1880s Parker built on the work of Shelton in oral expression and advocated the use of improvisation as a way to motivate children to engage in discussion. Somewhat later, Merrill expanded upon this idea and began to use drama as a way to teach literature (Landy, 1975, p. 50).

Dewey's "learning by doing" led to drama projects and to some use of free improvisation in many private schools (Courtney, 1968, p. 43). In England, Dewey's ideas led to a method developed by Caldwell Cook known as the "play way." In this method dramatic improvisation (play) was used to teach lessons in other subjects in a more "natural" way. The teacher did not impart instructions but was a "leader" in helping students develop their expressive abilities and their inherent self-discipline. The "play way" is still to be found in British infant schools and in many junior schools as well.

Much of the recent writing on dramatic education has been done in England. Brian Way proposed a cognitive theory of learning in *Development Through Drama* (1967). The individual develops "through the imaginative and emotional process, of relishing and enjoying inner resourcefulness and intuition" (p. 3). Drama in his view is living in the classroom. Initially it is aimed at developing the child's inner resources through activities of exploration and discovery. The views of Courtney (1968) also have a strong cognitive thrust:

> Dramatic imagination lies behind all human learning, both social learning and academic learning. It is the way in which man relates himself to life, the infant dramatically in his external play, the adult internally in his imagination. It teaches us to think, to examine and to explore, to test hypotheses and discover truth. (Courtney, quoted in Landy, p. 23)

Also in England, Dorothy Heathcote described drama as a learning process rather than a subject matter (see Wagner, 1966). She feels that it should not be labeled "creative dramatics," "role playing," "psychodrama," or "socio-drama" but should be considered a conscious employment of the elements of drama to educate. This she terms "volume building" within the student. She attempts to "plummet deep into feeling and meaning," to expand the child's awareness and thus to enable him or her to look into other areas of the curriculum. She allows children to make as many of the decisions as possible and to set the problems.

Through subtle guidance she enables the drama to come alive, each child using his or her own character in the decided upon situation. Questioning is her most important tool. Through it, she enables the student to find out what is fundamental and human in the situation.

In a recent publication, MacGregor, Tate, and Robinson (1977) described their aims in drama education in the following way: "The destination is the resolution of the problem of meaning or understanding which is motivating the work. To work in the arts is to tackle problems of understanding through representing them in symbolic forms" (p. 19). The teacher's role in this conception of drama is two-fold: to encourage the children to deepen and challenge perceptions of themselves and the world so that they gradually begin to make sense of the complexities and subtleties of experience, and to accomplish this through the symbol processes provided by the arts (p. 23).

Drama in the work of such educators as Cook, Way, Heathcote, and MacGregor and his colleagues is primarily used as a teaching instrument, a tool to advance the acquisition of subject matter competence, and cognitive or emotional development. Natural self-expression and improvisation are exploited as ways to advance specific educational goals that are often extra-aesthetic in nature. Somewhat later I will refer to another group of educators for whom self-expression becomes the end in itself.

The nineteenth century also saw the beginnings of a second tradition in drama education, namely the development of theatre experiences with a strong professionalist bias, where the function of instruction is geared to the production of a professional product. According to Curtis (1914), the "careful and conscientious study of a masterpiece" resulted in more and more elaborate performances for assemblies and presentations to parents (p. 55). Often this over-riding emphasis upon presentation did not allow the fuller possibilities of dramatic training to be explored. In the early 1900s the practice of allowing plays to be spontaneously developed out of the child's interest and inclination was recommended by such writers as Dewey, but the prevailing practice was to impose a teacher-selected script on the children. Landy (1975) described the situation in the following way:

> This emphasis on plays, proper to the domain of theatre, rather than on play, proper to the domain of dramatic education of children, was to dominate the development of the creative dramatics and children's theatre movement in the United States. (p. 52)

The emphasis on the product can be readily seen in Winifred Ward's *Creative Dramatics* (1930). Although this publication was one of the landmark contributions to the development of creative dramatics in the school, fully half of the publication is devoted to helping teachers with the professional problems of choosing the play for presentation and directing, costuming, and staging. In 1961, Geraldine Siks and Hazel

Dunnington attempted to clarify the goals of drama educators (see Landy, 1975). They collected and edited the contributions of twenty-five educators and attempted to develop the distinction between "creative dramatics" and "children's theatre." Landy summarized their efforts:

> Even much of the discussion of creative dramatics centers upon theatre, the creation of a product performed to an audience, rather than upon drama, a process of teaching/learning. There is continued emphasis upon adults as creators of scripts, direction, design, and more often than not, acting. (p. 57)

The 1970 *A Survey of the Status of Theatre in the United States High Schools* (Peluso, 1970) stated that "perhaps the most notable findings . . . are that most United States High Schools put on plays, but few offer theatre arts courses" (p. 55).

The Expressive Tradition in Theatre Education

In the early 1900s Alice Minnie Herts founded the Children's Educational Theatre. She published the results of her experiments with "free dramatic expression" in 1911 in a book with the same name. In the Introduction, Charles Eliot, President Emeritus of Harvard, describes her work as "imparting ethical instruction through stimulation of emotions that prompt to persistent personal action . . . at the same time . . . imparting to them the means of giving pleasure to other people in a safe and wholesome way." Eliot suggests that the processes of children's educational theatre be adapted to ordinary school conditions. Herts' program was one of freeing emotional tensions through the free interpretation of mood music, relaxing muscles, and stirring creative imagination. Her objectives were to "utilize the eager craving of man, woman and child to realize the meaning of lives totally apart from their own restricted environment—to see the abstract pictures of their imagination realized in concrete form." According to her, the responsibility for creating an atmosphere for free dramatic expression rests with the teacher. The situation in which the children are involved must be a happy one with lots of fun and laughter: "We create only in freedom . . . the event is play and, strangely enough, in play we do our most serious, successful work" (pp. 1-21). What Herts describes as teaching fits more closely into the current definition of "creative dramatics" rather than "educational theatre."

Curtis (1914) describes children's irresistible attraction to the theatre as a demand for the expression of personality, "a push of the ego which finds its vents vicariously" (p. 27). She describes an "almost epidemic" interest in dramatization as a part of primary school work which arises from interest in the child's nature (p. 38). In her view the dramatic instinct is a prime force in civilization; the need to give vent to pent up emotions, to express the joy of living, to put into material form ideas that vex the spirit—all these drive us to create, and by exploiting this instinct, the emotional needs and desires of children can be accommodated.

Earlier I referred to Ward's *Creative Dramatics* (1930) as an example of a leading text that devoted much attention to play production as a kind of pre-professional activity, but this does not do justice to the book's role in shaping the interest in creative dramatics as a school activity. The book was based on her work in the Evanston, Illinois Public Schools and at Northwestern University. Her aims were "psycho-social." She was concerned with the "development of creative self expression and growth in tolerant understanding of self and society" (pp. 52-53). She emphasized the making of plays by children to suit their needs and tastes. Her teaching focused on storytelling, pantomiming, and a process of helping the children arrive at decisions involving characters, story line and scene (pp. 30-34). She showed a particular concern for the adolescent "who can scarcely repress his feelings yet is ashamed to vent them. Without fear of ridicule he can express his feeling in one vivid experience after another" (p. 9). In 1947 Ward's *Play Making with Children* appeared and described creative dramatics as "controlled emotional outlet," while the arts are presented as offering the best opportunities among school activities for channeling emotions into constructive uses.

In the mid-forties Slade began his work in the Experimental Drama Centre in Birmingham, England. Slade believed that child drama was rooted in play rather than theatrical performance. This idea influenced the work of both Way and Courtney (Landy, 1975, p. 5). Courtney (1968, p. 46) noted that Slade was committed to the fact that dramatic play provided a child with a great safety valve—an emotional catharsis—and went on to say that in providing for emotional release, dramatic play also offered an opportunity to achieve emotional control and an inner self-discipline. Slade refers to his method as "planned emotional training" growing out of the child's natural personal and projected play (Slade, 1958, p. 1). In his view the teacher's role is that of a loving ally giving suggestions when the imagination fails but never showing the child how to do it (p. 2).

Isabel Burger published *Creative Play Acting: Learning Through Drama* in 1950. Her method also makes use of improvisation and characterization based on situations, characters, and emotions familiar to the child. She states that children should never be made to feel restricted by the imposition of rules of technique and that carefully worded questions can accomplish miracles with children (p. 97). "Becoming another character in a dramatic situation involves feeling deeply the emotions of someone else. Through this use of the complex emotional mechanism a boy or girl may get a healthy release from his tensions" (p. 5).

In 1963, the American Educational Theatre Association published *A Suggested Outline for a Course of Study in Theatre Arts at the Secondary*

Level which says that while in general drama is predominantly studied as literature, its curriculum emphasizes the psychological view that the primary aim of creative drama studies is to educate the emotions for controlled use (Teeter, p. iv). The teacher's role is to use creative activity to develop the students' latent techniques. The individual is led to discovery of inner resources and to the ability to express himself or herself through acting. In a similar vein, Tyas wrote that child drama is a voyage of self-discovery. The child is the captain, the adult is merely the navigator. Children need to discover what they can do and who they are, and opportunities for personal play safeguard this need (Tyas, 1971, p. xv).

The Objective Tradition in Theatre Education

Although Aristotle's *Poetics* is frequently cited as the first attempt to deduce a set of rational principles for the drama, there was little use of drama as an art form in education in classical times. To be sure, works of dramatic art were studied and important parts committed to memory but drama was not taught as an art form in and of itself. The reliance upon a set of rationally deduced rules as a basis for the writing and performance of dramatic works provided a basis for the teaching of the drama in the seventeenth and eighteenth centuries, but rarely was drama considered a part of the formal education of children. As late as the nineteenth century, the theatre and acting were thought to be socially inferior professions.

In spite of a pedigree dating back to Aristotle and seventeenth century French dramatic tradition, there are relatively few contemporary developments to report in the objective tradition. Garrard, for example, has developed a form of dance drama based upon Laban's analysis of movement. The four elements of movement (time, space, energy, and flow) become a technical frame for the support of spontaneous drama (see Courtney, 1968, p. 50). The California *Drama/Theatre Framework* mentioned earlier can also be viewed as an attempt to give structure to the teaching of theatre by dividing it into discrete categories, in this case the acts of originating, performing, producing, and responding. Objectives and activities for each of these processes are suggested in a kindergarten to twelfth grade sequence.

Conclusions

I have suggested that four main orientations in the history of aesthetics align themselves with specific theoretical orientations in psychology: (1) the mimetic tradition in aesthetics with psychological behaviorism; (2) pragmatic aesthetics with cognitive psychology; (3) expressive aesthetics with psychoanalytic psychology; and (4) objective aesthetics with Gestalt psychology. I have also suggested that these four alignments can serve as categories for grouping together distinctive teaching traditions in each of the arts, and using this assumption I have examined the teaching literature in four of the arts to find suitable examples of practices reflecting these alignments. *Figure 3* is an attempt to represent some of the more important examples of practices surveyed in this paper.

Some cautionary observations have to be tendered at this point. First, it was necessary to interpret some of the developments described in each of the arts somewhat freely. For example, music education never quite developed the kind of interest in self-expression that developed within the other arts. However, at the time that self-expression was the dominant approach to teaching in the other arts, music educators did develop methods that would allow children to improvise with musical materials. For this reason I described these developments as related events in the history of music education.

Second, in describing individual contributors to conceptions of teaching, I tended to classify persons in terms of their predominant emphasis. Thus I discussed Lownefeld and Read as contributors to an expressive view of teaching art, one that made use of constructs derived from psychoanalytic psychology; however, these writers were also strongly influenced by Gestalt psychology. It was also sometimes necessary to describe the contributions of certain educators as belonging to more than a single tradition. Barkan's early writings, for example, were pragmatic in their orientation and strongly influenced by transactional psychology. Later, under the spell of Bruner, he moved toward an objective stance in which the meanings of experience are facts awaiting discovery through disciplined inquiry. In describing Mursell's views, I placed them with developments in music whose emphasis lay with expressive or improvisational activity yet few of his psychological views came from psychoanalytic sources. He was more at home in the Gestalt tradition. Similarly in dance, one finds that certain leaders' (like H'Doubler) interests and ideas fit into more than a single category, and the same is true of Ward in theatre.

Nevertheless, the scheme does enable one to compare traditions of teaching in the several arts to see how particular concepts may have fared within a given artistic genre. My comparison underscores the following points:

1. The four main orientations in aesthetic theory, traditions with roots reaching back to ancient aesthetics, continue to influence teaching practices. Although these views came into prominence at different times in history, they are still to be found in contemporary teaching practices in some form. For example: The *mimetic* teaching tradition, once the major tradition, is still widely practiced in the several arts, particularly those characterized by performance. Children still learn to draw by copying, to play music by imitating the actions of their teachers, and to dance and act according to discrete models provided by instruction. The *pragmatic*

Figure 3

Conceptions of Teaching in the Arts

	Mimetic	Pragmatic	Expressive	Objective
Art	Walter Smith, 1871 Learning to draw by copying	Melvin Haggerty. Art in daily living, Report on the Owatonna Project Art conceived of as a tool for the solving of problems in the Progressive Era, 1930-1940	Self-expression becomes a dominant approach in teaching with Cizek, Lowenfeld, and Read, 1911, 1958	Arthur W. Dow develops a teaching approach based upon the elements and principles of design Bauhaus in Germany develops a rational approach to art instruction
Music	Lowell Mason, 1838 Singing school techniques strongly rote in their emphasis Emphasis on drill and practice, 1900-1925 Suzuki violin schools	Lowell Mason establishes performance as a major goal of music education, 1838 Throughout the Progressive Era music is correlated into Social Studies and the curriculum as a whole	Music does not develop a self-expression thrust, but does develop a series of approaches to improvisation in instruction: Orff, Kodaly, Manhattanville Music Curriculum Project	Gestalt theory in music focuses instruction on wholes, calls into question prevalent emphasis upon drill and practice Emphasis on structure also seen in curriculum development efforts of the 60s: Orff, Kodaly, MMCP, Reimer
Theatre	Classical theatre largely learned by role, Curtis, 1914	Pestalozzi developed a series of object lessons using plays as learning tools, 1830s Children's theatre develops a strong performance orientation, 1900-1970	The "play way," first introduced in England in the early 1900s; remains an important technique in the British infant schools	Theatre does not develop a strong objective tradition but in the 1960s some theatre educators begin to adapt Laban techniques to structure theatre instruction
Dance	Early dance forms learned by rote methods. Folk dancing, 1600s Aristocracy employs dance masters, 1600-1700s	Touring dance companies (Graham, Humphrey and Holm) and the Denishawn school establish a strong professionalist approach to dance education, early 1900s	Margaret H'Doubler though a strong advocate of a biological structure for dance education sees the dance as a way to develop the student as a person	Laban notation system introduced in the early part of the century provides a structure for the teaching of dance Strong movement toward non-literal or nonrepresentational dance

tradition in teaching was important in the ancient world where the arts were viewed as agents for moral education. It returned to prominence in the Progressive Era in the thirties and forties and enjoys currency today when the arts are seen as important ways to spur cognitive development. The *expressive* tradition came to the fore during the same period as a response to child-centered education. In the visual arts, its influence peaked in the late fifties; it continues to be a dominant emphasis in theatre education. The *objective* tradition began in the visual arts and music in the early decades of the twentieth century with teaching that emphasized the formal qualities of the arts and their organization. As notation systems developed in dance, this tradition was felt there also.

2. Although practices associated with some of these teaching traditions are sometimes seen as outmoded or old fashioned (for example, copying in the visual arts), arguments and circumstances can probably be found to justify any and all given practices. Rote learning tends to be discounted in favor of meaningful learning, yet methods that make use of rote learning, like those developed by Suzuki for the teaching of string playing, have been highly successful.

3. The view that there are compatible although not necessarily logical alignments among aesthetic traditions and psychological theories points to an interesting possibility—namely that some combinations of theory might result in "mis-alignments." Consider the teacher who says: "Now that you know the elements and principles of design (objective orientation), express yourself freely (expressive orientation)." Or the teacher who says, "Be freer with your use of clay. Let your feelings guide your expression (expressive orientation), forget about function (objective orientation), and while you're at it, look at pots in the Japanese Raku tradition to learn how to be loose (mimetic orientation)." In the last case we see a three-way contradiction in practice, and such mixed messages from teachers to students are not at all uncommon. It is my view that the four-fold view of teaching presented earlier might serve as a basis for evaluating teaching styles in terms of their compatibility with differing views of art.

4. Though all views of art and teaching are viable (not necessarily true or false), this paper is not an invitation to a willy-nilly kind of eclecticism. Views of art, of individuality, and of society are elements that come out of larger world views. Once a teacher recognizes these views it should be possible to express these relationships in theories and models that clarify the connecting links between content and method. Such a task is beyond the scope of the present paper.

Columbus, Ohio
September 1978

REFERENCES

Note: The reference list contains several entries that are not specifically cited in the text of the paper; they are included here because they are part of the necessary background for a discussion of the topic.

Abrams, M. H. *The mirror and the lamp.* Oxford: Oxford University Press, 1953.

Aristotle. *Politics and poetics* (Jowett and Twining trans.). Cleveland: Fine Editions Press, 1952.

Arnheim, R. *Art and visual perception.* Berkeley, California: University of California Press, 1964.

Art education today: Art education and the war. Teachers College: Columbia University, 1943.

Bandura, A., and McDonald, F. Influence of social reinforcement and the behavior of models in shaping children's moral judgments. *Journal of Abnormal and Social Psychology,* 1963, 67, 274-281.

Barkan, M. *A foundation for art education.* New York: Ronald Press, 1955.

Barkan, M. Transition in art education. *Art Education,* October 1962, 15(7), 12-18.

Barkan, M. Art education in the elementary school. *Report of the Commission on Art Education,* 1964.

Barkan, M. Curriculum problems in art education. In E. Mattil (Ed.), *A seminar in art education for research and curriculum development.* Cooperative research project #V882, Pennsylvania State University, 1966.

Beardsley, M. *Aesthetics from classical Greece to the present.* New York: Macmillan, 1966.

Boyle, J. D. (Ed.). *Instructional objectives in music: Resources for planning instruction and evaluating achievement.* National Commission on Instruction, Music Educators National Conference, 1974.

Broudy, H. S. The structure of knowledge in the arts. In S. Elam (Ed.), *Education and the structure of knowledge: Fifth annual Phi Delta Kappa symposium on educational research.* Chicago, 1964.

Brown, S. Has school art a place in modern life? *Teachers College Record,* February 1934, 35, 396-406.

Bruner, J., Goodnow, J., and Austin, D. *A study of thinking.* New York: John Wiley & Sons, 1956.

Bruner, J. On perceptual readiness. In J. M. Anglin (Ed.), *Beyond the information given.* New York: W. W. Norton Co., 1973, 7-42.

Bruner, J. *The process of education.* Cambridge: Harvard University Press, 1960.

Bruner, J. *Toward a theory of instruction.* Cambridge: Harvard University Press, 1966.

Burger, I. B. *Creative play acting: Learning through drama.* New York: A. S. Barnes & Co., 1950.

California State Department of Education. *Drama/theatre framework.* Sacramento, California: California Department of Education, 1971.

Cook, C. A. *Suzuki education in action.* New York: Exposition Press, 1970.

Courtney, R. *Play, drama, and thought.* New York: Drama Book Specialists, 1968.

Curtis, E. W. *The dramatic instinct in education.* Boston: Houghton Mifflin Co., 1914.

Dewey, J. Experience, nature and art. In Dewey, J., Barnes, A., et al., *Art and education*. Merion, Pennsylvania: Barnes Foundation Press, 1930.

Dorner, A. A. The background of the Bauhaus. In *Bauhaus: 1919-1928*. Boston: Charles T. Branford Co., 1959.

Dow, A. W. *Composition*. New York: Doubleday Doran & Co., 1929.

Dunnington, H. and Siks, G. *Children's theatre and creative dramatics*. Seattle: University of Washington Press, 1961.

Efland, A. Changing conceptions of children's artistic development. In E. Eisner (Ed.), *The arts, human development and education*. Berkeley, California: McCutcheon Press, 1975.

Eisner, E. *Curriculum ideas in an age of crisis*. An address to the Ohio Art Education Association. Columbus, Ohio, November 13-14, 1964.

Ellfeldt, L. *From magic to art*. Dubuque, Iowa: W. C. Brown, Co., 1976.

Erwin, M. E. The integration of the curriculum through the arts. *Educational Method*, January 1936, 15, 191-197.

Florida State Assessment Project in Art. Tallahassee: Florida Board of Education, 1972.

Glace, M. F. Individual development through art education. *Peabody Journal of Education*, September 1934, 12, 78-85.

Green, H. Walter Smith, the forgotten man. *Art Education*, 1966, 19(1), 3-11.

Haggerty, M. *Art, a way of life*. Owatonna Art Education Project, University of Minnesota Press, 1935.

Herts, A. M. *The children's educational theatre*. New York: Harper & Bros., 1911.

H'Doubler, M. *Dance: A creative art experience*. New York: F. S. Crofts & Co., 1940.

Hoyt, R. Isadora Duncan. In D. Hering (Ed.), *Twenty-five years of American dance*. New York: R. Orthwine, 1951.

MacGregor, L., Tate, M., and Robinson, K. *Learning through drama*. London: Heineman Education Books, Ltd., 1977.

Marks, J. E., III. *America learns to dance*. New York: Dance Horizons, 1976.

Maslow, A. H. Peak experiences in education and art. *Theory into Practice*, June 1971, 10(3), 149-153.

Mason, L. *Manual of the Boston academy of music*. 1851.

Mathias, M. Art in the integrated program. *School Arts Magazine*, February 1936, 35, 324-331.

McMurray, F. Pragmatism in music education. In N. B. Henry (Ed.), *Basic concepts in music education*. Fifty-seventh yearbook of the National Society for the Study of Education, Part II. Chicago: University of Chicago Press, 1958, 30-61.

Munro, T. Franz Cizek and the free expression method. In *Art and education*. Merion, Pennsylvania: Barnes Foundation Press, 1930.

Munro, T. The Dow Method and public school art. In Dewey, J., Barnes, A., et. al., *Art and Education*. Merion, Pennsylvania: Barnes Foundation Press, 1930.

Murray, R. L. *Dance in elementary schools*. New York: Harper Bros., 1953.

Mursell, J. L. *Education for musical growth*. New York: Ginn & Co., 1948.

Nadel, M. H., and Nadel, C. G. (Eds.). *The dance experience*. New York: Praeger Publishers, 1970.

Nicoliades, K. *The natural way to draw.* Boston: Houghton Mifflin Co., 1941.

Nye, R. E., and Nye, V. T. *Music in the elementary school* (4th ed.). New York: Prentice-Hall, 1977.

Pearson, R. *The new art education.* New York: Harper and Co., 1941.

Peluso, R. *A survey of the status of theatre in the United States high school.* United States Office of Education, November, 1970.

Perkins, D., and Leondar, B. (Eds.). *The arts and cognition.* Baltimore: Johns Hopkins University Press, 1977.

Kilpatrick, F. (Ed.). *Explorations in transactional psychology.* New York: New York University Press, 1961.

Korzenik, D. Role-taking and children's drawings. *Studies in Art Education,* 15(3), 17-24.

Krathwohl, D. R., Bloom, B. S., and Masia, B. B. *Taxonomy of educational objectives, Handbook II: Affective domain.* New York: David McKay Co., Inc., 1964.

Kraus, R. *History of the dance in art and education.* Englewood Cliffs, New Jersey: Prentice-Hall, Inc., 1969.

Kreitler, H., and Kreitler, S. *Psychology of the arts.* Chapel Hill, North Carolina: Duke University Press, 1972.

Krevitsky, N. Can dance be nonobjective? In G. Lippincott (Ed.), *Focus on Dance-I, 1960.* National Education Association, 1960.

Landy, R. J. *Dramatic education, an interdisciplinary approach to learning.* Unpublished doctoral dissertation, University of California, Santa Barbara, 1975.

Leonhard, C., and House, R. W. *Foundations and principles of music education.* New York: McGraw Hill, 1972.

Lippincott, G. (Ed.). *Focus on Dance-I, 1960.* National Education Association, 1960.

Lowenfeld, V. *The nature of creative activity.* New York: Harcourt Brace & Co., 1939.

Lowenfeld, V. *Creative and mental growth* (1st ed.). New York: Macmillan Co., 1947.

Lowenfeld, V., and Brittain, L. *Creative and mental growth* (6th ed.). New York: Macmillan Co., 1976.

MacDonald, S. *The history and philosophy of art education.* New York: American Elsevier Publishing Co., Inc., 1970.

Plato. *The Republic* (Jowett trans.) New York: Modern Library Books, 1941.

Popovitch, J. E. Development of creative dramatics in the United States. In G. Siks and H. Dunnington (Eds.), *Children's theatre and creative dramatics.* Seattle: University of Washington Press, 1961, 115-123.

Raebeck, L., and Wheeler, L. *Orff and Kodaly adapted for the elementary school.* Dubuque, Iowa: W. C. Brown, 1972.

Read, H. *Education through art.* New York: Pantheon Press, 1944.

Reimer, B. *Development and trial in junior/senior high school of a two year curriculum in general music.* Englewood Cliffs, New Jersey: Prentice-Hall, 1967.

Reimer, B. *A philosophy of music education.* Englewood Cliffs, New Jersey: Prentice-Hall, 1970.

Rich, A. L. *Lowell Mason: The father of singing among the children.* Chapel Hill: University of North Carolina Press, 1946.

Rogerson, B. The art of painting the passions. *Journal of the History of Ideas,* 1953, *14,* 68-94.

Russell, J. *Creative dance in the primary school.* London: MacDonald & Evans, Ltd., 1965.

Schaeffer-Simmern, H. *The unfolding of artistic activity.* Berkeley: University of California Press, 1948.

Schaper, E. *Prelude to aesthetics.* London: George Allen & Unwin Ltd., 1968.

Shaw, A. A taxonomical study of the nature and behavioral objectives of creative dramatics. *Educational Theatre Journal,* 1970.

Sheets, M. Phenomenology: An approach to dance. In Nadel and Nadel (Eds.), *The Dance Experience.* New York: Praeger Publishers, 1970.

Sherman, H. *Drawing by seeing.* New York: Hynds, Hayden and Ellridge, 1947.

Slade, P. *An introduction to child drama.* London: University of London Press, 1958.

Smith, R. A. Aesthetic criticism: The method of aesthetic education. *Studies in Art Education,* 1968, 9(3), 12-31.

Smith, W. *The drawing book.* Boston: James R. Osgood Co., 1872.

Surette, T. W. A general view of music education for children. In S. Hartman and A. Shumaker (Eds. for Progressive Education Association), *Creative Expression.* New York: John Day Co., 1932.

Teeter, R. W. *A suggested outline for a course of study in theatre arts at the secondary school level.* American Educational Theatre Association, Inc., 1963.

Tellstrom, T. A. *Music in American education, past and present.* New York: Holt Rinehart & Winston, Inc., 1971.

Thomas, R. *Manhattanville music curriculum project.* USOE No. 6-1999 and V-008.

Thompson, B. L. *Fundamentals of rhythm and dance.* New York: A. S. Barnes Co., 1933.

Todd, A. Denishawn, cradle of American Dance. In D. Hering (Ed.), *Twenty-five years of American dance.* New York: R. Orthwine, 1951.

Turner, M. J. *New dance: Approaches to non-literal choreography.* Pittsburgh, Pennsylvania: University of Pittsburgh Press, 1971.

Tyas, B. *Child drama in action: A practical manual for teachers.* New York: Drama Book Specialists, 1971.

Viola, W. *Child art.* Peoria, Illinois: Charles A. Bennett, 1946.

Wackwith, M., and Lurry, L. Art in the core curriculum: A case study. In *Art Education Today.* New York: Teachers College, Columbia University, 1951-52.

Wagner, B. J. *Dorothy Heathcote: Drama as a learning medium.* Washington, D.C.: National Education Association, 1976.

Ward, W. *Creative dramatics: for the upper grades and junior high school.* New York: Appleton Century Co., 1930.

Ward, W. *Playmaking with children.* New York: Appleton Century Crofts, Inc., 1957.

Way, B. *Development through drama*. London: Longmans, Green & Co., Ltd., 1967.

Wilson, B., and Wilson, M. An iconoclastic view of the imagery sources in the drawings of young people. *Art Education*, 1977, *30*(1), 5-12.

Winslow, L. *The integrated school art program*. New York: McGraw-Hill, 1939.

Richard L. Loveless / *A Response to Efland*

Creating New Myths in Art Education

I am going to try to respond to the work of Professor Efland the only way I know how! I simply do not have the eloquence of his scholarship. I am going to describe for you some events as a point of departure for developing some ideas. I will begin by relating to you a personal story which I consider to be a description of a successful teaching process.

I was sitting on the front porch of an old house in Tampa, Florida, about six or seven years ago. It was a mid-July, and if you've even been in Florida in July, you know that its pretty hot and humid. There was a guy who lived in the neighborhood who was about twelve years old; his name was Crazy Moses! He got his name because he had the distinction of being able to get attention from all of his friends in the neighborhood by appearing to be crazy and, well, he had several methods of doing that. He would roll his eyes way back behind his eyelids and start frothing at the mouth, and then he would go into a body stance, which by all appearances would have you believe that he was completely out of touch with reality. Several weeks earlier I had had a chance to experience one of his crazy-making academy award performances, and had decided to call his bluff! Picking him up physically and setting him on the hood of my car, I told him he could get away with that phony act with his friends, but not ever again with me! If he intended to get any attention, he would have to find a better way. Whereupon he demonstrated for me a very unusual high shrill whistle he could make, and that, we agreed, would be his signal anytime he was coming to see me.

Now, a week later, I was sitting on the porch rocking and waiting for something to happen, and I heard that familiar whistle in the distance. Sure enough, it was Moses, and this time he had his dog with him. He was a mangy grey-black dog, and his name I soon learned was Trix. Moses walked up to me and said, "Hey Mr. Love, you wanna see how my

RICHARD L. LOVELESS is *Associate Professor of Art and Music Education at the University of South Florida.*

dog Trix minds me?" I said, "Gee, that's really exciting, I would like to see that!" So he walked across the porch and he called his dog, "Trix! You all come over here," and the dog ran across the porch to him and sat down at his heels. Moses didn't say anything. He just stood there, inflated his chest as well as his cheeks, and held that pose for a minute. I said, "Moses, that's the smartest dog I've seen in at least a month." He said, "Yeah, I'll show you some more." He walked to the other side of the porch and said, "Trix, you all come over here!" The dog went back across the porch and sat by his heel, and Moses repeated the same display of elated pride. I said, "Moses, I think that's the smartest dog I've seen in at least a year!" Now, he started to move toward an old screen door on the house, one that didn't have any screen on it. He went through the door and called his dog, and the dog followed him and sat by his heel for the third time. He inflated his chest, and I said, "Moses, I don't think I've ever seen a dog that smart in all my life."

So he went inside the house and then came out a few minutes later after discovering a barrel of clay in the back room. He said, "Hey Mr. Love, you mind if I use some of that mud in there?", and I said, "Yeah you can use some of that mud in there, but you can't put your fingers in it until you get a good idea." And he said, "But I don't know, I don't know what to make with it." I said, "Now Moses, don't you stand there one minute and show me how smart your dog is, and the next minute tell me how dumb you are." I said, "Go back in there and get an idea." He said, "But if I use that mud I can't make it look like a dog," and I said, "What?" He said, "I won't be able to make it look like a dog," and I said, "That's your problem, that's not my problem. If that's what you want, you take Trix in there, put him up on the table and make him mind you in the clay!"

So a few minutes later I went in, and I watched this piece that was developing. There was a beautiful form—it didn't look a bit like Trix, it had ears that flopped down, where Trix's ears were half-chewed off; it had a beautiful tail and Trix didn't even have a tail; and to top it all off, he had put a smile on the face. And so I praised him and talked to him about his work, and told him I thought he had been very successful in expressing his feelings about his dog and that I really believed in his work. About three or four weeks later, I was leaving the place late, late at night. I was kind of down from a day where not much had happened, and as I was driving away, I heard a familiar shrill whistle. I looked in the rearview mirror and saw Moses running down the street yelling, "Mr. Love, Mr. Love, don't go, don't go, I have something I want to tell you!" I stopped the car as he ran up alongside and short on breath he said, "I just wanted to let you know that I think you're a nice man!" And not having my senses together I said, "Boy, what a way to end the day, but I really don't know why you said that." His response to me was, "Because you're the only one who listens to me besides my dog!"

Now, it's a good story! A few weeks after that, I went to consult at M.I.T. for the National Science Foundation who were doing a seminar there hoping to identify what successful community arts programs were doing that could be translated to community science centers. Philip Morrison, the astrophysicist, began the conference by saying, "There are only three components to any significant scientific experience. One, it has an aesthetic component; two, you have to change your perceptions in the act of doing something; and three, it has to have affect." So I discovered that as an artist I knew what he was talking about—in fact, Moses and I both knew about that!

Now, what I want more than anything out of what I have to say is not to be misinterpreted. I am supportive of, and completely overwhelmed by, the eloquence of what Arthur has described here: the relationships between aesthetic theory, psychological orientations, and the various teaching traditions in the arts. I am not here to question assumptions, the categories, or the historical interpretations he has applied to the teaching traditions of the several arts. A few years ago I heard Harold Taylor make a statement about the Carnegie Unit in Education. He said, "It's a way of dividing up knowledge so you don't have to think about it!" Now, he was saying it in a negative way—that if you were able to divide knowledge neatly up into its individual parts, it would not guarantee that you would be able to see the relationships that exist between the parts and thus have a comprehension of the whole. Now, I am not advancing this as a negative criticism of Professor Efland's paper. I simply choose this idea to illustrate what I think is a caution! My concern is that when we start to seriously translate these ideas to the teaching process, and particularly to the training of the arts teacher, rhetoric of this sort presents a *singular theoretical view*, which by its very nature avoids the "creative artist" as a distinct model, equally valid in producing *multiple theoretical meanings* for implementing teaching skills. I was glad to hear, or at least I was encouraged to hear, the response that Arthur's students made to the paper because I think inherent in that response is the thing that we have to be careful about. (This remark is in reference to a comment Professor Efland made, that after reading the first part of his paper to some of his graduate students, they asked him which of the various matchings he thought were the best ones, and his response was that he really didn't know.)

I personally view the teaching of the arts as a creative process, not too unlike the way I involve myself when I create a work of art. Now, while in theory we have to separate all of these things to talk about them—and in truth we can only talk about one thing at a time—in the process of making art, as well as in teaching, we have to tacitly internalize these speculative patterns, coordinating them spontaneously as we engage each experience. Taking this as an assumption, I would like to relate this to one of the points that Arthur made when he was describing the "mimetic process" of teaching in the visual arts. He is saying that copying is a source of learning about art through drawing. He further suggests that much of what is learned about art is self-taught and that a lot of people who teach themselves essentially do it by copying. I would like to translate that metaphorically to the training of teachers. Most students tend to begin to teach based on copying models of teachers they have had. Once they get out into the schools and into the real world of teaching, what they need most are models for teaching themselves to expand their potential as artist-teachers. And it's here that I really worry and become concerned. I am getting now to the reality of what we have to do when we train teachers. I see undergraduates who are going to become new teachers—if I am lucky—for about eighty-eight hours out of a lifetime. If I see them for the two courses I teach, I see them for forty-four hours (not even a weekend) when they are freshmen, and forty-four hours when they are seniors. All of which means: that's all the time I have to help them develop some method of self-learning to use once they get out of the university and into the classroom.

Now, I recognize that where the student learns this process of how to teach isn't just in my class during those eighty-odd hours. It happens in the studio courses, it is affected when Twyla Tharp brings her dance company through town, it happens in education courses and during internships. It happens in so many different places; I really have little control over who will influence students the most in the way each defines his or her unique potential as a teacher of the arts. If we can view the work that Professor Efland has presented as providing one alternative theoretical model among some others to inform the future teacher of the arts, I see it as a very valuable historical contribution to the philosophical literature of arts education. My particular concern is that in trying to train novice teachers to balance logical and intuitive decision-making processes in the classroom, some may be tempted to over-simplify Efland's interpretation of these explicit categories into shortcuts for prescribing teaching methods. The risk is one of assuming that each novice will in time be able to develop a tacit pragmatic grasp of the "overlapping realities" that cut across the distinctly coded match game that Efland has created. My experience over some twenty years of observing teachers in the arts as they continue to train themselves after schooling would not cause me to be optimistic about taking such a risk!

It is here that I should like to depart for a moment from my rather spontaneous initial verbal response to Efland's paper and elaborate on a few other things that I feel need to be said.

For some time now it has been a concern of mine that we in the arts tend to talk too much to each other; we read the same literature and, for the most part, look for *consensus* rather than *diversity* in developing alternative approaches to teaching processes in the arts. Since its very beginning, our country has guarded the rights of individuals and groups to retain private identities while seeking some acceptable balance between cultural diversity and pluralism.

Perhaps it is time to create some "new myths" regarding potential models for advancing teaching processes in the arts. Where are the contemporary myths? Must they always be vestiges of the distant past, filtered through the sieve of traditional philosophical inquiry, perhaps less appropriately suited to what is now an information-rich society? It may just be that new myths about art are reflected aesthetically in the processes of those twentieth century visionaries (not always "artists") who are capable of responding to changing information and newer technologies so that old theories are defied, and new ones are invented. If this is indeed the case, it not only changes the nature of art itself but reshapes the image we have of the aesthetic process into something "future-oriented" in its implicit meaning rather than an event, object, or process measured and verified by some acceptable prejudice from the past. If we believe that means and ends are open to deliberation and choice, then the "images" we create of the future will become our reality, so that as we invent ourselves we invent the future.

Let me briefly illustrate my point in this fashion. I was first formally introduced to drawing by a rigid, unfeeling ninth-grade art teacher. She chose to impose on me and the class a Renaissance mathematical system for defining space—more easily recognized in curriculum guides as "perspective." She led me to believe that successful drawing was based on my ability to choose a *horizon line* and to establish imaginary vanishing points—one, two, or three depending on which form she wanted me to replicate that day, the railroad track or the ice cube. Since that exercise took eight of the thirty-six, forty-minute periods I was to be in her art class that year, the following six weeks with speedball pens and "old English lettering" hardly offered any challenges to dream about the future.

In contrast to that memory, I have been reading the work of the contemporary anthropologist, Magoroh Maruyama (1976), who is now conceptualizing the first extraterrestrial community. In anticipating this new stage of civilization he suggests that we will have to think in terms of hitherto unknown cultural options. "We will be in a position to invent new cultural patterns and new social philosophies and then choose materials, conditions, and community design to fit the desired cultural goals and philosophies." In further differentiating alternatives, he describes "heterogeneity" as the key to future survival in such new environments. A "homogenistic" view places ultimate importance on the search for "general rules" and "universal criteria" (sound familiar?) and the belief that there is one best way applicable to everybody. In the heterogenistic view, by way of contrast, diversity in goals and design is basic. "Heterogeneity is the very source of growth, enrichment, resource diversification, evolution, symbiotization, and survival. Traditional Western logic preaches the ideology of unity by similarity and regards differences as sources of conflicts. But the new scientific logic is 'symbiosis thanks to diversity'." (Maruyama, 1976, p. 274)

One state of mind that Maruyama has described as a danger in space is "solipsism syndrome." Solipsism is the name for a theory that everything exists in your imagination and there is nothing at all outside of your brain. You learn to cope with reality precisely because reality is different from your imagination. If reality is the same as your imagination, you cannot escape falling into solipsism. As a philosophical theory solipsism is internally consistent and cannot be disproved. But as a psychological state it is highly uncomfortable.

Well, you ask, what has all of this discussion about extraterrestrial communities and the danger of solipsism have to do with contemporary myths? In search of means to alleviate the tendency toward the solipsism syndrome, Maruyama identified four conditions needed for survival. Guess what one of them happens to be? The need to experience a *horizon line*, to feel that there is something beyond the horizon which gives you the feeling that the world is larger than what you see. So out of the Renaissance tradition where the *horizon line* became a *symbol of the past* and the *imaginary key* to a controlled process for creating an *illusion of space*, it becomes a *symbol of the future for the visionary of today, a real key* for survival to a controlled process for bringing order, as well as aesthetic pleasure, to the *world of outer space*. Now I simply ask, which of these myths about the horizon line, in C.P. Snow's terms, "has the future in its bones"? Let me conclude by restating these premises: (1) that "symbiosis thanks to diversity" should be pursued equally with ideologies based on unity by similarity (Efland's work) as modes of inquiry regarding the nature of art and the teaching process of the arts; and (2) that the teacher of the future, if he or she is to develop modes for self-learning, needs to develop skills for identifying and inventing new myths for arts education—ones that are in sync with contemporary conceptual frameworks, making experience and learning in the arts more "future oriented." Perhaps by doing this, we can better realize Maslow's dream, that education-through-art could become a paradigm for all of education, because it seems to be a good education in potential!

I've chosen my new myth, what's yours?

Tampa, Florida
July 1978

REFERENCES

Maruyama, Margoroh. Designing a space community. *The Futurist*, 1976, *10*(5), 273-281.

Laura H. Chapman

The Bearing of Artistic and Educational Commitments on the Teaching of Art

In this paper I will describe four orientations to the teaching of art, will indicate the kind of content and curriculum forms that may be supported by each orientation, and will suggest how the expectations embodied in the orientations and plans might influence the teaching process. My stance is analytical and speculative; it is intended to suggest lines of inquiry that might be fruitful if we wish to understand the teaching process as it is shaped by what teachers hope to accomplish with children and youth in the course of a year in school. Although the analysis is interlaced with a bit of descriptive information, the thrust of the paper is theoretical. The case materials are drawn from the visual arts, and while the discussion is dominated by references to art studio activities, the use of these illustrations should not be construed as an endorsement of studio activity as the major aim or as the exclusive means for art education. The references are cogent, however, in the light of typical patterns of instruction in schools.

What happens in classrooms in the name of "arts education" cannot be interpreted without some reference to the goals toward which teachers of art see themselves working, to the cultural content they regard as "art," and to the interpersonal relationships which best accommodate their artistic and educational commitments. It is not the case that teachers, scholars, or parents will agree on the central values of arts education. Even teaching, as Gage (1964) has observed, is "not a single, unitary phenomenon" (p. 273). There are usually different premises for elementary and secondary education, for general and vocational education, for programs aimed at appreciation versus those directed to skills in performance. Even within these broad instructional contexts one can find different patterns of belief about the value of art and the role of the teacher in the cultivation of the student.

LAURA H. CHAPMAN *is author of* Approaches to Art in Education, *Senior Editor of* Studies in Art Education, *and a member of the editorial advisory boards of* Review of Research in Visual Arts Education *and* School Arts.

That the teaching of art is a value-centered and intentional enterprise is obvious; less obvious is the role that the teacher's beliefs may play in determining the curriculum made available to students, and how those beliefs may enter into the process of teaching. These considerations are of special importance in the visual arts where instructional materials in the form of texts and workbooks are rarely used as the primary source of content, objectives, and learning tasks. One cannot assume, as is true in many subjects, that art teachers can or do choose among carefully researched curriculum materials (few materials of this kind are available) and then serve chiefly as "supplementors" or "facilitators" of student interaction with the pre-structured, published materials (Gage, 1978, p. 78). Teachers of art, in comparison with other teachers, are relatively free to decide what to teach and toward what ends.

Few studies in art education address the role of the teacher's beliefs as they bear on instruction. Day (1974) has offered sample rationales for use in staff development, and Eisner, Laswell, and Wieder (see References) have developed a scale for assessing "tough" and "tender" orientations to teaching art, but neither of these efforts have been extended to a point of illuminating relationships between beliefs and the form or content of instruction. Moreover, there is a marked tendency in research on teaching to equate the teaching process with classroom interaction during a lesson or a class period without regard to the broader time and curriculum structures that may govern the pace of instruction. Philip Jackson's *Life in Classrooms* (1968) should serve as a reminder that the significance of schooling is as likely to be found in the larger patterns of a day, a week, or a year as in the more easily observed dynamics of a single lesson.

What follows is an account of some probes I have made in an effort to map relationships between rationales for teaching art, the form and content of curricula, and how the expectations built into rationales and plans might shape the teaching process. Although I have mustered some bits and pieces of data on prospective art teachers in order to support the discussion, the information is offered to illustrate a direction for theory-building and further inquiry, not as empirical research. If the teaching of art differs from teaching in other fields, surely the difference is due to the intent, content, and curriculum forms that teachers choose as vehicles for student encounters with "art."

Rationales for Teaching Art

Almost every prospective teacher has, or soon develops, some implicit notion of what counts as "art" in education and why art should be offered in schools. Whether the beliefs of the teacher are consciously held and well-reasoned or held at the level of simple maxims, they are manifested in situations where choices must be made.

One of the problems in determining the structure of the teacher's beliefs is that many general claims about the importance of teaching art seem to function as slogans for which agreement can readily be obtained but which yield little information about the priorities teachers might assign to one "good" versus another "good." For example, most teachers will agree that it is important to introduce students to the elements and principles of design *and* that it is important to nurture imaginative personal expression in art. If the teacher is forced to rank these aims in relation to several other aims of equal validity and apparent importance, to which aims might the teacher give priority? Further, do the priorities teachers assign to these and other statements about art education reflect any consistency in thought or attitude that might be interpreted as a "rationale" for teaching art or, in Gage's terms (1978, p. 70), an "implicit theory of teaching"?

For some years I have administered to prospective art teachers a brief scale intended to profile the coherence and dominance of teachers' beliefs with respect to four hypothetical orientations to teaching. The scale requires one to use each of four ranks to rate the relative importance of four sentence completions for a given statement. The key statements treat such issues as the mission of schools, the nature of art and aims of art education, characteristics of good teachers, and methods of instruction considered most suitable for a junior high or beginning high school art class. Each sentence completion is pre-coded as relevant to a particular educational tradition and to teacher attitudes or practices that might be supported within that tradition. The statements to be ranked reflect broad values or concepts associated with experimentalism, existentialism (here called personalism), classical realism (here called idealism), and scientific realism (that is, the technological and empirical tradition in education).[1] Attitudinal and practical items thought to be reasonably coherent with the broader values and concepts were adapted from Cosgrove (1959) and organized around the constructs "others," "self," "criteria," and "tasks." The sentence completions are randomly arranged under each key question. There is no meaningful total score for the assessment; the sum of the ranks assigned to items in each orientation "subtest" reflects the coherence and strength of the teacher's endorsement of statements for each orientation.

The instrument lacks any of the precision required for systematic research, but I wish to cite results from administering it to twenty-seven juniors majoring in art education in order to: (a) present the statements that operationally define the four orientations, and (b) illustrate how the orientations bear on curriculum planning undertaken by the same group of students. It will be obvious that I am most interested in the problem of description itself, especially the problem of describing value-orientations that may influence the way teachers conceive of their work.

The following narratives of each orientation are constructed from specific items on the orientation test that attract positive endorsement (rank 4) and appear to be useful in discriminating among those who score highest and lowest on each of the subtests.[2] In spite of the difference in the length of each description (due to the lack of refinement of the scale), I believe the descriptions have some face validity.

The Idealist Orientation

The person who scores high on this subtest regards the school as a separate and distinct institution that is not obliged to adjust its programs to social trends or to merge its mission with needs and interests in the community. Learning is viewed as a process of acquiring new knowledge and accommodating it so that one is disposed to approach things in a more systematic way.

The concept of art as formal order is endorsed. Studies of design and composition are considered the foundation of a good art program and are viewed as the major means through which self-expression is achieved.

The art teacher is seen as a person who should be well-informed, thoroughly knowledgeable in the subject of art. The best art teachers make art seem important, not a frill; they do their best at whatever they do. If placed in a secondary school (teaching Art I), the preferred method of teaching would be imparting information to the whole class first, followed by discussion. When asked what they would do if a principal criticized their personal appearance, those scoring high on this subtest checked the sentence: "I doubt if it would happen, I'd adjust beforehand."

The rationale is brief but cohesive in its emphasis on order, separateness, control, conceptual knowledge, and formality.

The Realist Orientation

The prospective teacher who scores high on this subtest sees the school as an institution that should accept social change and prepare students to meet predicted trends in society. The school should set an example for the community and yet be open to suggestions from members of the community. Learning is viewed as an observable change in behavior that is brought about by instruction.

The concept of art as skillful performance and keen observation (especially of nature) is preferred. A good art program emphasizes mastery of media and basic factual information. There is special interest in nurture of the talented.

Those who score high on this subtest indicate that teaching art is their *first* choice of occupation (as opposed to other art-related occupations). Art teachers should be practical, know their strengths and weaknesses, and be concerned with their improvement as teachers. The best teachers make their subject interesting, so students are eager to learn; students downgrade teachers who can't get the subject across. If placed in a secondary school teaching situation, the favored method of teaching would be total group instruction with specific grading standards for each activity. Classroom routines would be handled in a manner that is arbitrarily fair; for example, rotating assignments for clean-up.

The Personalist Orientation

Individuals who score high on this subtest see the school as an institution that inhibits the expression of individuality. Traditional school programs might well be abandoned if students can be educated in other settings. Schools should encourage students to explore alternative social arrangements and should try to involve students directly in social change. Learning is seen as a motivation to achieve a self-selected goal, even if others do not think the goal is important.

The concept of art as creative self-expression is favored. A good art program nurtures self-expression by developing the student's ability to "play" with ideas and to combine them in imaginative ways. It teaches that art is a matter of personal taste, it promotes skills in solving problems independently, it nurtures an appreciation for the creativity of individual artists.

Those scoring high on this subtest indicate that they would really prefer to be studio artists and they would like to teach in a school system where they could continue their studio work (as opposed to a system that might offer other attractions such as a friendly, supportive staff). Criticism from school officials, especially if it touched on the teacher's personal appearance, might be sufficient cause to try to find another teaching position. The art teacher is seen as a person who should be innovative, up to date. The best teachers make every student feel important as a person; students downgrade teachers who make students compete with each other too much. If placed in a secondary school, instruction based on dialogue with individual students would be preferred. Students would evaluate their own work on their own criteria and grading would be based on individual growth. Routines such as clean-up would be self-monitored.

The Experimentalist Orientation

The school is viewed as integral to the community and under obligation to assume initiatives to keep programs from becoming isolated from members of the community. If students are to solve social problems in their adult lives, they must be involved in cooperative efforts to solve problems in their present lives.

The concept of art as communication is embraced. Art is a sharing of ideas and experiences, a way of responding to everyday life creatively. A good art program relates art to ordinary life. If art history is introduced, it should be related to problems students encounter in their own studio work.

The greatest satisfaction in teaching is the pleasure of being with children and youth. Art teachers should want to learn more about their students and make it possible for students to feel free to express their opinions. Sarcasm and favoritism are the reasons for which students most often downgrade teachers. If placed in a secondary-school position, instruction would center on activity or interest groups. Routines would be handled by volunteers.

Judging from the items producing the highest correlations with each subtest, those who score high on the idealist subtest are drawn to questions that deal with the *status* of art and the qualifications of those who teach art; the experimentalist viewpoint is developed around questions that treat the mission of schools and the *ends* of education. The items most clearly associated with high scores on the personalist subtest are *methods* for interacting with students; those defining the realist orientation deal with *what* to teach. Although the whole of the test is designed to assess viewpoints on means, ends, content, and criteria, there was no prior anticipation that such fundamental concerns might, in themselves, differentiate among the orientations.

A scatterplot of scores on the subtests resulted in the expected fourfold clustering of responses from the forced ranking of statements. Of interest are the particular configurations among the subtests: experimentalist with personalist (high positive), realist and idealist (low positive), experimentalist (high) and idealist (low), and personalist (high) and the realist (low). Even without the informal confirmation of the scatterplot, a study of the rationales would suggest possibilities for teachers to engage in "practical eclecticism" by selective agreement with the values here keyed to idealism and to realism (art as a subject for study), and with those keyed to the personalist and experimentalist orientations (concern for human development). The emphasis on dialogue and imaginative play within the personalist orientation appears to be "at odds" with the interest in skill development in the realist orientation; the idealist's focus on the serious study of art, especially design, is "distant" from the experimentalist's interest in art for everyday living.

Although these patterns of association among the several orientations are, in part, an artifact of the forced-choice response format, there is some indication that patterns of endorsement may be related to other preservice experiences. For example, prospective teachers who had taken the test were asked to check, from a list of objectives for art education in Ohio elementary schools, those which they felt least prepared to teach. Persons scoring high on the realist and idealist subtests checked the fewest objectives. Would not expressions of greater self-confidence in teaching be expected from those who are most inclined to teach for cognitive or technical mastery? Among the seven students who scored highest on the realist subtest and lowest on the personalist subtest, all had entered the teaching program with work experience in commercial art or with a record of exhibitions of their work, and three held offices in the student chapter of a national professional association in art education. Is it possible that having demonstrated one's capability as an artist, one can then freely claim that teaching art is a "first choice" in occupation? Among those who scored highest on the personalist subtest, six had earned reputations as emotionally complex students and four had a strong interest in art therapy (one has since completed training as an art therapist). Beyond this, it is worth remarking that no systematic relationships were found between grades and orientation scores, and retrospectively, no easy judgments can be made about the relationship of such scores to "success" in teaching. There is some indication that those who score high on the personalist and experimentalist subtests seek advanced degrees in art education earlier than their classmates and that students who score high on the realist and idealist subtests become active in local art teacher organizations and are known as teachers who offer good "solid" art programs.

While probes and parallels such as these are tentative at best, they suggest that inquiry into the patterns of belief among art teachers—the differentiation of beliefs (vertical structure), their degree of generalization (horizontal structure), and importance relative to other beliefs (centrality)—may be one path for explaining some of the differences in the intent, content, and methods of teaching found among teachers of art (Bem, 1970, p. 12).

The Form and Content of Instructional Plans

If high scores on the subtests reflect the central tendencies in a teacher's beliefs, one would expect to find some relationship between subtest scores and the art programs teachers envision as desirable and as practical. Both the form and the content of programs should differ. "Form" is here defined as the structure of a curriculum—its pace, the variety of activities offered to students, the options provided to them, the frequency of encounter with selected content, and the idiosyncratic features of the program. It is within such formal structures that smaller units of instruction occur during a school year. "Content" refers to such aspects of art as media, techniques, and processes; art forms or product types such as sculpture, painting, and printmaking; aspects of design such as line, color, shape, balance, repetition; subjects or themes such as landscape, still life, or peace/war; and the stylistic framework of the activity—representational, surrealistic, and so on.

Obviously, what a teacher may project in a plan may not be realized in a particular situation. Nevertheless, to the extent that plans reflect expectations, they are benchmarks for describing the difference between anticipated and actual practice and they may have some utility in predicting some characteristics of the teaching process (Good and Brophy, 1973/1977). An analysis of plans may suggest what conditions teachers would interpret as facilitating or interfering with their work, and it may provide one avenue for studying the relationship between the teaching process, the curriculum, and a particular setting for instruction. Let me illustrate some of these possibilities by reporting on an informal study of the curriculum plans developed by the prospective teachers from whom I had also obtained orientation test scores some eight weeks earlier.

As a final project for an art education course, prospective teachers were asked to plan a curriculum in art for the seventh grade, spanning the typical ninety hours of instructional time allotted for art at this grade level. They were asked to consider the fact that for most students, these ninety hours would probably be the first and last point of instruction from a specialist teacher in art. The hypothetical seventh graders were described as heterogeneous with respect to age, sex, and other background factors; and one could not assume that the students had acquired any common skills and knowledge from the elementary grades. The budget for expendable supplies was fixed at $300.00 for 300 students. A list of available tools and equipment was provided. Unfortunately, these conditions are not a far-fetched representation of the circumstances under which art teachers may work. The intent was to force hard decisions and to determine how well the prospective teachers could respond to criteria for curriculum development treated in the course.

The curriculum plans were presented in the manner illustrated in Figure 1. The character of the planned activity is discerned by reading columns. Entries in each category reflect an hour of instructional time; a blank space (or arrow) indicates a continuation of the same content to the next class period (here scheduled every other day). "Options" or "choices" to be made by students are noted. If a unique activity were planned for each class, each plan would have a minimum of 90 x 5 descriptors.

Several indices of prescriptiveness can be developed from an analysis of plans. First, the number of entries mark shifts in emphasis within the ninety hours allocated for instruction. Not every feature of content changes from day to day so that one can describe the relative pace of activity for each content feature or for all of them. In studio activity, for example, the same medium might be used for several days but the art forms, themes, or stylistic features might shift. In the present analysis, multiple entries in the same cell were usually treated as independent entries. The pace of activity might be interpreted as an index of anticipated "demand" for learning.

Second, variety in content can be described by noting the number of different descriptive entries in each category. In the present analysis, descriptors were not pre-structured on any basis except for style, where students were encouraged to use terms such as representation, expression,

Figure 1

Sample Page: Hypothetical Ninety-Hour Curriculum for the Seventh Grade

	Art Form	Media	Subject	Design	Style	Notes	Aims
Monday	Drawing	Conte crayon, newsprint	Figure	Gesture, over-all movement	Expressionist	About 10 short drawings, also slides of master drawings	Studio Expression, Art History
Wednesday		Pencil, white paper		Contour, edges	Abstract	Contrast "slow" visual study with gesture drawings	Studio Expression
Friday		Chalk (white & black on gray paper)		Value, form	Representation	Work with dramatic lighting to develop form	
Tuesday	Painting	Tempera	Still life	Tints, shades, monochromatic color	Representation	Translate value into color, first stage	
Thursday							

fantasy, and other style labels if historical style labels seemed inappropriate to the activity. The descriptors educed from the plans are shown in *Table 1*. The analysis of plans would be facilitated and made more reliable by developing sub-categories for the coding of entries. (The meaning of the major content categories can be established with teachers rather easily after about fifteen minutes of practice in coding art activities.)

Table 1

Content Categories Established from an Analysis of Plans for a Hypothetical Ninety-Hour Seventh Grade Art Program

N = 27 Juniors Majoring in Art Education

MEDIA (53)	f[1]	N	fr[2]	SUBJECTS (32)	f	N	fr
Discussions, slides, demonstrations	80	17	13	"Designs"	128	23	18
				Figures, people	97	25	22
Tempera	76	22	22	Optional	76	24	18
Pencils	75	23	16	Landscape	50	17	12
Pen and ink	63	24	16	Actual scene or object	46	15	10
Paper, assorted	61	21	12				
Clay	60	25	18	Work of an artist	43	14	9
Ink and brush	50	22	4	Still life	36	19	12
Charcoal	50	22	11	Portraits	36	19	8
Watercolor	49	24	16	School environ-ment, outside	30	13	9
Yarn	37	19	11				
Found objects	30	20	7	City, buildings	28	15	7
Tissue paper	28	16	6	Animals, birds, insects	24	16	5
Optional	25	14	7				
Cardboard	24	17	5	Plants, trees	24	12	5
Wood	21	15	5	Illustration of story or poem	23	19	4
Papier-mâche	21	14	6				
Linoleum	19	16	3	Sensory stimuli, touch, sound	20	4	4
Crayon	19	13	3				
Chalk	18	13	4	Letters, words	19	10	3
Wire with string	18	11	3	Other arts, dance, music, plays	18	12	4
Ink, varied tools	17	12	0				
Acrylic paint	17	11	3	Machines or mass-produced objects	17	9	5
Plaster	17	15	2				
Felt markers	17	6	5	Social commentary	17	5	1
Burlap, felt	16	11	4	A mood or feeling	17	10	5
Cloth, dyes	15	13	2	A medium or pro-cess	15	6	5
Perception games	15	6	3				
Film, photos	12	6	1	Self, aspirations or past history	14	7	4
Metal foil	11	11	0				
Magazine cutouts	10	7	2	Interiors	13	5	4
Mixed 2-D media	9	2	2	Student's own art, evaluation of	13	6	4
Craypa	7	4	2				
Vegetables	5	4	1	Imaginary world, creature	13	8	3
Wire	4	3	1				
Field trip	4	3	0	Personification of an object	10	7	2
Written work	4	3	1				
Ink, colored	4	3	1	Environmental changes, actual	10	1	1
Oil paint	3	3	0				
Cellophane slides	3	2	1	Seasons, holidays	10	7	2
Conte crayon	3	2	0	Lettering a quo-tation	7	5	1
Music	2	2	0				
Silk screen	2	2	0	School environment inside	7	4	1
Wax	2	1	0				
Ink with stick	1	1	0	Community plan-ning	7	4	1
Fingerpaint	1	1	0	Earth sculpture	5	4	1
Litho crayon	1	1	0	Toys, kites	4	3	1
Colored pencil	1	1	0		877	349	192
Styrofoam	1	1	0				
Fresco	1	1	0	$\overline{X}$	32	13	7
Egg tempera	1	1	0				
Snow	1	1	0				
Video	1	1	0				
	1008	496	219				

$\overline{X}$ N = 27   37   18   8

[1]f = frequency
[2]fr = frequency of repeated entries

ART FORMS (34)	f	N	fr
Drawing, final	142	26	25
Painting	93	23	21
Sculpture	86	27	23
Discussion of seeing	81	16	12
Drawing, sketches	70	20	15
Collage, montage	53	23	13
"Designs"	35	14	11
Graphic design, posters, cards	33	12	7
Prints, varied	24	10	5
Prints, relief	22	12	7
Optional	21	10	6
Collage and ink	20	11	5
Weaving	18	13	3
Prints, mono and surface	13	9	1
Models, interior, architectural	13	9	3
Containers, clay	12	11	1
Wall hanging, rug	12	7	2
Photographs, slides	10	6	2
Mobiles	9	8	1
Art exhibit	9	7	1
Jewelry	9	8	1
Stage a play or media event	6	4	1
Models, package or product	6	5	0
Mural	6	6	0
Masks	5	4	1
Written work	5	3	2
Mosiac mural	3	3	0
Photo collections	2	1	0
Stitchery	1	1	0
Candles	1	1	0
Candy	1	1	0
Puppets	1	1	0
Decorated window	1	1	0
Room arrangement	1	1	0
	824	307	170
$\overline{X}$	31	11	6

DESIGN (27)	f	N	fr
Color mixing	196	25	23
Shape	173	19	15
Line	164	24	19
Proportion	108	20	17
Texture	92	21	20
Composition	75	19	13
Form	74	17	14
Materials, qualities of	72	16	11

DESIGN	f	N	fr
Value, tone	67	22	18
Imagery, motif	65	16	12
Optional	64	13	11
Overlap	44	17	13
Perspective	37	14	8
Balance	36	14	8
Contrast, emphasis	35	12	6
Space, position	27	9	9
Pattern	25	11	5
Figure-ground	23	11	7
Unity, harmony	23	6	5
Gesture, movement	21	11	3
Repetition	18	8	5
Mass	17	9	7
Function	17	9	5
Abstraction	13	8	4
Color for mood	11	7	1
Directionality	9	5	2
Role of designer	4	2	2
	1510	365	263
$\overline{X}$	56	14	9

STYLE (17)	f	N	fr
Optional varied or personal	221	27	27
Geometric, cubist	167	27	25
Naturalistic	166	27	26
Expressionistic	82	25	20
Impressionistic, pointillism	30	14	8
Surrealistic or fantasy	30	16	8
Linear, decorative	13	7	4
Contemporary functional	10	5	2
Op or Pop	10	7	2
Genre, narrative	5	3	1
Greek, Gothic, Medieval	5	4	1
Renaissance	3	1	1
Prehistory	3	2	1
Western tradition, general	2	2	0
African	2	2	0
American Indian	2	2	0
Egyptian	1	1	0
	752	171	126
$\overline{X}$	28	6	5

Third, a measure of cross-referencing or explicit "reinforcement" of content is the number of repeated entries in a given category. Line, for example, may be treated in the context of drawing or in the context of sculpture. The pace of instruction and the frequency of repeated entries, taken together, are indicative of program "depth"—sustained or recurrent attention to selected aspects of art.

Fourth, one can develop a picture of a "typical" program. Normative description, in turn, provides a basis for identifying the locus and degree of idiosyncrasy in selected programs. The "novelty" of a given program can be ascertained by noting (a) the entries omitted from a given program that are typically included in other programs, and (b) the entries infrequently mentioned in typical programs. One might set the range for "typicality" in several ways. In the present analysis, a tally for novelty was made if the plan failed to mention an entry cited by 73 percent of the class or if the plan included a descriptor used by fewer than 73 percent of the class.

Finally, a measure of "planned unstructuredness" is obtained from the number of entries marked "optional" or "choice."

From these several dimensions one can characterize the overall form and emphasis in programs, the duration of a typical learning activity, and the kind of instructional demands that teachers project for themselves and students. One could refine the general technique outlined here so that it might be used for self-reports by in-service teachers or might be combined with interaction analysis to reflect both the content and the form of teaching. Even though the analysis of the junior-level plans is crude, the results are worth reporting, not only to illustrate what a typical plan provides by way of instructional content, but also to demonstrate that the plans designed by students who score high on each of the orientation subtests are, in some respects, translations of the rationales to which they subscribed.

A Typical Plan

Only six of the twenty-seven plans reflected a substantial concern for art history and art criticism. *Table 1* shows that the vocabulary of the teachers is most particularized for media, followed by subjects, art forms, design, and style. Aspects of design are most frequently prescribed ($\overline{X}$, 56 per plan), followed by media ($\overline{X}$, 37 per plan), subjects ($\overline{X}$, 32), art forms ($\overline{X}$, 31), and stylistic descriptors ($\overline{X}$, 28). Equally distributed over ninety hours, these frequencies would produce a shift in design content for about every hour and one-half of instructional time; in media, about every two and one-half hours; and a shift in subject, art form, and style, about every third hour. Given the range of descriptors in the plans, the average duration of a content-coherent instructional activity would be about three hours.

A typical program would introduce students to 18 media, 14 features of design, 13 subjects, 11 art forms, and 6 styles. Distributed equally over 90 hours, students would be likely to encounter 12 major units of instruction of 7 or 8 hours duration. Of the 18 media noted in a typical plan, 8 might be encountered in a context different from the original one, 7 of the 13 subjects might be re-encountered, 6 of the 11 products might recur, 9 of the 14 aspects of design might enter into more than one activity, and 5 of the 6 styles might be emphasized more than once. A typical program might treat 6 or 7 artistic problems in depth, with 10 or 11 hours of instruction for each such unit.

Prospective teachers were least inclined to prescribe the stylistic features of activities. During a year of instruction, a typical plan offered only eight hours for unspecified stylistic work, four hours for options in design, three for subjects, and two hours, respectively, for choices in media and product types. Very likely the college students, more than in-service teachers, felt compelled to make entries to fulfill the expectations for the assignment.

If one were to ask what a typical student might be required to study in some depth in the seventh grade, our hypothetical seventh grader would probably be involved with sculpture, drawing (sketches and completed work), painting, and collage. He or she would probably use clay, watercolor, pen and ink, pencil, and tempera paint to create works portraying the human figure, still life, landscapes, "designs," or a subject of the student's choice. The aspects of design most likely to be emphasized are color mixing, line, value, texture, and proportion. Stylistic considerations would encompass naturalism, geometric abstraction, expressionism, and surrealism. One should keep in mind the sense of urgency inherent in the assignment of only ninety hours for instruction and in the budget provided in the hypothetical situation. Even so, the "picturing" of instruction in terms such as these is a healthy corrective for the great expectations and grand claims we are inclined to make for art education.

Relationship of Rationales to Plans

An informal comparison of plans submitted by prospective teachers scoring high on each subtest suggests that the orientations may influence the way they envision an art program. Profiles of differences among the plans are presented in *Table 2*.

Idealist Plans

Persons who score high on this subtest develop plans with the highest frequency of entries. The salient features of the idealist programs are the rapid pacing of instruction, recurrent attention to design concepts, and narrow range of art forms. Specific entries show that the idealist favors subjects described as "designs" or "collage designs" based on still life or on actual scenes at school. Exercises in lettering are also emphasized to a

Table 2

Means on Program Features for Total Group
and High Scores on Orientation Subtests

Pacing	Group*	I**	R**	P**	E*
Subject	32.48	33.00	31.28	30.51	31.14
Medium	36.33	39.14	31.42	37.42	34.42
Design	57.44	69.85	57.14	53.71	45.42
Product	30.40	45.57	30.00	32.28	24.57
Style	28.11	30.42	33.85	27.14	27.14
Total	36.80	40.57	35.54	36.22	32.71
Variety					
Subject	11.62	8.22	12.00	11.57	11.71
Medium	17.59	17.57	15.42	18.14	17.42
Design	13.03	13.85	13.71	12.00	13.42
Product	11.11	10.28	11.42	11.14	13.14
Style	5.44	5.85	6.28	4.42	4.71
Total	11.75	11.62	11.77	11.45	12.08
Reinforcement					
Subject	6.48	6.00	5.85	8.71	6.42
Medium	7.92	8.42	6.42	8.71	8.00
Design	9.03	10.42	9.71	8.42	9.00
Product	5.96	6.14	6.00	5.42	6.28
Style	3.66	3.14	3.71	3.42	3.57
Total	6.61	6.82	6.33	6.93	6.65
Novelty					
Subject	3.74	2.14	4.14	4.00	4.28
Medium	4.74	4.00	5.28	5.14	5.28
Design	3.22	1.28	2.42	3.57	3.57
Product	2.37	3.14	2.00	1.85	1.71
Style	.77	.71	.85	1.28	.57
Total	2.97	2.22	2.94	3.42	3.08
Options					
Subject	16.00	25.00	14.00	11.00	14.00
Medium	3.75	.00	6.00	5.00	4.00
Design	12.75	9.00	12.00	13.00	17.00
Product	2.75	2.00	2.00	3.00	4.00
Style	.77	.71	.85	1.28	.57
Total	17.55	22.60	14.60	16.50	20.60

*Group = 21 students scoring highest on each subtest. Six students scored at the extreme of two subtests: two on PE, two on RI, and one each on PR and EI.
**N = 7 for each orientation.

greater degree than in other programs. Shape, pattern, overlap, contrast, and unity are the aspects of design most frequently mentioned. Sculpture is the chief means for exploring three-dimensional form: clay, wire, and papier mâché are the preferred media. The crafts are not emphasized. Subjects treating the self, moods and feelings, and the inner life are infrequently mentioned.

The concept of art as a serious, knowledge-based, "no frill" subject is translated into a highly structured fast-paced program with relatively little variety and novelty. Activities are centered on design.

Realist Plans

The dominant features in the realist programs are found in the variety of activities offered, the stylistic control exercised by the teacher, and the sustained attention given to selected media. Realist programs favor work in the crafts. Activities in weaving, stitching, jewelry, clay containers, mask-making, and puppetry account for much of what is distinctive in these programs. Subjects and themes are most frequently centered on natural forms, trees, plants, the figure, and seasonal changes. Aspects of design relevant to pictorial representation are emphasized to a greater degree than in other programs, especially perspective and color for atmospheric effects and moods. Realism, surrealism, and analytical cubism are more frequently cited as descriptors of style than in other orientations. The themes of skill, craftsmanship, careful observation, and mastery of media are supported by program patterns and content choices found in the realist plans.

Personalist Plans

These plans are noteworthy (a) in their display of idiosyncracies with respect to all content features except product types, (b) in the primacy of media and style as points of control in determining the character of activities, and (c) in the sustained "in-depth, few-option" approach to subjects and themes in art. The personalist emphasizes subjects and themes that deal with sense experience, the self, dreams and imagination, and the interpretation of stories. The concept of art as self-expression is echoed by more frequent stylistic references to expressionism than are found in any of the other plans. This stylistic preference is also evident in the fewest mentions of representational devices such as shading, proportion, and perspective, as well as the fewest references to "designs." The variety of media made available to students is associated with opportunities for choice among media. This pattern is not found in any of the other orientations.

Experimentalist Plans

The most dominant aspects of these programs are the "slow" pace of instruction, the relatively limited options, and the use of art forms and style as points of control in planning. Experimentalist and idealist plans represent extremes in the pacing of instruction. They are similar in their emphasis on stylistic options. Specific entries show that, more than the others, the experimentalist plans emphasize drawing, painting, and architecture; and graphic, interior, and product design. The treatment of design is distinct in its attention to the role of the professional designer and to functional or "applied" design. These choices support the concepts of art in everyday living and art as communication as portrayed in the rationale. Subjects in art activities more frequently call for memory, interpretations of themes, and reflective thinking than direct observation. This preference is echoed in few stylistic entries for representational accuracy and geometric abstraction. Experimentalist values are also evident in the highest number of entries for student discussions, written evaluations, and the "culminating" activity of exhibiting completed art work.

In a further analysis of program characteristics, simple scatter plots were made to examine the direction of association between each of the program features. These are described in *Table 3*. Even though the information from the pilot study is meager, the program features seem to operate in different ways within each orientation. For example, reinforcements of content that might lead to mastery of concepts and skills are greater in the idealist and realist orientations. If a slower pace of instruction facilitates attention to individuals, the development of the "self" of the student might be more likely under the pace allowed by the experimentalist, personalist, and realist orientations. If student satisfaction is associated with program novelty, the experimentalist and the realist programs would seem to favor that result. With regard to content, the idealist tends to "think" of program planning in terms of design, the realist in terms of media, the personalist through attention to subjects, and the experimentalist through art forms. If such patterns of thinking are fairly stable, it seems probable that teachers with a "strong" orientation along one or another of these lines would develop teaching methods to accommodate their interests.

Relationship of Orientations and Plans to Teaching

Orientations are expressions of value, plans embody expectations. Expectations are not always fulfilled: They must be reasonably consonant with the actualities of life in school. Dialogue with thirty-eight eighth graders is not easy, especially if they have been scheduled into the same art class because they are slow readers, and especially if the art class is held just before lunch. Expectations must be communicated to students, and rather consistently over time—if the messages inherent in them are to be received and acted upon. Even when daily instruction is possible, not all students attend school regularly or attend the same school for the whole year. One can be mentally absent while being physically present,

Table 3

Pilot Study: Relationships Among Program Features
for Each Orientation to Teaching Art

Orientation	Pacing	Variety	Reinforcement	Novelty	Options
Idealist	High	Low			
	High		High		
	High			High	
	High				Low
		Low	High		
		Low		Low	
		Low			Low
			High	Low	
			High		Low
				Low	Low
Realist	Low	High			
	Low		High		
	Low			High	
	Low				Low
		High	High		
		High		High	
		High			Low
			High	Low	
			High		Low
				Low	Low
Personalist	Low	Low			
	Low		Low		
	Low			Low	
	Low				Low
		Low	Low		
		High		Low	
		Low			High
			Low	High	
			Low		High
				Low	Low
Experimentalist	Low	High			
	Low		Low		
	Low			High	
	Low				Low
		High	Low		
		High		Low	
		High			Low
			Low	High	
			Low		Low
				Low	Low

whether teacher or student. And students are not passive: some are as highly skilled in the arts of manipulation as any Machiavellian teacher; and for some students the expectations of the teacher may be quite simply out of reach. If there is utility in the study of teacher orientations and plans, it is not limited to judging the teacher's effectiveness in carrying out the plan (Berliner, 1977), assuming the plan has sufficient merit in the first place. The utility should be found in the degree to which one might predict the conditions under which a teacher might flourish or be stymied.

The following speculations are based, in part, on the information developed to this point, and in part, on a theory of social power set forth by French and Raven (1959) and extended by Steiner (1963). The theory distinguishes among five bases of interpersonal influence: coercive, reward, legitimate, expert, and referent. Space does not permit anything more than a brief suggestion of the relevance of such bases to the teaching process. For the purpose of discussion, it is useful to continue the analysis as if teachers were "true believers" in each of the several orientations and as if they would endeavor to secure for themselves classroom conditions and interaction patterns that would be "psychologically" consistent with their beliefs and expectations (Abelson and Rosenberg, 1958; Bem, 1970, p. 13).

Expectations and Problems: The Idealist

The idealist expects to move through the school year at a fairly rapid pace. The short-term character of instruction probably reduces the need for the teacher to make special requests for the scheduling of classes beyond the customary hour-long blocks of time allocated to art instruction from about the third grade on. Because the envisioned curriculum does not require the use of expensive materials, tools, equipment, and space, the lack of such material resources might not be a serious handicap to the teacher. In these and many other respects—willingness to conform to school expectations in dress, preference for group instruction, little program variety, few options—the idealist orientation and plan is well suited to the many school settings with inflexible schedules, restricted budgets for art, and an academic curriculum structure.

Because the idealist is concerned with the status of art as a "serious" subject and with the role of the art teacher as a dependable source of knowledge, the most probable expectations for students are that they perceive the teacher as a person who has a legitimate right to teach art, and that they regard the art that is taught as "legitimate" art. If these patterns of acceptance are not established with the student beforehand—for example, through parental, peer, or other reference groups—then the teacher must "earn" the right to teach art. If the teacher expects to deal with the most formal and inherently abstract facets of art and in a highly structured program, it seems obvious that some students will have difficulty in art and the teacher might well perceive as "difficult" those students who do not keep up, who do not take art seriously, who show disrespect for the teacher, or those who have a poorly developed concept of design or orderliness. These apparent difficulties can be solved in two fundamental ways: endeavoring to change the basis of interpersonal influence and changing the curriculum. In both cases, the teacher's expectations must be amenable to change and the teacher must be capable of carrying out the change.

One way for the teacher to cope with the difficult student is to increase the specificity of requirements for satisfactory performance and to attach penalties for infringements (coercive influence). A second way is to "sweeten the pot" of content by selecting activities with fewer requirements attached to them. A third strategy is to make it evident to the students that the teacher is an expert in the kind of art that the student wants to learn or that the teacher is an expert in some other field of interest to students, not necessarily art. Because expertise is independent of status and role, the teacher may "reach" students for whom art (or schooling or teachers) has little status. A fourth strategy is to disclose to students dimensions of one's self as a person, not simply as a teacher or as an expert. The premise is that the student will find some aspect from the multi-faceted self of the teacher thus revealed that has sufficient intrinsic appeal to cause personal identification (referent influence).

Expectations and Problems: The Realist

The realist expects to have access to physical resources for teaching the crafts. Special tools, equipment, and supplies are required for the teacher to be effective. Scheduling patterns that do not provide for the systematic development of art work could be a problem for the teacher, especially if a complex technique is involved. Under such conditions, the realist might search for "low technology" short-term craft activities (for example, "stained glass" windows from cellophane paper) or might try to persuade the school system to invest in proper equipment and expanded blocks of time for art studio instruction, as seen in the vocational focus of many secondary programs.

The plans developed by those who scored highest on the realist orientation seem to anticipate that students are not skilled in observation, are impatient when using media, and are weak in design. Skills in art are to be developed through sustained effort. Effort counts.

The most probable basis for interpersonal influence is the student's perception of the teacher as an expert in art. Such influence hinges on the student's wanting to know something that the teacher knows. By definition, expertise involves a high level of mastery; it is based on a kind of authority that is readily separated from role and status, and consequently may permit the teacher to "reach" students for whom the role of "teacher" has little status. The hidden hazard in any display of expertise is that the novice may be overwhelmed by it, with the result that the novice feels that an insurmountable distance exists between present abilities and those to be achieved. In order to demonstrate that expertise is approachable, the teacher might reveal to students that experts are not "perfect" or might make a point of letting students know that they may be expert in areas where the teacher is not (seeking referent influence). The teacher might endeavor to pre-structure activities so students are guaranteed a success (seeking influence by immediate reward), or might insist that some students are simply unteachable.

Expectations and Problems: The Personalist
The personalist expects to offer a program in which subjects and themes are explored through various media and art forms. The particular media and art forms are of less importance than the student's opportunity to encounter a variety of media. Because low-cost supplies can have high expressive potential, neither budgets nor extraordinary spaces for teaching are absolutely essential. Scheduling is a different matter. Large classes and inflexible schedules are especially problematic for the teacher who is committed to dialogue and individualized instruction. One might expect that the teacher faced with both conditions might argue first for a reduction in class size, and second for time to help students outside of formally scheduled classes. The personalist orientation and plan is probably best suited to schools with flexible scheduling or open classrooms.

Because the personalist is primarily concerned with the "self" of students, the most probable expectation of the teacher is to achieve referent influence with the student; that is, a personal identification with the student. The teacher is likely to see as "problems" those students who are insensitive, unwilling or unable to move beyond stereotypes; who are psychologically "distant," or unable to make choices. Referent influence is difficult for the teacher to establish, since it originates from the student's "feeling of oneness" with the teacher (Steiner, 1962, p. 122). It is doubtful if one can deal with any degree of authenticity with the personal and expressive dimensions of art by the use of coercion or simplistic rewards. It may be meaningful to suggest that the teacher display his or her expertise as "a knower" of feelings and themes as experssed in life and in art.

Paradoxically, the process of identification may result in emulation of the teacher. A potential problem for the teacher is that the student may uncritically accept what the teacher says, engage in imitative behavior, and consequently, become less "individual." If we are to believe Bandura's (1971/1977) analysis of the "modeling" process, the teacher cannot achieve significant referent influence by "getting down to the student's level." The teacher must have some attributes that are valued but not possessed by the student. Further, those characteristics most likely to be imitated by the student are those evident under conditions where students observe the teacher's behavior but do not fully experience the consequences of it. If the teacher induces the student to undertake some activity or line of thought that touches on the inner life, and if the consequences of doing so are not satisfactory from the student's point of view, and if this happens with any degree of consistency, the teacher's "credibility" as a model is seriously diminished.

It seems unlikely that many students outside of a therapeutic setting will consider it legitimate for the teacher to probe for "public" expressions of self that might be directly and forcefully revealing of the "private" self—especially if the teacher should undertake such inquiries with adolescents, or at the beginning of the school year when expectations for decorum are greatest, or if the expression is to be put on display, and if students see themselves as unskilled in art. Taken together, these hazards may contribute to what Efland (1976) has called the "school art style" in the studio art of children and youth—a simplistic treatment of thematic content and media, so selected as to assure that students produce the qualities of "looseness" and "spontaneity" that many teachers seem to equate with creative self-expression.

Expectations and Problems: The Experimentalist
The experimentalist does not want to rush through the school year. Uninterrupted time is needed for sustained attention, especially for activities that require collaborative effort and discussion of the relevance of art to life. Traditional studio supplies are likely to be of less importance than easy access to community resources (field trips and visitors to schools) and other means to demonstrate that art *in* school is related to art *outside* of school. In the absence of such resources, the teacher might improvise by taking advantage of films, role-playing, and other surrogates for the real world.

The experimentalist hopes to establish an atmosphere in which students feel free to express their opinions. Favoritism is to be minimized. Fairness in the allocation of praise and in the distribution of duties and penalties is essential to the teacher's success. Because fairness is usually judged in comparison to "what others got" in the same or similar situations, the teacher is likely to make visible (public) both the expectations for students and the teacher's judgment of their performance. In practice, the teacher might solve this problem by addressing comments more to the group than to individuals, or might use private conferences to communicate the most significant comments to individual students.

These descriptions of potential problems and strategies for dealing with them are based on the assumption that there is a "psycho-logical" affinity between the teacher's expectations and the bases of influence a teacher would attempt to establish in a classroom. Expectations, of course, may be unreasonable and plans are just that—anticipations of action, not actions taken. When the outcomes of the teacher's actions prove over a period of time to be inconsistent with his or her expectations, some reorganization of the teacher's beliefs, or plans, or modes of interaction is likely to occur. Clearly, empirical studies are needed to determine the degree of interdependence among the teacher's beliefs, the curriculum offered to students, and modes of classroom interaction. Studies of the stability of such factors and of the relationship among them are needed as well. If the teaching of art differs substantially from teaching in other fields, the differences must surely be linked to the "content-bound" expectations of the teacher.

Observations on the Issue of Teacher Effectiveness

Much of the research on teaching is based on the assumption that the aims and content of instruction are implicit in the "learning tasks" set forth in texts, workbooks, related published instructional materials, and achievement tests. It is typically assumed that the aims and content of instruction, so defined, are not at issue in research; rather, it is the teacher's skill or method of involving the student in learning tasks that is of primary interest (Gage, 1978). Teaching in the visual arts, especially studio-based instruction, occurs in a cultural and educational context that gives to the art teacher a remarkable degree of freedom to determine the aims, content, and form of the curriculum. The use of standardized achievement tests in the visual arts is not only rare, it is actively criticized (Eisner, in press). It is typical for the art teacher to make significant decisions about the aims, content, means, and evaluative techniques for the students' program of studies. For this reason, assessments of teacher "effectiveness" are likely to be trivial unless they include some judgment about (a) the quality of instruction offered—its worthwhileness, representativeness, appropriateness, and fundamental accuracy—and (b) the conditions under which the art teacher is required to work.

In general, too little attention is paid to teaching as a long-term and large-scale enterprise with results that are not immediately evident in the moment during which we think we are assessing its effectiveness. Nor do we have an adequate understanding of the "careers" of art teachers with respect to their early development, to the impact of teacher education programs on their views, and to how those views are modified by experience in the field.

Fundamental to virtually every inquiry in art education is the value orientation from which it is framed. In studies of the teaching process, it is suggested that ways be found to map the value orientations of teachers (A), to determine how these orientations may bear on the curriculum offered to students (B), and to study the bases of interpersonal influence in the classroom (C). An understanding of the dynamics in A, B, and C is essential if we wish to assess how and in what degree teachers bring about student learning in art. In teaching—as in art—intent, content, and form are essential considerations. One need not accept the particular constructs and analyses that I have offered here to recognize the need for this kind of inquiry.

Cincinnati, Ohio
July 1978

NOTES

[1]Items were constructed from the author's experience and "practical" commentaries on philosophy in Phenix, P. H. (Ed.), *Philosophies of education*. New York: Wiley, 1961; and Burns, H. W., and Brauner, C. J. (Eds.), *Philosophy of education: Essays and commentaries*. New York: Ronald Press, 1962.

[2]Item analyses were made using: Fan, C-T. *Item analysis table*. Princeton, New Jersey: Educational Testing Service, 1952. The table provides estimates of item discrimination based on the high-low 27 percent group method of analysis. For the pilot study, an item with r.45 (N = 27) was considered eligible for discussion.

REFERENCES

Abelson, R. P., and Rosenberg, M. J. Symbolic psycho-logic: A model of attitudinal cognition. *Behavioral Science,* 1958, *3,* 1-13.

Bandura, A. Analysis of modeling processes. In H. F. Clarizio, R. C. Craig, and W. A. Mehrens (Eds.), *Contemporary issues in educational psychology* (3rd ed.). Boston: Allyn & Bacon, 1977.

Bem, D. J. *Beliefs, attitudes, and human affairs.* Belmont, California: Brooks Cole, 1970.

Berliner, D. C. *Instructional time in research on teaching.* Paper presented at the meeting of the American Educational Research Association, April, 1977. San Francisco, 1977. (Mimeographed)

Cosgrove, D. J. Diagnostic rating of teacher performance. *Journal of Educational Psychology,* 1959, *50,* 200-204.

Day, M. Rationales for art education: Thinking through and telling why. In G. W. Hardiman and T. Zernich (Eds.), *Curricular considerations for visual arts education: Rationale, development and evaluation.* Champaign, Illinois: Stipes, 1974.

Efland, A. The school art style: A functional analysis. *Studies in Art Education,* 1976, *17*(2), 37-44.

Eisner, E. W. The state of art education today. *Art Education,* 1978, *31*(8), 14-23.

Eisner, E. W., Laswell, B., and Wieder, C. *What do prospective art teachers believe about the teaching of art?* Unpublished manuscript. Stanford University.

French, R. P. Jr., and Raven, B. The bases of social power. In D. Cartwright (Ed.), *Studies in social power.* Ann Arbor, Michigan: Institute for Social Research, 1959.

Gage, N. L. Theories of teaching. In E. R. Hilgard (Ed.), *Theories of learning and instruction.* Sixty-third yearbook of the National Society for the Study of Education. Chicago: University of Chicago Press, 1964.

Gage, N. L. *The scientific basis of the art of teaching.* New York: Teachers College Press, 1978.

Good, T. L., and Brophy, J. E. Teachers' expectations as self-fulfilling prophecies. In H. F. Clarizio, R. C. Craig, and W. A. Mehrens (Eds.), *Contemporary issues in educational psychology* (3rd ed.). Boston: Allyn & Bacon, 1977.

Jackson, P. W. *Life in classrooms*. New York: Holt, Rinehart & Winston, 1968.

Steiner, E. An educational theory model: Graph theory. In E. S. Maccia, G. W. Maccia, and R. E. Jewett, *Construction of educational theory models* (Cooperative Research Project 1632, U.S. Office of Education). Columbus: The Ohio State University Research Foundation, 1963.

Bennett Reimer / *A Response to Chapman*

Difficulties in Studying How Values Affect Teachers' Actions

Laura Chapman is among those aesthetic educators who believe very deeply that value commitments are at the core of the art education enterprise and that value systems can and should provide the direction, the point, the impetus for productive work. Her own research over the years I have known her, which stretch back to the earliest days of the CEMREL Aesthetic Education Program in the late sixties, has used a variety of techniques but always as means toward larger ends, rather than, as so often occurs in education research, ends in search of some point. Because I share her orientation I have valued her contributions, have learned from them, and have been changed by them—sometimes, I must say, painfully changed.

Her present report is another instance of her concern for clarifying how values affect actions, and I am more than a little delighted that this topic has appeared so explicitly at this conference, giving it the prominence I believe it deserves, particularly when the conference is devoted to teaching the arts and aesthetic education. Her paper, at the same time, illustrates how difficult it is to devise techniques for quantifying what is essentially qualitative, and how equally difficult it is to avoid logical missteps on the very rocky path leading from philosophical premises to their conclusions in specific practices. My comments will focus on these difficulties because we must consider how to overcome them. I am not, therefore, being critical of this particular study so much as using it as an opportunity to reflect on the issues it raises so well. I particularly want to avoid over-analysis of a project that is intended to be provocative rather than definitive. There is nothing so unfair (or, I might add, so boring) as to pick apart the little pieces of an endeavor not designed to be a model of technique, and there is nothing so stifling for education research as to insist on technical polish before it is called for. I fully accept Dr.

BENNETT REIMER *is John W. Beattie Professor and Chairman of the Music Education Department at Northwestern University.*

Chapman's disclaimers about the level of precision in what she has reported and offer my comments in the same rather freewheeling spirit.

The first and perhaps most fundamental difficulty in probing the practical consequences of value orientations is to select—from the many types and levels of value positions—types that are sufficiently coherent as to afford genuine options, and a level sufficiently close to the actualities of teaching and learning as to be clearly related to observable practices. When the types are so broad as to suggest general orientations to life, based largely on personality in the sense of a more or less constant subjective set toward life, and when the level is so inclusive that education style is but one of many possible categories, of which art education style becomes one of several possible sub-categories, the chances are that whatever follows in a study will be built on sand.

I would not have chosen the four positions used as the basis for Dr. Chapman's project because they are, I believe, somewhat too all-encompassing. While I am comfortable with some of her descriptions of their applicability to education decision making, and to expectations, and to problems, I am very uncomfortable with many others, which strike me sometimes as *non sequiturs,* sometimes as false distinctions, and in a few instances as contradictions. There are so many inherent difficulties in teasing out convincingly the relations of belief and action that we must, I am afraid, be somewhat more modest in our attempts to do so, perhaps by starting with smaller, tighter problem areas and gradually generalizing as knowledge increases. What we want to avoid is that this important, this essential kind of inquiry be reduced to the "non-event" status of so much research in the field of education. Better, I would suggest, a somewhat smaller "event" than a too large "non-event."

The second difficulty in studies of the sort Dr. Chapman reports is to find subjects who in fact embody a discernible value orientation. I respectfully submit that she is incorrect in her comment that "almost every prospective teacher has, or soon develops, some conception of what counts as 'art' in education and why art should be offered in schools." I would say, in fact, that it is the exceptional prospective teacher or teacher in service who does so. She is extremely optimistic to assume that her twenty-seven tender juniors have (a) thought through, and (b) committed themselves to anything like a consistent philosophy of education or art education, however they have been subjected to the "high-low 27 percent group method of analysis," which guarantees nothing about either their beliefs or what they understand of the consequences of their beliefs. After all, how would they possibly have become articulate spokesmen for and practitioners of this or that value system in either education or art education? In such matters a youngster comes to college as a philosophical *tabula rasa,* and what is typically inscribed thereon in four years is a welter of confused, contradictory, totally unsystematic philosophic inputs from a college faculty that exemplifies these qualities in its own level of development and that also reflects the philosophic disarray of the arts education profession, especially, one might say, at this point in its history. Further, it is the exceptional four-year undergraduate program that provides even a single course devoted to the development of philosophic understandings about the arts in education, even if one course were sufficient to address such an issue. Now it may well be that Dr. Chapman's program is of this exceptional sort—knowing her I would not be surprised. But of course my concern here is the general context in which studies of this kind must be undertaken.

The next difficulty I want to mention stems directly from the previous one. Even if one were to assume that a solid philosophic position had been developed, the process of extrapolation from theory to practice is fraught with hazards. It is no simple matter to translate a philosophy into the myriad bits and pieces of the teaching process even when one is a trained specialist in this particular area—let alone a preservice or in-service teacher. So many judgments are required, so many alternatives exist, so many gaps appear where philosophy does not provide answers—yet action must be taken. We simply cannot take as valid data about the relationships between theory and practice, the choices made by students or teachers in settings not very carefully constructed or strictly controlled and very modestly interpreted. To use this study once more as illustrative: Only six of the twenty-seven instructional plans the students developed "reflected a substantial concern for art history and art criticism." I do not believe this is a reasoned application of the particular rationales to which the students were reported to have subscribed, but simply reflects the typical training of art education majors, who are seldom taught how they can use what they have learned from history courses or other content courses as an integral component in the teaching of media classes. Needless to say this situation generalizes to music education and any other art education. The point is that curriculum choices made and teaching processes used are often quite unrelated to a stated philosophy. This is regrettable and, I believe, surmountable to a large extent, but this reality must be firmly in mind when a research study tangles with it.

Still another set of conditions making it difficult to trace the consequences of beliefs is the inevitable dilution of a philosophic stance when it finds itself immersed in the realities of a school setting. Studies confined to college students not yet in service will tend to suffer from all the ills I have mentioned plus the unavoidable fact that the situation is artificial. Studies going into the field, in addition to the same ills, are also infected by that overwhelming factor of context, which, according to practically the entire literature on education change and innovation is by far the most powerful factor influencing any particular philosophy or program or practice. This is not the time to review that literature. Suffice it to say that whatever consistent value system a teacher holds, it will be subjected to the stresses and strains of a host of factors inherent in the school as a complex social system, including the characteristic gestalt of a particular school setting, the many diverse expectations in operation there, its special history as a school, and the interrelations among the faculty, between the faculty and administration, and between the school and the community it serves. Add to this mix, all of it pulling and pushing at the teacher's orientation, the value systems of the students as both individuals and reflectors of their families and community, their interests and lack of interests, their expectations, their differences in skills and learning abilities both within individuals and across individuals, and the holes punched into a philosophy now begin to make it look like Swiss cheese. The *coup de grâce*, as Dr. Chapman mentions as one of her own concerns about her study, is the very limited time that finally becomes available for actual instruction, so that only a very thin slice of that holey Swiss cheese is left to nourish the student body. No wonder it is difficult to trace a philosophy to measurable or even discernible pupil outcomes.

A further point on this matter. Philosophies are generally not static, as Dr. Chapman reminds us. They change as teachers change, they grow with their growth, they ebb and flow in the individual's commitment, so that it is often difficult to pin down a person's philosophy at any one point in time. As if this were not enough, Dr. Chapman makes the rather startling assertion that "if we expect teachers to reach all or almost all students, the teacher must be capable of functioning as an eclectic." Now if this were so, research of the sort she has reported would be irrelevant if not impossible. Much more significantly, every teacher would hold the very same philosophy—that called "eclecticism," which seems to have been defined as a process of switching philosophies as one is presented with differing students. I want to suggest that if a philosophy has to be abandoned in favor of another because it does not meet some student's need, and then the other has to be dropped in turn, and so on, we are seriously misconstruing what philosophies are and what they do. A philosophy can and should provide a coherent context for teaching and learning. To the extent it is so limited that it cannot give a meaningful direction to actions, it is probably not a "philosophy" but a "Method" (with a capital M), with which we in music education seem to be uncommonly afflicted. Eclecticism, I further submit, is often little more than a refuge for sloppy thinkers, who are not eclectic in having forged a hard-won unity from diverse sources but instead are only conceptual ragamuffins. That particular philosophical condition is not the *solution* for education—it is, perhaps, its major *problem*.

One final point about the complexities of studies of this sort. While the hidden biases of the researcher are a matter of concern in all research, they are particularly so in this kind of work because so many interpretations must be made as the study proceeds. It is very hard—perhaps impossible—to keep one's own beliefs from coloring various aspects of a study, including its design, its treatment of data, its interpretation of findings. We cannot, after all, free ourselves from our own opinions and proclivities whenever we don the hat of researcher, and perhaps this is just as well. Yet we must be careful. For example, in her discussion of one of the curriculum plans, the "Idealist," Dr. Chapman gives the following as a descriptive statement: "The content favored does not invite exploration of the life of feeling so much as it requires the patterning of shape and form." I would like to argue that exploration of feeling in art takes place precisely through "the patterning of shape and form," and can take place in no other way than by shaping and forming materials to achieve expressive results. Is the Idealist, then, unconcerned with feeling or very deeply and genuinely concerned with feeling?

In another place Dr. Chapman offers this comment, which contains what seems to be a fact: "Taken together, these hazards may account for the simplicity with which many teachers actually treat the most potent dimension of art, its thematic essence." Now if "thematic essence" is regarded as the most potent dimension of art, judgments about curriculum choices and teaching activities will reflect this belief. Those who would reject such a notion, arguing that thematic references are absent from much art, including most music, and are, even when present, always means rather than ends, are likely to interpret data quite differently. I am not interested here in arguing through these points of aesthetic contention; I raise them to illustrate that even in work so keenly intelligent as Dr. Chapman's, debatable assumptions lurk below the surface. This is not a criticism—it is simply a reminder that in doing this kind of work and studying what others have done we must exercise special care to be aware of unstated value orientations.

In her concluding remarks Dr. Chapman offers the following counsel, which is gradually becoming more accepted in education research as its wisdom is understood. She says, "In general, too little attention is paid to the teaching process as a long-term and large-scale enterprise with results that are not immediately evident in the moment during which we think we are assessing its effectiveness." The implications of this insight stretch to all corners of the research enterprise. It reminds us to think in more global terms about matters that are infinitely complicated. A major part of our lives as human beings in general and educators in particular is spent in trying to define and refine what we believe and to act more in consonance with our developing beliefs. Research that clarifies our understandings of this fundamental process is of central importance to education. Despite its difficulties we must persist in doing it, recognizing all the while that nothing is more "long-term" and "large-scale" than forming life values and applying them in action. We should not expect such studies to yield definitive results; it is simply not that sort of topic. Dr. Chapman's work is evidence that progress can indeed be made—that ideas can be clarified, that techniques can be developed, that information can be sifted, that insights do appear when, as she demonstrates, persistence and intelligence and a bit of courage are brought to the task.

Evanston, Illinois
July 1978

James Hanshumaker

The Art of Recognizing Artistic Teaching in the Arts

or

*Problems in Developing Principles or Methods
of Recognizing Exceptional Skill in
Teaching That Which Is Beautiful,
Appealing, or of More Than
Ordinary Significance*

If, after reading these titles, you feel a sense of hopelessness, chaos, and frustration, then the titles will have succeeded in communicating the confusion surrounding the central questions forming the basis of this paper. What are the characteristics of excellent arts teachers? How can we recognize excellence in arts teaching when we see or, more importantly, when we *sense* it? In this instance, reference to sensory input is deliberate for, like making qualitative judgments about art works, determining quality in the teaching of the arts is dependent upon impressions created by what we see, what we hear, possibly by what we smell—but most certainly by what we feel. Thus problems of making qualitative judgments about arts teaching are interlocked with the characteristics of those who make such judgments and with the very difficult task of describing the synthesis of intellectual and sensory input upon which qualitative judgments of any kind must be made.

For purposes of clarification, let us compare the task of the critic judging the quality of artistic output with the task of a critic whose job is to judge the quality of teaching in the arts. Put in these terms it becomes apparent that such a task should not be assigned to just anyone. Perhaps the most callous examples of uninformed criticism occur when the critic is asked to judge an art form about which he or she knows little or nothing. Thus, for example, music critics are often asked—and, what is worse, they accept the assignment—to review

JAMES HANSHUMAKER *is Professor of Music and Education at the University of Southern California.*

performances of dance. If the resultant reviews miss the artistic point, they would certainly have fared no better in the hands of the drama critic whose experience is limited to what passes for dance in a musical comedy. It seems the most successful arts critics have extensive experience which provides a basis for comparison and which includes direct knowledge of the artistic process.

Unfortunately, assignments to judge quality in teaching are frequently made in the same manner as assignments which befall arts critics. Persons who have little or no experience (including students or parents) are asked to make such judgments, as are psychologists, school principals, and general "supervisors." Small wonder that what results both in the literature and in practice is confusing and frequently misses the point. Those who presume to judge the quality of arts teaching must themselves be experienced teachers with extensive direct experience in the arts process being taught. Even then such paragons of virtue face the dilemma confronting all critics: the necessity to objectify, describe, and compare the characteristics forming the basis of what in reality is a subjective judgment.

Just as the arts critic must make separate judgments about the art work and the manner of its execution, so the arts-teacher-critic must make such judgments about the content of arts teaching as well as the manner of execution—or perhaps performance—of the teacher. In education this is a more crucial issue than it may be in a concert. While a deft performance of Leschetizky's piano arrangement for the left hand of the Sextette from *Lucia di Lammermoor* may represent a questionable but forgivable triumph of technique over substance, all the mastery and technique of a superb teacher, when applied to insignificant content, may well result in nothing more profound than the peculiar American phenomenon called the marching band. Other such examples abound in educational settings.

The principal of a local junior high school provides enthusiastic reports of the quality of arts teaching in the school as represented by a yearly production which occupies both the days and nights of all the arts teachers and their students for an entire semester. The resultant "Broadway Musical," conceived in its original form for mature professionals, is psychologically, physically, and artistically damaging to thirteen and fourteen year olds upon whom pleading, cajoling, and psychological threat ultimately work their magic. The production bears no resemblance to the original, is painful (except for parents of the cast) to watch and hear, and is, in fact, a triumph of misguided effort in that the children manage to get through it at all.

At the insistence of its artist-teacher, a university school of music turned out artistically and musically satisfying performances of operas by both Wagner and Strauss. Unfortunately *Friedenstag* proved to be the final undoing of a gorgeous but youthful dramatic soprano voice, which has not been heard since.

In recent years, student evaluations of teacher performance have found great favor at educational institutions as decisions regarding tenure and merit salary increases are made. Usually, a form or rating sheet is devised on which students are asked to exercise judgment regarding characteristics presumed to be indicators of teaching excellence. The trend toward student evaluation grows out of the 1960s when students sought reform of educational practices many considered to be archaic and detrimental. Although much good, particularly in matters of curriculum, was generated in this manner, there is considerable doubt about the ability of students to assess critical components in their own education.

Rodin and Rodin (1972) reported their research in which they compared student ratings of teachers with student mastery of subject matter. In their words:

> There are two ways to judge teaching through the medium of students. The objective criterion of teacher effectiveness is based on what students have learned from the teacher. The subjective criterion is based on student evaluations of teacher effectiveness. The objective of this study was to assess the validity of student evaluations by means of a comparison between the objective and subjective criteria of good teaching. (p. 1164)

After testing the validity of student ratings in an undergraduate calculus course (a far easier task than assessing artistic or aesthetic development), the Rodins concluded:

> present data indicate that students are less than perfect judges of teaching effectiveness if the latter is measured by how much they have learned. If how much students learn is considered to be a major component of good teaching, it must be concluded that good teaching is not validly measured by student evaluations in their current form. (p. 1166)

Their conclusion was further supported in an evaluation of two modes of studying music theory and music history conducted by the writer (1977). In an attitude survey, one group of students gave consistently high marks to their teachers and rated highly their own mastery of subject matter. After a comparison of group test scores, it could only be concluded that this group of students simply didn't know what they didn't know, nor were they able to assess accurately the effectiveness of their teachers, at least in relation to their own acquisition of skills and information.

Examination of a form (see *Figure 1*) used for such evaluation may reveal the answer to this disparity. Many of the items on the form deal with teacher characteristics that seem to be important regarding student likes and dislikes. Items 4, 6, 8, and 9 fall into this category. Many others ask students to make judgments in matters in which they have little background or experience: items such as 2, 12, 14, 15, 16, and 17.

Figure 1

UNIVERSITY OF SOUTHERN CALIFORNIA SCHOOL OF MUSIC

Student's Evaluation of a
Classroom Course and Instruction

PLEASE PRINT

To the Student: University policy regarding promotion and retention places high
priority on the documentation provided by student response to a class. These
forms represent the only comprehensive procedure available for this purpose. In
addition, you are in a position to convey to your instructor much helpful information
which will enable him to make the course of greater value in the future. This report
is not to be signed.

Date_____

Course Title and No._____

Instructor's Name_____ Required Course? Elective?

Circle the approximate percentage of class meetings you have attended:

   100%-80%   80%-60%   60%-40%   40%-20%   20%-0%

Circle the appropriate rating number
LOW   HIGH

I. Value of the course to me

    1. What was your level of interest in the course?   1   2   3   4   5

    2. To what degree do you think the course helped
        you in the acquisition of knowledge and/or skills?   1   2   3   4   5

    3. To what degree do you think the course furthered
        your interest in this area?   1   2   3   4   5

II. Instructor's attitude and behavior toward students

    4. Rate the instructor's willingness to listen to
        suggestions for the course (but not necessarily
        accept them).   1   2   3   4   5

    5. How would you rate the instructor for

        a. reasonableness?   1   2   3   4   5

        b. fairness?   1   2   3   4   5

        c. objectivity?   1   2   3   4   5

    6. Has the instructor been available for appoint-
        ments or during prescribed office hours?   1   2   3   4   5

Of the remaining items, only 5, 7, 10, 11, and 13 have any relation to teaching effectiveness and assess characteristics with which students may have sufficient experience for making a valid judgement.

So while student evaluations of teachers may provide valuable insights for teachers about how they and their instructional practices are perceived, such evaluations are of little value in identifying the specific characteristics of excellent arts teaching.

Attempting to judge the quality of arts teaching is a highly complex process requiring extensive knowledge of the specific field, considerable teaching experience, knowledge of materials, pacing, sequence, learning theory, and philosophical and psychological foundations of both art and education. But, even assuming the individual has all such attributes, the

III. Instructional Effectiveness

7. How would you rate the instructor's
    interest and enthusiasm in the course?   1   2   3   4   5

8. How would you rate the instructor in being
    reasonably prompt in:

    a. Starting the class?   1   2   3   4   5
    b. Dismissing the class?   1   2   3   4   5

9. How would you rate the instructor in:

    a. Clearly defining the course's content at
        the beginning of the semester?   1   2   3   4   5
    b. Being consistent with his definition of
        the course's content throughout the semester? 1 2   3   4   5

10. How would you rate the instructor in making
    course assignments:

    a. Sufficiently in advance   1   2   3   4   5
    b. Clear in content   1   2   3   4   5

11. How would you rate the value and appropriateness
    of the assignments?   1   2   3   4   5

12. How would you rate the instructor in the degree
    to which he was well-informed and up-to-date
    in the field?   1   2   3   4   5

13. How would you rate the instructor's skills in
    communication?   1   2   3   4   5

14. How would you rate the classroom procedures
    utilized?

    a. Organization of lecture material   1   2   3   4   5
    b. Variety of teaching techniques used   1   2   3   4   5
    c. Opportunity for class discussion   1   2   3   4   5

15. How would you rate the textbooks and/or
    repertoire used?   1   2   3   4   5

16. How would you rate the fairness and validity
    of the tests used in the course?   1   2   3   4   5

17. How would you rate the fairness and validity
    of other bases for grading that were used in
    the course, such as reports, papers, and par-
    ticipation in class discussion?   1   2   3   4   5

18. What is your overall evaluation of this course? 1   2   3   4   5

19. Please write any other comments that might
    be helpful to the instructor in evaluating
    his course.

arts-teacher-critic will finally be forced to recognize the shortcomings of either language or mathematics as descriptors of excellence in arts teaching. Just as the arts critic is finally forced to recognize the inadequacy of language in describing The Artistic Experience, arts-teacher-critics must be prepared to fuse what they know with what they sense in order to synthesize a subjective impression of the quality of artistic teaching which transcends verbalization. This job is made even more difficult because arts teaching involves the complex act of bringing about desired change within an artistic mode. Such change involves an internalized process which does not lend itself to the more common forms of verbal or numerical description and assessment.

This is not to say that artistic change does not result in some change in observable (aural or visual) behavior. It does suggest, however, that only relatively gross behavioral change can be described verbally or numerically with any precision, since that which is truly "artistic" is essentially nonverbal or nonnumerical in nature. Thus, while it is possible to objectify and describe gross characteristics of a performance (number of wrong notes performed or whether the actors do or do not know the lines of a play), it is not possible to describe the really subtle characteristics which distinguish an artistic performance from a routine one. While the techniques and devices utilized in the created art work can be described in verbal or numerical ways, the personal significance or aesthetic impact on the viewer or listener cannot. Since teaching is a form of performance, it seems likely that verbal and numerical descriptions of teaching performance will be useful in objectifying gross behavior but not in describing characteristics of excellence. While it is possible to "stand back" from a specific lesson or teaching sequence and to describe techniques and devices used by the teacher, it is far more difficult to describe the subtle nonverbal impact of the total experience on students.

Literature on Characteristics of Good Teaching

Given the problem of developing principles or methods of recognizing exceptional skill in arts teaching, what can be learned from an examination of literature and other printed documents? Precious little in most instances, although much has been written on the subject. The mundane quality of many articles appearing in professional journals may be illustrated by examining "Whom Shall We Fire?" written by H. Ogden Morse and appearing in the NASSP Bulletin (1977). After exposing the staff problem faced by schools in an era of declining enrollments, the author suggests the following areas—which I shall discuss in the order in which they are presented—as bases for judging quality of teaching:

1. Knowledge of Subject Matter

Morse suggests that it is important for teachers to know the subjects they teach in order to gain the respect of students. While this idea can hardly be faulted, I suggest that it is important for teachers to know the subject they teach in order for students to learn anything. Further, this is so gross a characteristic that it provides no basis whatever for assessing excellent teaching. In the arts, at least, mastery of subject matter and related skills must be taken for granted as a prerequisite to the privilege of teaching, not as a basis for determining excellence in teaching.

2. Control

Although admitting that the noise level of a class is no criterion for assessing teacher control, the fact that Morse even mentions it points up what are problems for many teachers, but special ones for arts teachers. One problem results from the fact that ill-educated individuals are asked to make judgments about teaching excellence. Another involves the criteria such individuals, particularly in public schools, use in making such judgments.

Too often judgments of teaching quality are made by the principal of a school or by parents or other lay persons. Such individuals often compare the effectiveness of the teacher to the amount of noise in a room or the amount of uniformity in student activity at a given moment. This is disastrous for excellent arts teachers because: (1) sound is the most likely product of much artistic activity and (2) all arts activity is individual and the most effective learning may take place during a multitude of simultaneous activities under the supervision of an arts teacher. Experienced arts teachers would instantly recognize and value the learning taking place and be all but oblivious to the resultant noise or activity. Also indicative of the public school lay mind is the criterion which measures teacher excellence in relation to nonteaching, nonartistic activities. Favorites seem to include whether the roll book is kept accurately or whether the teacher greets clerically oriented staff meetings with enthusiasm. The irrelevance of such criteria becomes readily apparent in the following citation by Sheridan (1972) in a study of factors influencing music teachers to transfer or leave the profession:

> It would seem that fewer of the transfer or drop-out teachers believed uniform fitting to be without at least minor problems, although a greater percentage of the continuing teachers felt this to be a problem or a serious problem. Most instrumental music teachers experience some difficulty when it comes to uniform fitting. (p. 84)

While there is no question that the excellent teacher of the arts plans and effectively directs student activity, what often passes for a measure of control may have nothing to do with what students learn and may even inhibit student learning in the arts. Neither control, as commonly used by artistic lay persons, nor the many nonartistic nonteaching activities peripheral to the teaching function constitute meaningful criteria upon which to recognize excellence in arts teaching.

3. Effectiveness

After admitting that this is a difficult area in which to make judgments, Morse goes on to admit, albeit by default, the difficulty of even defining the term. One element to be considered, he suggests, is the quality of students' performances. This is probably the most promising suggestion in this or most similar articles on the subject of judging teaching quality. The proof of the pudding is in the eating and the proof of excellent teaching in the arts is in the quality of student performance and products. This is not a new idea, but it provides little help for or insight into attempting to define the characteristics of excellent teachers who are responsible for consistently high-quality student performance.

Another element of effectiveness, according to Morse, lies in the teacher's relationship to students. This is one of those marvelously open-ended criteria which abound in such literature and which tell us absolutely nothing. Suppose a student-teacher relationship results in a pregnancy. Is the student-teacher relationship a good or a bad one? Like judging the quality of such a criterion in the first place, the answer probably depends on personal viewpoint—whether you are the impregnator or the impregnatee—and on perceived desirability of the outcome of the relationship.

The teacher's contribution to the department and school is another element in what Morse calls effectiveness. Again there is no evidence to suggest a relationship between this element and teaching excellence nor does he define what such a contribution might be. If the implication suggests an intense and involved institutional commitment, it must be pointed out that many excellent arts teachers have no institutional commitment at all. Some of the most effective student performances and products I have witnessed were brought about by teachers who don't give a fig about either department or school.

4. Growth Potential

When applied to younger teachers and more precisely defined, this criterion might have some use in prediction, although it is doubtful that it is useful in defining characteristics of excellence in arts teaching. Morse, however, suggests the following as "other areas to consider": willingness to listen, willingness to evaluate new ideas, willingness to adapt to changes in program or structure, and commitment to "certain" standards. This, of course, sounds like text from an administrative bible. If applied to, perhaps, the most famous living violinist-teacher, a dismissal would probably result. This teacher, whose pupils are prominent violinists throughout the world, is seldom willing to listen to ideas about violin playing, seldom evaluates new ideas about either violin playing or teaching, insists that changes in program or structure *adapt to him*, and is committed to precise well-defined (rather than "certain") standards. Perhaps Mr. Morse would be willing to suggest to the administration that he not be allowed to teach!

5. Personality

Here, as elsewhere in much of the literature, the term used is so broad and so global that little of benefit accrues to the reader with serious intent. Morse makes reference to teachers "with negative personalities," whatever that means. In any event, research seems to confirm that selected personality characteristics as defined in so-called personality tests or inventories bear scant relationship to teaching success measured in terms of pupil achievement.

By using Morse's article as an illustration, I do not wish to imply that there is no literature worth reading on the subject. There are some helpful articles but they are far outnumbered by those of little value. Essentially, a statement made by Getzels and Jackson (1963) still seems to be true: "Despite the critical importance of the problem and a half century of prodigious research effort, very little is known about the nature and measurement of teacher effectiveness" (p. 574).

The Artist as Teacher

Surely, the controversy over the artistic quality of those who teach is as old as arts teaching. Quite simply put, this argument revolves around the rather sophomoric statement that "those who can't do, teach." Many teachers take instant offense at such a suggestion and the inference that their personal artistic performance is suspect. While it is probable that a teacher with no artistic experience will have difficulty in developing suitable strategies for the artistic education of others, there is little evidence to support the thesis that high level artistic output alone will produce a good teacher. It must be pointed out that "doing" and "teaching" are entirely different processes.

John M. Peterson (1975) points to this problem as it is found among architects:

> One widely held assumption among architects is that the best designers are the best judges of their own and others' work. This is extrapolated further in architectural education to suggest that the best designers are also the best teachers. There is little in the literature to support such views. (p. 147)

A large segment of the artistic community assumes that there is a direct link between the quality of the teacher's artistic performance and the quality of teacher performance as teacher. While I doubt that any artist or arts teacher could, or would, seriously challenge direct personal experience in an appropriate art process as a requisite to teaching that process, the argument hinges on matters of degree, quality, and extent of such experience. One thing is certain: The excellent arts teacher must have an imaginative vision of excellence in artistic output as exemplified by the artistry of recognized models. If the teacher is to teach the process of becoming an artist, then there is no substitute for "having been there." The teacher who works with those who wish to know artistry through their own creative or re-creative performance must know what it means to achieve such an end. In this respect, experience is not only the best teacher, it is the *only* teacher.

The matter of currency of artistic activity by arts teachers is another question. While the enthusiasm of a teacher is probably stimulated by continued involvement in the process being taught, it is not at all certain that there is any relationship between successful teaching and the degree to which the arts teacher *maintains* activity of a high artistic level. To be a staunch advocate of artistic currency as a characteristic of excellence in arts teaching, one must discount figures such as Gregor Piatigorsky and Lotte Lehmann, among others, whose excellence as teachers increased as their personal activity as artists declined both in quantity and quality.

While there is no substitute for artistic experience in the background of the excellent arts teacher, there is also no substitute for continuing enthusiasm for teaching and the desire to improve personal performance as a teacher. Many are the ills that have befallen unsuspecting students whose artist-teachers are motivated by the prospect of a steady income, security between professional engagements or shows, or the disappointment of personal professional rejection.

Martin Engel (1976) brings precision and clarity to the problem:

> It simply won't do for professional artists to castigate the teaching profession for its lack of artistic mastery. Indeed it has a moral obligation to enhance those very skills now recognized as grossly insufficient. Half a job is no job at all, for a professional artist who can't teach is as useless as a teacher who has no skills in or feel for the arts. (p. 175)

How one views the level and extent of "doing" as a characteristic of the excellent arts teacher is actually a matter of perspective. From the perspective of the nonteaching creator or performer, there may indeed be some truth to the argument that "those who can't do, teach," particularly if one is willing to include teachers like Nadia Boulanger, Rosina Lhévinne, and Stanislawski among the "can't doers"!

The Trouble with Competence

As Vincent O'Keefe has duly noted (1976), competency-based teacher education or CBTE is one of the more recent approaches to identifying the essential characteristics of arts teachers. Proponents of CBTE argue that these characteristics can be identified through observing specific behaviors of teachers. Behaviors judged to be incompetent or inappropriate are noted, and modules of instruction designed to modify undesirable behavior are instituted. Behaviorists argue that by "chaining" appropriate behaviors, a poor teacher can be made into a better one. Teacher effectiveness is likewise measured by assessing the competence of students as predefined by specific teaching objectives stated in behavioral terms. Thus, for example, if it is determined that instrumentalists should be able to play the D-major scale at a given rate of speed and *if* 80 percent or so can perform this task, then the teacher would obviously be judged competent to teach scales to instrumentalists.

One problem, among several, is that competency based programs lead to just that—*competence*. As any artist will attest, the term "competent" used to describe an artist or artistic product is not a complimentary one. At best, it is a polite way of describing mediocrity. To use such an approach to set standards for excellence in teaching is absurd. Such thinking is the reason why state certification requirements are always couched in minimal terms and why mediocrity too often characterizes the performance of teachers.

Although not a proponent of CBTE, Robert W. Travers (1975) provides a description exposing the artistic as well as the teaching problem:

> Competent teaching is assumed to consist of a collection of modular skills, and effective teaching performance presumably consists of a chain of these modular performances. This kind of conception of behavior has been promoted widely by operant psychologists who have long attempted, rather unsuccessfully, to account for complex behavior in terms of chains of components. (p. 419)

The reduction of teaching performance to a set of behaviors may well produce characteristics similar to those described in a recent article by Wyszpolski (1978) appearing in the *Los Angeles Times*.

> At Marineland the trainers are hired to establish and maintain a personal rapport between themselves and the animals with which they work. To refine an animal for show purposes the trainer must reward it with something it wants (usually fish) when it performs a desired response on cue. In other words the animal learns through operant conditioning, or behavior modification. It has been remarked that, for all their avowed intelligence, these creatures are still trained as animals, and not as potential comrades. (p. 58)

A major problem in arts education is that too many teachers have been trained rather than educated and, like the whales, perform on cue without the least idea of why they are doing what they are doing.

Excellent teaching, like an excellent performance or an excellent painting, consists of more than the execution of a chain of prespecified behaviors. Implied competence can only be seen as the starting point or the foundation for either teaching or artistic excellence. In Gestalt terms, if either teaching performance or artistic product consists merely of the sum of its parts, then it undoubtedly may be competent, but it most certainly will be neither excellent nor artistic. Artistry is surely more than the sum of its behavioral parts and artistry, not competence, is the whole point of excellent teaching.

Eisner (1975) comments further on the mentality which approaches education from a business or industrial viewpoint with emphasis on cost-benefit ratio.

> If one is removed from the complexities, vicissitudes, and uncertainties of the classroom, a simple, neat, and efficient view of schooling likely will appeal. There is nothing wrong with a technological approach to a task, if the task fits the approach. It fits in manufacturing refrigerators, clocks, and automobiles. . . . One should, I believe, raise the legitimate question of whether such a model is appropriate for education. (p. 175)

As one searches the CBTE movement in vain for some sign of concern for quality in teaching, the faddishness of the American educational establishment as it grabs for straws in the wind hits full force. Eisner again comments:

> I cannot help mentioning a paradox in this country concerning art education. At the same time that state departments of education and local boards of education mindlessly pursue the path to efficiency with demands to prespecify in behavioral terms classroom objectives ... at the same time that teachers are being subjected to evaluation to weed out, supposedly, the incompetent ... The National Endowment on the Arts supports artists to teach in the schools with essentially no interest whatsoever in careful evaluation. On the one hand, innuendoes are circulated that art teachers are not competent to teach art while artists, working without a stitch of educational training, are looked to as providing the real artistic leadership in American schools. (p. 176)

Competency-based programs are good as far as they go. They just do not go far enough. Competence in teaching, like competence in art, is not good enough. In one way or another, American education has set its goals on competence for many years and now suffers the mediocrity of attainment.

In any search for characteristics of excellence in arts teaching, mere competence must be presumed and the gross behaviors identified in CBTE must be givens. While CBTE might identify the behaviors necessary to make a poor teacher into a mediocre one, reliance on such an approach for identifying the characteristics of excellence is likely to produce little more than yet another attempt to turn the sow's ear into a silk purse.

Characteristics of Excellence in Arts Teaching

To begin, let us assume that the basic characteristics necessary to teach the arts are in place. Some of these are:

1. Teacher "knowledge-of" and experience in the art to be taught, including techniques necessary to the creation or recreation of art works.

Engel (1976) contrasts the distinction between "knowledge-of" and "knowledge-about":

> The former is an internalized state and involves the conceptual integration of information, values, and attitude. The latter, knowledge-about, is simply thinking in an objective, logical framework. In the arts, ... "knowledge of" or understanding, is the essential condition, so devastatingly absent among most teachers of the arts. (p. 8)

This may seem to be a large order, but it simply is not possible to describe characteristics of excellent teaching if this "basic" is absent.

2. An enthusiastic attitude toward the art and the teaching of that art.

3. Ability to communicate in modes appropriate to given artistic ends.

Communication should not be thought to exist only in a verbal mode. In many artistic learning situations the arching of an eyebrow or a body movement and its manner of execution may be more communicative than the most skillful and fluent verbalization.

4. The consistent selection of *artistically significant* goals for instruction.

Such goals may be technical, analytic, or perceptual in nature but attainment of the goal should provide the student with a technique, a skill, or an insight which is intrinsically artistic or which contributes to the creation, performance, or perception of something artistic. Artistically significant goals are not social or political in nature nor are they centered upon techniques or facts as ends in themselves.

5. The consistent selection of artistically significant instructional goals *which are commensurate with the developmental characteristics of students.*

Having described the basic characteristics without which no arts teacher should be given full responsibility for teaching, we are now at the point where characteristics of excellence in arts teaching can be discussed. After surveying the relevant literature, J. T. Sandefur (1972) developed a model for the evaluation of teachers which is currently being tested. In an interim report, Sandefur and Adams (1976) identify general characteristics drawn from "thematic clusters" found in the literature. Without putting them in a hierarchy they will be presented here as a framework for recognizing excellence in arts teaching.

It is interesting to note that the characteristics identified by Sandefur can all be described as *pervasive* or *holistic* rather than as isolated or specific behaviors as prescribed by the purveyors of CBTE. Such pervasive behavior tells us much more about the nature of characteristics of excellence in arts teaching although the psychometric approaches associated with CBTE will undoubtedly be useful in validation studies which are currently under way. In most instances, the items identified by Sandefur and Adams deal with either teaching style or personal characteristics. (The italicized portions of the following discussion are derived directly from Sandefur and Adams, 1976.)

1. *Good teaching utilizes the maximal involvement of the student in direct experiential situations.*

Jerome Bruner (1960 a and b) is the foremost advocate of experiential learning in our time. This process, the so-called "discovery" approach, is described in detail in his books. When the discovery approach is applied to the arts, the student is placed in the midst of an experience with the problem of explaining it. In this setting, the teacher's initial role is to pose questions or create problems whose answers or solutions will lead students to discover principles for themselves. The extended role of the teacher is to confirm these principles, thus developing the students' confidence in their own abilities to retain and apply the principles in similar situations. Hobgood (1970) comments on this approach:

> What the great teachers of the arts have seemed to grasp instinctively is the necessity to engage the student's sensibility fully. The point has special significance for the talented individual, in whom nonrational powers have as much importance as rational powers and who thrives on attention to that individuality which is at once his gift and his problem. In short, *the student in the arts gains most from under-going experiences of some intensity at the moments when significant learning should take place.* (pp. 49-50)

a. *Good teachers attempt to foster problem-oriented, self-directed, actively inquiring patterns of learning behavior in their students.*

b. *Good teachers elicit pupil-initiated talk and allow more pupil-initiated exploration and trial solutions.*

c. *Good teachers elicit independent thinking from their students.*

d. *Good teachers involve students in decision-making processes in active, self-directing ways.*

e. *Teachers who are interested in student involvement are less prone to dominate the classroom with lectures and other teacher activities.*

On this point, Hobgood (1970) offers further eloquent discourse directed toward teachers of theatre history and dramatic literature. Moreover, his comments seem to have great relevance for teachers of comparable specialties in the other arts.

> Teachers of these vital areas in theatre study seem frequently to resent student disinterest in their work, even to the point of suspecting that their colleagues in performance and production are undermining their efforts. But the plain matter of fact is that the presentation of theatre history and literature is typically dull and unimaginative, charged with presuppositions and traditional prejudices that may well boggle the mind of a discerning student. A notable grievance is warranted against instructors who rely upon lecture presentations despite their lack of talent as performers—for the effectiveness of a lecture lies, particularly before performance-sensitive students of theatre, in the dynamics of persuasive presentation as well as in the merit of organization. Lectures which are mere recitations understandably offend the sensibilities of an aware student, rendering the subject so treated as dry compilations of undramatic information.
>
> At all events, the teacher of theatre who fails to realize how crucial it is to manage the classroom so that memorable experiences occur there is, in an important sense, deferring to the authority of a textbook, making unnecessary and probably patronizing demands upon student attention, or resigning himself to an impactless endeavor for whose sometimes fortunate outcomes he should take small credit. (p. 49)

2. Good teaching encourages maximal "freedom" for the student.

a. Good teachers use significantly more praise and encouragement for the student.

b. They accept, use, and clarify students' ideas more often.

c. They give fewer directions, less criticism, less justification of the teacher's authority, and less negative feedback.

d. They use a relaxed, conversational teaching style.

e. They use more divergent questions, do more probing, and are less procedural.

f. They are more inclined to recognize the "affective climate" in the classroom and are responsive to student feelings.

g. Teachers with low dogmatism scores are more likely to use indirect methods than those with more closed-minded attitudes.

3. Good teachers tend to exhibit identifiable personal traits broadly characterized by warmth, democratic attitude, affective awareness, and a personal concern for students.

a. Good teachers exhibit characteristics of fairness and democratic behavior.

b. They are responsive, understanding, and kindly.

c. They are stimulating and original in their teaching.

d. They are responsible and systematic.

e. They are poised, confident, and emotionally self-controlled.

f. They are adaptable and optimistic.

g. They are well-versed in subject matter and give evidence of a broad cultural background.

As I suggested earlier, any attempt to determine distinguishing qualities of excellence in arts teaching faces the same problems confronting attempts to make such distinctions between artistic performances or products. While the items defined by Sandefur and Adams provide a useful framework upon which to make such distinctions and help to move us beyond consideration of the foundation necessary for excellent arts teaching, they still lack the scientifically determined precision so dear to the academic mind. Just as we ultimately rely on experience and our ability to *sense* excellence in art works and performances, so we must ultimately trust experience and the *intuitive process* as we attempt to develop a *feel* for recognizing exceptional skill in teaching that which is beautiful, appealing, or of more than ordinary significance. Or as Louis Armstrong is supposed to have said when asked to define jazz: "If you have to ask, you'll never know." Those who attempt to define excellence in arts teaching many ultimately have to say the same.

Los Angeles, California
May 1978

REFERENCES

Note: The reference list contains several entries that are not specifically cited in the text of the paper; they are included here because they are part of the necessary background for a discussion of the topic.

Asch, R. How creative are your art lessons? *Instructor*, 1976, *86*(2), 128-130.

Bruner, J. S. *On knowing: Essays for the left hand.* Cambridge, Massachusetts: Harvard University Press, 1960. (a)

Bruner, J. S. *The process of education.* Cambridge, Massachusetts: Harvard University Press, 1960. (b)

Eisner, E.W. Toward a more adequate conception of evaluation in the arts. *Peabody Journal of Education*, 1975, *52(3)*, 173-179.

Engel, M. The continuing education of teachers. *Art Education*, 1976, *29*(5), 4-8.

Frey, P. The ongoing debate: Student evaluation of teaching. *Change*, 1974, *6*(1) 47-48; 64.

Getzels, J.W., and Jackson, P.W. The teacher's personality and characteristics. In N.L. Gage (Ed.), *Handbook of research on teaching.* Chicago: Rand McNally, 1963.

Gray, C.E. The teaching model and evaluation of teaching performance. *Journal of Higher Education*, 1969, *40*(8), 636-642.

Gray, J.J. A little more dialogue please and a lot less rhetoric. *Art Education*, 1976, *29*(6), 25-29.

Hanshumaker, J., Michael, J., and Michael, W. *Evaluation of the core and existing theory programs: Preliminary report.* Unpublished paper. University of Southern California, 1977.

Hobgood, B.M. The concept of experimental learning in the arts. *Educational Theatre Journal*, 1970, *22*(1), 43-52.

Hodge, L.R. Recording classroom nonverbal behavior for effective teacher evaluation. *Contemporary Education*, 1975, *46*(3), 189-193.

Hunter, M. Teacher competency: Problem, theory, and practice. *Theory Into Practice*, 1976, *15*(2), 162-171.

MacGregor, R.N. Evaluating student teacher experiences in art education. *Art Education*, 1974, *27*(2), 15-18.

Mittler, G.A. Evaluating teaching and learning in art. *The Clearing House*, 1977, *50*(6), 252-255.

Morse, H.O. Whom shall we fire? *NASSP Bulletin* (National Association of Secondary School Principals), 1977, *61*(406), 76-79.

O'Keefe, V. CBTE: Shaking old wive's tales out of teaching. *Music Educators Journal*, 1976, *62*(6), 72-75.

Peterson, J.M. Jury criticism and design ability: Factors in evaluative judgments in design. *Perceptual and Motor Skills*, 1976, *42*(3), 147-154.

Rodin, M. and Rodin, B. Student evaluation of teachers. *Science*, 1973, *177* (4053), 1164-1166.

Sandefur, J.T. *An illustrated model for the evaluation of teacher education graduates.* Washington, D.C.: The American Association of Colleges for Teacher Education, 1972.

Sandefur, J.T., and Adams, R.A. An evaluation of teaching: An interim research report. *Journal of Teacher Education*, 1976, *27*(1), 71-76.

Sheridan, R.L. Factors influencing tenured senior high school instrumental music teachers to transfer or leave the profession. Unpublished doctoral dissertation, University of Southern California, 1973.

Teacher education in music: Final report. Washington, D.C.: Music Educators National Conference, 1972.

Travers, R.M.W. Empirically based teacher education. *Educational Forum,* 1975, *39*(4), 417-433.

Wyszpolski, B. Marineland animals: Privilege or prison. *Los Angeles Times* (Calendar), May 21, 1978, 58.

Joseph F. Dominic / *A Response to Hanshumaker*

Remarks on Artistry as a Criterion for Evaluating Teaching

> *To make a start*
> *out of particulars*
> *and make them general, rolling*
> *up the sum, by defective means—*
> *Sniffing the trees,*
> *just another dog*
> *among a lot of dogs.*

These lines from *Paterson: Book I* by William Carlos Williams suggest the conceptual struggles inherent in his beginning a series of poems that would be held together by their relationship to the idea of community. For Williams the intellectual as well as artistic problem was how to locate an imaginative framework for his poetry that would depart from the familiar genre discovered repeatedly by poets before him. The lines cited above also suggest the poet's struggle with attempts to enlarge meaning by moving from his particular experience to discoveries of more general patterns in human experience.

The title of James Hanshumaker's paper suggests a similar kind of conceptual problem but on a smaller scale. He deals with the evaluation of arts instruction by first locating an analogy which compares the task of evaluating the performance of the arts teacher with that of the critic of an artistic performance. He thus begins with a rather narrow cut across issues that fall under the general category of art as performance. In fact, he suggests that arts teaching be viewed as performance.

Like the previous analogy, this one falters because, unlike the effects produced by applying bow to strings or embouchure to wind instrument, the cause and effect relationship between teacher behavior and learner outcome is not always apparent. Where the analogy may be most apt, however, is at the level where students' motivation to learn is matched by their understanding of the gap between their present performance and an ideal one. At this educational level, usually the university, the student can also expect instruction toward such mastery.

JOSEPH F. DOMINIC *is Research Associate at the National Institute of Education.*

The analogy, though, enables us to think productively about the complex demands made upon the teacher of the performing arts; however, it also takes us far afield from fundamental evaluation problems in arts instruction. The first of these problems is a definitional one, namely, how do we define the various processes which we call arts instruction and how do different goals affect such definition? If, as Dr. Hanshumaker suggests, the goal of arts instruction is to "teach the process of becoming an artist," then how can we effectively accommodate the variety of goals which motivate arts education in the early grades? There the term "artistry" is an awkward criterion for the students who are just beginning to learn the fundamentals of "making art." In these processes we actually know very little about what kinds of learning accompany students' efforts to approximate the ideal through what they produce.

My point is that the term "artistry" may not be the most productive criterion for determining successful arts instruction at all educational levels. In the early grades, especially, instruction in the arts is conceived of in ways as various as the curricula from which it emanates. There the purposes of instruction are often confused as much by conflicting theories of instruction as they are by the narrow preferences of the teachers. Elliott Eisner (1978) makes a good attempt to clarify some of the confusion surrounding goals and methods of arts instruction:

> The arts have a much more organic orientation to rationality, where what is an end and what is a means are far from clear and where the speed of arriving at a destination is not always regarded as a virtue. (p. 14)

This observation takes us closer to another source of frustration in arts instruction, namely, that it has not had the benefit of adequate research to inform its development. Using the label "aesthetic education" to describe much of what passes for arts instruction in the schools, Howard Gardner makes the following observation about the contributions of research:

> In my view, research on aesthetic education has yet to come of age. To be sure, there are important studies and competent researchers. But as yet there is neither an experimental paradigm nor a theoretical framework that has been widely accepted. The marrow of the field is missing. Our wager is that the crucial character of artistic knowledge and education will most clearly emerge if the arts are seen as a symbol-using endeavor, calling for certain kinds of cognitive skills. (p. 275)

Dr. Hanshumaker advertises his task as an attempt to frame important issues in the evaluation of arts instruction. He, therefore, rightly points to the inadequacies of current methods which include student evaluation forms, checklists of teacher personality traits, and various attempts to correlate teacher behaviors with successful learner outcomes in arts instruction. By anchoring much of his discussion, though, to the notion of artistry as the important criterion for teacher effectiveness, he creates categories of meaning that are frequently as ephemeral as the notions which he criticizes.

"Whom Shall We Fire?", an article in the NASSP Bulletin (1977) by H. Ogden Morse, is used by Dr. Hanshumaker to illustrate the conceptual looseness prevalent in theories of what evaluation should be. There is more compelling theoretical work, however, on issues related to evaluating instruction than the Morse piece. A useful collection of articles can be found in the March-April 1978 edition of the Journal of Teacher Education. These articles deal with a variety of conceptual issues and methodologies aimed at producing better evaluation of the preservice teacher.

Dr. Hanshumaker also deals with the limitations of competency-based and performance-based evaluative concepts. He observes that these methods are "good as far as they go" but concludes that "they don't go far enough." He rightly argues that excellent arts instruction should consist of more than the execution of a chain of "pre-specified behaviors"; however, the major limitation that he sees in such systems is that competency, as a concept, is inadequate for characterizing the aims of the artist. This point is more or less a play on words, though, rather than a satisfying argument, for competency-based evaluative methods do not necessarily remove artistry from their range of concern. If used imaginatively, such methods could prescribe levels of teacher activity that would serve to identify bases for effective arts instruction.

Near the end of his paper, Dr. Hanshumaker concentrates more specifically on what he sees as an appropriate framework for the evaluation of arts instruction. He begins by identifying five characteristics which he feels are essential to good teaching in the arts. The first two, "teacher knowledge-of and experience in the art to be taught" and "an enthusiastic attitude toward both the art and the teaching of that art" are hard to quibble with. The other three characteristics, however, admit large degrees of abstraction when we try to specify just what might be called for on the part of teachers at different grade levels.

Viewing these characteristics as a foundation, then, Dr. Hanshumaker cites the work of J.T. Sandefur and R.A. Adams (1976) as a framework for considering the process of evaluation of teaching in the arts. Their work extends much previous research on teacher behaviors and skills which have been shown to effect certain kinds of outcomes. The list of behaviors which they have assembled seems to be generalizable for instruction in all subjects and doesn't have special significance for arts instruction alone. What these characteristics have to recommend them, as Dr. Hanshumaker points out, is the degree to which they encompass the larger issues of context. What he does not do is discuss these characteristics in terms which enable us to see how they might be incorporated into an evaluative system developed specifically for arts instruction.

It seems to me that in this whole area of teacher behaviors and characteristics, one piece of work that is applicable to evaluation of arts instruction is that of David McClelland at Harvard (cited in Pottinger, 1978, p. 31). He is working on a model for evaluating instruction which seeks to be more than a descriptive identification of individual teaching behaviors (for example, frequency and range of tasks performed). Rather, this model would view instructional competency as it is related to behaviors that are often covert and which often precede and even cause much of the teacher's successful behavior. Such an evaluative model, for example, would try to account for less evident behaviors and attitudes, such as the teacher's motivation in certain instances, diagnostic listening abilities, thinking clearly under stress, empathy, and flexibility in teaching style. Because arts instruction, however it gets defined at various grade levels, involves particular kinds of teacher planning, knowledge, and behavior, the evaluation model just cited could help to separate those aspects of teacher effectiveness into more understandable events. What is needed, moreover, is an evaluation approach in the arts which goes beyond a concern for teacher behaviors to the whole environment of learning and the role of arts instruction in that environment.

Washington, D.C.
October 1978

REFERENCES

Eisner, E. *The state of art education today.* Paper prepared for the National Endowment for the Arts, January 1978.

Gardner, H. Sifting the special from the shared. In S. Madeja (Ed.), *Arts and aesthetics: An agenda for the future.* St. Louis: CEMREL, Inc.: 1977, 267-278.

Morse, H.O. Whom shall we fire? *NASSP Bulletin,* 1977, 61(406), 76-79.

Pottinger, P.S. Designing instruments to measure competence. *Journal of Teacher Education,* 1978, 29(2), 28-32.

Sandefur, J.T., and Adams, R.A. An evaluation of teaching: An interim research report. *Journal of Teacher Education,* 1976, 27(1), 71-76.

Lee S. Shulman

Research on Teaching in the Arts: Review, Analysis, Critique

The purpose of this paper is to discuss the major themes of the conference on Research on Teaching in the Arts. I will review the relationships among subject matter, pedagogy, and research in this field. The particular questions that most affect the conduct of fruitful research in this important area will be examined.

The role I have been asked to play is both made easier and more difficult by my own marginality to the arts. The handicaps of marginality are clear to everyone. Nevertheless, there are also virtues. These include a relative freedom from certain biases and preconceptions that typically render clear characterization of familiar settings extremely difficult.

I therefore view my role as akin to that of the traditional ethnographer. As an outsider I am seeking the indicants of a strange culture through examination of its rituals, lore, patterns of interchange and intercourse, social grouping and barriers, uses of language within and between groups, and conflicts and resolutions. Conflicts, in particular, reveal patterns of value and commitment otherwise veiled by ritual and other forms of socially patterned behavior. My goal, therefore, is similar to that stated by Clifford Geertz (1973) as the purpose of anthropology, to discern the "webs of meaning" of those who work in the fields of art and aesthetic education, as well as those who would venture forth into those fields in order to teach and to investigate.

This expository and interpretive activity cannot function through retelling alone. These comments may be analogous to the Talmudic view of the four levels of Biblical exegesis: *p'shat*, explication of the plain meaning of the text; *d'rash*, interpretation of plain meanings; *remez*, broader inferences based on discerning nuances or "hints" from the text; and *sode*, barely bridled speculation soaring effortlessly from the text and

LEE S. SHULMAN *is Professor of Educational Psychology and Medical Education, and Director of the Institute for Research on Teaching at Michigan State University.*

tethered but loosely, if at all, to its sources—normally the level of exegesis assigned to the Kabbala or mystical literature. The reader should be forewarned that there will appear little interpretation of the first kind, much interpretation of the second and third kinds, and occasional forays into the dangerous altitudes of the fourth.

The Plot, Characters, and Essential Tensions

This first brief section will proceed somewhat dramaturgically by review of three central elements in this conference: plot, characters, and essential tensions. The plot was rather straightforward. We began with a review and discussion of the field of research on teaching. We learned that relatively little research has been conducted on the teaching of the arts in particular. We then examined the same question from the perspective of the arts in themselves and the literature dealing with the relationships between the art forms and their appropriate pedagogies. Next there was a review of the forms of research that might most appropriately be applied to the teaching of the arts, with special reference to those approaches involving teachers as collaborators. We then examined specific instances of arts teaching and its evaluation, in order to instantiate some of the more abstract discussions conducted earlier. In the course of examining these specific examples, there were sharp disagreements among participants regarding what constitutes "good arts education." The most significant disagreements occurred between specialists in the subject matter and educational practitioners. This conflict was not readily resolved and remains a source of tension. We thus have a plot which, like many academic discussions, has built up to a crisis which awaits resolution.

There appeared to be four distinctive sets of characters in this drama. These were (a) theorists of the arts and aesthetic education; (b) practitioners in teaching the arts, who were primarily teachers and administrators, not always arts specialists; (c) researchers on teaching, both general and in the arts; and (d) a group which I characterize as "the fourth world"—teacher educators, developers, educational consultants, and the like. The characters inhabiting the first three worlds brought distinctively different perspectives on the problems of this conference to the dialogues which ensued. Moreover, it appeared that while the manifest dialogue was carried on, each group of participants was muttering to itself *sotto voce* in the following manners:

"How can you claim to be able to study the processes of teaching in the arts if you cannot tell the difference between good art and poor art?" (Implicitly directed at the researchers and practitioners by the arts theorists and specialists.)

"So much abstract and sophisticated talk about the beautiful, the aesthetic . . . Where is the real world of chalk dust, hall passes, and active children?" (Implicitly directed by practitioners to the arts theorists and researchers.)

"All this mysticism with descriptions couched in esoteric aesthetic terms ... How is it possible to investigate the processes of art education as a means for improving it, if these experts will not formulate clearly what they really mean?" (Implicitly directed by researchers to other participants.)

These characters and their questions defined the essential tensions of the present conference and, I suspect, the durable dilemmas of research and teacher preparation in the fields of aesthetic education. I shall now turn to a more focused examination of the character of those tensions.

Significant Perspectives: Subject Matter, Practice, Research

Each of the first three constituencies—subject matter specialist, practitioner, researcher—represents one of the three central elements, the relationships among which define many of the issues in this field. These three elements are (1) the subject matter or *contents* of arts/aesthetic education; (2) the processes of *pedagogy* in arts/aesthetic education; and (3) the processes of *research* in arts/aesthetic education. It was generally assumed that we should strive for accord among those elements, ensuring that they are consistent with one another. The grounds for that expectation and the conditions under which consistency among elements should be defined constituted the basis for much of the debate.

Accord of Content and Pedagogical Practice

The first important assertion was that the contents of arts education ought to be, in some fashion, congruent with the processes of pedagogy in the arts. We first saw this in Efland's (1979) scholarly contribution, where he attempted systematically to link conceptions of art and conceptions of pedagogy. We again observed it in Chapman's (1979) study of the relationships between conceptions of art education held by neophytes and the ways in which they planned a hypothetical teaching unit. This commitment to the importance of consistency between the content of art and the process of pedagogy was the breeding ground for the most popular metophor of the conference, "the teacher as artist."[1]

The general acceptance of the notion that both teacher and learner in the arts must perform artfully—that is, creatively, inventively, independently (in some art forms), collaboratively (in other arts)—is brought into the sharp focus of controversy with Rosenshine's (1979) interpretation of the major findings of contemporary research on teaching (see also, Rosenshine, 1976). Rosenshine reported in his summary of the results of research on teaching that the form of teaching most conducive to pupil achievement of basic skills was "direct instruction." Direct instruction was defined by Rosenshine quite precisely. It bore little resemblance to the arts educator's preferred view of the teacher and learner as artists. Both Rosenshine and others recognized that generalizations from research on teaching reading and arithmetic to the teaching of the arts must be made cautiously. However, in the absence of countervailing evidence from other studies, the existing body of research must be taken seriously. A problem had been set. Could we continue to claim the need for accord between the nature of art and the teaching of art when a growing body of evidence appeared to point to the superiority of direct instruction for achieving a wide range of instructional goals?

I shall not now provide a critique of Rosenshine's conclusions. Others have already done so (for example, House, Glass, McLean, and Walker, 1978). Whether or not his conclusions are well-gounded in this particular case, they provide us with the opportunity to examine critically the assertion that effective instruction in a subject matter must always be congruent with the manner in which mature practitioners of the subject field—be they artists, scientists, or mathematicians—accomplish their mature daily work. Despite its intuitive appeal, the assertion is more readily offered than defended.

During an earlier part of my career I was actively involved in what became known as the "learning by discovery" controversy (Shulman and Keislar, 1966). There were many aspects to this controversy. One recurring question was whether one needed to learn *by* discovery in order to learn *to* discover. Did didactic, guided instruction doom the pupil to rote learning? Was discovery teaching the only road to higher cognitive accomplishments and creative thinking? Much of the curriculum revolution of the 1960s in mathematics, science, and the social studies was predicated on the assumption that there must be congruence between instruction and intended achievement. Since the post-Sputnik era aimed to produce a generation of creative American scientists, the new curricula were intended to teach science and scientific reasoning by discovery.[2]

Do we have a body of research that reflects on this question? I am ignorant of any such work in the arts. However, there is some fascinating research in the learning of mathematics and science which is suggestive. Groen and Resnik (1977) have been studying the teaching of computational algorithms to first and second graders (see also Woods, Resnick, and Groen, 1975). One of their striking findings was that pupils heuristically transform algorithms they have been taught into new algorithms which they invent.[3] That is, learners act upon the content of instruction and transform it in their own terms. It appears both unnecessary and inaccurate to assume a one-to-one correspondence between what is taught and what is learned. It appeared that the pupils studied by Groen and Resnick had learned spontaneously to transform algorithms into new forms which made better sense to them. They had learned to discover, if you will, from didactic instruction. Similar research has taken place in the teaching of science to older youngsters

(Finley, 1977) in which strategies for classifying rocks were taught in one fashion, but inventively transformed in application.

More examples can be drawn from our general experience. Chess masters typically learn their craft through carefully studying the games played by other masters. Moreover, they not only study the games, they replay them move by move and commit them to memory. Yet, they do not simply learn to mimic what they have memorized. They are capable of transforming the mimetic to the pragmatic. Were they not so able, they could rarely win a chess game.

I do not present these examples as sufficient evidence to refute the assertion that there should be congruence between the content of subject matter and pedagogical practice. I firmly believe that the relationship between the two elements is far more complex than typical educational polemics would allow. However, I believe these few examples are adequate to give pause to those who argue in principle that mechanistic drill-and-practice instruction necessarily sabotages subsequent creative, aesthetic performance. This is a question which must be examined through careful empirical study of artists, teachers, and pupils complemented by the sort of careful philosophical analysis which does not confuse disciplined inquiry with persuasive rhetoric.

Accord of Content and Research

Participants in the conference were appropriately on guard against the thoughtless importation into the study of arts and aesthetic education of research paradigms and methods more appropriate to other domains of teaching and experience. They were especially cautious regarding the employment of the psychological methods of research on teaching using experimentation or systematic categorical classroom observation schedules in the study of arts education. We thus saw the conference turn toward the more recently popular approaches of descriptive ethnographic research on teaching as alternatives to the more traditional methods. Pitirim Sorokin (1956), an outstanding sociologist of an earlier era, warned his fellow social scientists againt the inappropriate consequences of "quantiphrenia"—a madness in which the insane attempt to put numbers on all manner of phenomena. Similarly, we were advised to seek those modes of research which are themselves more artful than scientific. We were told that in studying arts education we must strive for the goal of "researchers as artist." Therefore, to the extent that the various forms of ethnography appear more subjective and artful than do the experimental and psychometric traditions of educational research, it is argued that ethnography is the approach of choice for the student of arts education.

I am not particularly comfortable with the insistence that researchers become artists for investigations of teaching in the arts. An extreme form of that position would demand that research on teaching mathematics be legitimate only when conducted using differential equations, and research on the teaching of history be properly pursued only in retrospect. Moreover, I find the rich case study and evocative research report as useful for understanding science teaching as it is for appreciation of arts instruction. Here again, the rhetorical call for congruence between the content of the subject matter and the mode of inquiry must be treated critically. It is not the subject matter alone which ought to determine the proper mode of investigation. It is a combination of the subject matter, teaching, learning, and instructional setting which together guides the questions asked in an inquiry. These questions properly determine the appropriate research methodology. One ought not extract a single element, such as subject matter, and demand that all other facets of the inquiry flow from it. It is one thing to seek accord among the elements. It is quite another to demand that one of the elements achieve hegemony over all others and define the terms for the congruence. I thus conclude this section with the admonition that those who study arts education use the specific questions they address as the basis for selecting modes of research rather than base that choice on a consideration of the nature of the subject matter alone.

Accord of Pedagogical Practice and Approaches to Research

A recurring theme of the meeting was the continued search for alternatives to the experimental, psychometric, and quantitative observational models that have heretofore characterized research on teaching. Though I too have participated in criticism of these models of research, I would hope we can recognize the distinction between error and insufficiency. These methods are not, in principle, improper for the understanding of educational processes. They become problematic when we insist on treating them as sufficient for answering all the questions that educators might ask. As Schwab (1958) argued persuasively in his analysis of "the corruption of education by psychology," the problem of any theoretically grounded approach to education is its necessarily narrow perspective. Alternative approaches to educational research methodology, such as ethnographies, will tell us different things about teaching. They will not necessarily tell us more.

There is a tendency to view ethnography as a monolithic, undifferentiated method of research. It is important to recognize that ethnography is a generic envelope in which we place a number of very different modes of investigation. Ethnography is a family of inquiries easily as diverse as psychology or philosophy. It would be a grave error to generalize from the particular approaches to ethnographic research on teaching reflected in the papers by Tikunoff and Ward (1979) or Bussis, Chittenden, and Amarel (1979) to the entire field of school ethnography. These fine papers were commissioned to speak to the role of teacher collaboration in research on teaching; I am sure they did not intend for all ethnographic research to be seen as instances of teacher collaboration, nor for the particular forms of collaboration reported in their papers to be viewed as necessary features of all ethnographic inquiry. As Erickson (1979) has clarified, the approaches to ethnography are themselves diverse and multipurpose.

What is shared by most approaches properly called ethnographic is their interest in characterizing subjective experience. They wish to capture the ways of seeing the world held by the participants in situations rather than as characterized "objectively" by outside observers. Thus it is that Margaret Mead dubbed anthropology a form of "disciplined subjectivity." Since it is difficult to be disciplined about one's own subjectivity in one's own culture, anthropologists have typically gone to strange cultures and alien lands to pursue their investigations. When attempting to do ethnographic research in one's own culture, as is the challenge for our contemporary educational ethnographer, problems are posed by the very familiarity of the researcher with the phenomena. The ethnographer's challenge, then, is to "make the familiar strange" (Erickson, 1973) or to "make the commonplace problematic" (Smith, 1978).

A goal of school ethnographies is to capture the ways in which the participants in school situations experience and cope with the features of those settings. This perspective will be an important element of any developing approaches to the proper study of arts education. There are other research approaches which also study the experiences and expertise of practitioners and those learning to practice. Many of these are well represented through an examination of a strategy of research advocated by the philosopher David Hawkins (1966) in his apt phrase, "wisdom of the practitioner."

Wisdom of the Practitioner

In 1966 Hawkins published a paper entitled "Learning the Unteachable," a phrase which may characterize much teaching in the arts. In this paper he introduces his conception of the wisdom of the practitioner.

> Our efforts are being made, I believe, in an historical situation where the best practice excels the best theory in quite essential ways; this fact defines a strategy we ought to follow.

> There have often been times in the history of science when the personal knowledge of practitioners was significantly deeper than anything embedded in the beliefs and writings of the academically learned. Indeed, science has never started in a social vacuum, but has grown typically out of the interplay of *Theorizein* and those practically achieved mappings of nature embodied in the working arts. (p. 3)

Thus, one reason for carefully studying the thought, strategies, and motives of teachers is that the practical wisdom of the teacher may well exceed that of the putative expert in important ways which, properly understood, can increase our understanding of pedagogical expertise. However, the concept of the wisdom of the practitioner takes us beyond the concept of teacher as model of skilled performance.

We begin with the assumption that teachers are, in the broadest sense, adaptively sensible. That is, when there is a substantial discrepancy between some observer's judgment regarding what a teacher ought to do and the observed performance of that teacher, it is our first inclination to ask "What is it about the total set of circumstances in which this teacher is engaged that would make the observed activities of the teacher sensible?" Or alternatively stated, "In terms of what goals and definition of the situation would the behavior under observation be adaptive?" To answer such questions requires us to investigate the teacher's goals and plans; the thoughts, motives, and anxieties experienced by the teacher in the course of instruction; the problems faced by the teacher and the strategies employed to deal with them; and the characteristics of individual teacher satisfaction and disappointment.

This approach to the study of teaching is consistent with principles enunciated years ago by many mathematics educators regarding the proper attitude that teachers ought to hold with regard to observations of pupil error in learning mathematics. They suggested that when we observe a pupil making a mathematical error we not immediately leap to correct that particular miscue. Rather we should raise the question of what possible system of mathematics that pupil might have in his or her head that would lead him or her to consider the offered response both proper and legitimate. In the final analysis, we are more interested in influencing the mentally retained mathematics concepts that generate student responses to mathematical problems than we are with merely shaping and judging specific overt mathematical responses. Similarly, we are most interested in understanding and influencing the pedagogy in the mind and in the heart of the teacher that generates the variety of particular teacher behaviors, rather than in merely characterizing and counting the behaviors themselves.

As a strategy of research, the wisdom of the practitioner suggests that we identify examples of experts working in context and study intensively the strategies they employ, the problems they sense and confront, and the modes of practice that appear to achieve their purposes for them.[4] This is a mode of research on teaching that characterizes much of the work of my colleagues at the Institute for Research on Teaching (Shulman and Lanier, 1977). Another research group with which I work (Elstein, Shulman, and Sprafka, 1978) has been studying the problem-solving processes of physicians in order to develop a more accurate and comprehensive understanding of medical diagnostic reasoning. As is often the case in such research, we discovered that the manner in which experts perform their tasks is not identical to that prescribed by textbooks in the field nor even with the typical self-report provided by practitioners themselves. Hence, it is important to note that one studies the wisdom of the practitioner by observing what they do, as well as by asking them how they manage. The self-report alone may contain significant distortions of actual practice. In order to build a comprehensive theory, however, it is as important to know what the practitioner *thinks* he or she is doing as it is to know what he or she is actually doing.

This sort of research has also been conducted to study the character of expertise in chess (deGroot, 1965); among trust investment officers (Clarkson, 1962); and it is reviewed more generally in Shulman and Elstein (1975). Closer to the topics of this volume, the character of expertise has been studied in architectural design by Eastman (1970), in musical composition by Bahle (reported in de Groot, 1965), and in still-life painting by Getzels and Csikszentmihalyi (1976).

A highly similar research strategy is even to be found in the work of historian of science Thomas Kuhn (1977). How does one make sense of the writings of early scientists who did not share the perspective on nature held by contemporary scientific scholars? Kuhn reports his frustrated efforts to understand Aristotle's concept of mechanics in physics. He reports being troubled by the serious inaccuracies of Aristotle's observations and interpretations.

> When dealing with subjects other than physics, Aristotle had been an acute and naturalistic observer. In such fields as biology or political behavior, his interpretations of phenomena had often been, in addition, both penetrating and deep. How could his characteristic talents have failed him so when applied to motion? How could he have said about it so many apparently absurd things? And, above all, why had his view been taken so seriously for so long a time by so many of his successors? The more I read, the more puzzled I became. Aristotle could, of course, have been wrong—I had no doubt that he was—but was it conceivable that his errors had been so blatant? (p. xi)

Kuhn then describes his insight in recognizing that he had to read Aristotle in his own terms rather than from the perspective of contemporary physics. When he came to understand Aristotle's physics in the light of the more general Greek worldview, the incongruities in the work of that ancient philosopher dissolved.

> Trying to transmit such lessons to students, I offer them a maxim: When reading the works of an important thinker, look first for the apparent absurdities in the text and ask yourself how a sensible person could have written them. When you find an answer, I continue, when those passages make sense, then you may find the more central passages, ones you previously thought you understood, have changed their meaning. (p. xii)

In these passages we see Kuhn doing history of science in a manner analogous to the ethnographer, the information processing psychologist, and the student of the wisdom of practice. All are attempting to understand the ways in which reality is constructed and defined in the minds of particular persons, whether living or dead.

A particularly illuminating example of such research with teachers is contained in Yinger's (1977, 1978) studies of teacher planning. This study involved planning activities and subsequent teaching performance of a single teacher over a five-month period.

One of the important virtues of research of this sort is that discrepancies between what experts say they are doing and how they actually accomplish their craft are made explicit and problematic for the experts themselves. Since many experts are engaged in the business of teaching others their form of expertise, discrepancies between what they say about what they do and how they actually perform become of great pedagogical interest. This is especially important when the experts have difficulty articulating the manner in which they perform. We encountered an example of this in the deliberations of the present conference when experts in aesthetic education made evaluative statements regarding instances of teaching they observed, but found it difficult to explicate the principles and standards they were employing to make those judgments. The teachers whom they observed were also making such implicit judgments. By clarifying and juxtaposing the two underlying "wisdoms"—that of the subject matter expert and that of the teacher—we might have been able to identify the grounds for disagreement and deal with them directly.

I have up to now been arguing that the wisdom of the practitioner identifies one strategy we ought to be following in the study of expertise in teaching. What are the specific arguments in favor of this approach? First, we claim with Hawkins that the expertise of teachers regarding instruction is likely to be greater than that of the extant theories in our field in significant ways. Second, we have asserted that an understanding of how teachers cope with the realities of teaching can guide our perspectives on a wider range of influences on pedagogical practice than our more limited theoretical purviews can typically provide. Thus the psychologist, subject matter specialist, group process theorist, or educational administrator will only focus on a portion of the total reality to which the teacher in practice must accommodate. Third, when our theories are based on the study of practice, we are likely to find less difficulty in intelligent dissemination of that knowledge back to practitioners. Since the research will have been an attempt to understand practice in its own terms, there ought to be less need to translate the alien language of the researcher into the common sense everyday language of the practitioner. Finally, research conducted with the practitioner as co-investigator and in the language of practice is more likely to reflect the currently more equitable distribution of power between researcher and teacher. Research conducted *with*, rather than *on*, teachers is therefore likely to encounter less resistance from teachers both in its conduct and subsequent interpretation.

One argument that has been leveled against this research approach is its susceptibility to the naturalistic fallacy. That is, there is the danger of equating what *is* with what *ought to be*. In so doing, we may treat the status quo as the standard for excellence and forgo opportunities for improving practice. Perpetuation of the status quo is unlikely to be a problem for several reasons. We typically study a number of practitioners in such research rather than only one. There is sufficient natural variation among practitioners to render improbable the specter of a monolithic, internally consistent current mode of operation emerging from our descriptions. Indeed, the differences among the teachers and within the same teacher across situations, in both knowledge and strategies, become significant sources of new thinking about teaching. Composite models of practice built up from the individual features of particular teachers are likely to be more instructive than the work of any single practitioner alone. Moreover, these descriptions are scrutinized critically by the teachers themselves as well as by experts in the appropriate subject matter and social science research fields in order to understand more fully both their virtues and limitations.

In summary, this approach seeks as its goal *research-into-practice*, in both senses of that properly ambiguous phrase. Research grows out of the disciplined investigation of practice and practitioners, using their concerns, problems, insights, activities, and traditions as its starting point. Yet its mission is incomplete and its promise unfulfilled, until research has returned to that same domain of practice by informing judgments, increasing knowledge, and improving teaching and learning.

This concern for the development of research-based theories of practice dedicated to the understanding and ultimate improvement of practice brings us to a question which received serious attention during the entire span of these meetings. What are the ways in which research can inform practice? This question is typically formulated in terms of the problems of dissemination, to which we now turn.

Research and Practice: Conceptions of Dissemination

In the course of these meetings we have examined, both explicitly and implicitly, several distinctively different conceptions of dissemination. Given the assumption that research and practice are two separate activities in which members of different professions engage in relative isolation from one another, how does the knowledge produced by the research profession become accessible to those who teach?[5]

The work of Tikunoff and Ward (1979) as well as that of Bussis, Chittenden, and Amarel (1979) dealt with the dilemma of dissemination through refusing to accept the basic dichotomy. That is, they argued that researchers and teachers ought to produce knowledge jointly, thereby becoming a single community of discourse. By becoming members of a single knowledge-producing and knowledge-using community, they would remove the need for translation and dissemination across present boundaries. Tikunoff and Ward especially argue that their approach is not only effective but practical on a large scale. It appears more prudent to claim that the involvement of teachers as co-investigators in research on teaching produces a new type of research enterprise and concomitantly new forms of pedagogical knowledge, with special personal outcomes for the particular teachers involved. I suspect that the basic dichotomy between the research community and the community of practice will remain even after substantial numbers of teachers have gained entry into the research community via research collaboration. Therefore, the problem of dissemination will remain.

The concept of dissemination most popular in the field of education comes to us from analyses of the diffusion of technological innovations in health and agriculture. In this conception, what is normally disseminated is a tangible product or object which can be employed by individuals to achieve certain purposes. We are constantly reminded of the success of agricultural extension agents in helping farmers grow more and better crops. Thus the road from the discovery of new forms of hybrid corn, special fertilizers or weed controls to their use by farmers is clear and impressive. Why cannot educational innovations be similarly disseminated?

It seems clear that even those educational innovations most directly analogous to technological products are not as readily disseminated. These are the materials and media of instruction that typically accompany new educational programs or curriculum packages. In great measure, this is because the teacher who must use these materials is unlikely to see them as unequivocally helpful. The classic dissemination model depends upon the recipient accepting the goals for which the innovation has been developed. For example, attempts to diffuse contraceptive loops in India failed dramatically compared to the successful diffusion of hybrid corn. There was no question in the minds of farmers that they wanted to grow more, but there were serious questions in the minds of parents about whether they wanted fewer children. It is for this reason that research, such as Chapman's, on the relationships between conceptions of arts education and teachers' goals and plans for instruction is very important. It therefore appears that dissemination for education is less like that of new technologies and more a question of modifying prevailing views of practitioners.

Dissemination for changing prevailing views is likely to be quite different from the diffusion of technological innovations. It appears to be more similar to the spread of ideology or of religion. The growth of Islam or the more recent spread of the peace movement may be more helpful analogies to the processes of educational dissemination. If research is to influence practice we may have to find a set of processes for significantly influencing the prevailing views of practitioners regarding both the goals and methods of instruction. The model of the agricultural extension agent for whom the goals of farming are rarely problematic is unlikely to be helpful.

Yet another view of dissemination holds that neither specific products nor prevailing views are translated and communicated. Rather the process of research produces opportunities for teachers to reflect on their own practice, thus becoming more aware of what they actually do as well as the meanings and interpretations which can be brought to bear on their actions. But how can research provide such opportunities for teachers who are not themselves personally engaged in the research process?

I believe that research informs practice through the provision of instances, of concrete examples of both practice and values which reflective teachers can employ as contrastive mirrors against which to compare their own efforts. In this regard, research is a rich source of such instances, albeit not the only one. In general, judgment is informed and behavior changed through contact with great works of art, the aphorisms of philosophers and saints, and the exhortations of evangelists and politicians. From research-grounded sources, judgment can be informed by the publication of the surgeon-general's reports, the announcement of test-score declines, research reports on the effectiveness of direct instruction, concrete case studies of children learning to read or of pupils learning to go to school, or detailed evocative descriptions of teachers accomplishing complex curricular integrations across the school day or week.

I thus conclude that our thinking about the translation of research into practice must itself be informed by the recognition that we are not engaged in a single activity but in several. We are diffusing specific materials and media of instruction, we are attempting to influence prevailing views, we are providing opportunities for critical reflection, and we are creating instances of practice and its purposes which can inform the judgments of teachers. Our programmatic efforts at dissemination must therefore reflect the multiplicity of forms and goals which the concept of dissemination demands.

Dissemination within Research: Problems of Generalizability

Rosenshine, among others, has raised the specter of non-generalizability with regard to many of the newer forms of research described in this meeting. Unlike the more traditional quantitative methods from either psychology or sociology, it is claimed, ethnographic research, case studies, clinical and information-processing approaches lack clear canons for demonstrating the generalizability of research findings. We therefore are unable to generalize the research conclusions safely beyond the boundaries of the immediate research sample itself.

I believe we can refute that claim through examination of the assumptions underlying generalizability in the quantitative approaches. Experimental psychologists argue that by randomly selecting samples from a defined population, generalization back to that population is legitimated. This is the claim for generalizability typically made by sociologists employing survey samples as well. However, in a now classic paper, Cornfield and Tukey (1956) have demonstrated that it is nearly impossible to achieve the theoretical claim of true random selection from a total population. Therefore they have argued that it is necessary for every researcher to provide readers with a clear and detailed description of the characteristics of individuals and research settings so that the reader can supply the degree of generalizability. Thus even for quantitative research, the question of generalizability typically becomes a matter of judgment rather than an absolute product of research evidence.

Generalizability of this sort is a problem for philosophy of science since the goal of science is typically theory development. We are concerned with how samples have been drawn from populations and settings in order to be able to make valid statements about aspects of nature or human behavior. In both qualitative and quantitative research we are confronted by a similar problem. We must ask ourselves, in the words of David Hamilton (1978), "What is this a case of?" This is true whether we are dealing with research that is experimental, correlational, or ethnographic. The bridge between the reported phenomenon and the limits of its generalizability cannot be built by the logic of method but only by the logic of human judgment. Moreover, in examining the usefulness of research for the improvement of teaching, we must extend our concept of generalizability to include the impact of research findings on the development of teachers—a form of pragmatic rather than scientific generalizability.

The Elusive Criterion

One of the most important questions repeatedly raised during the conference, and skillfully evaded by participants, dealt with the criterion problem in arts and aesthetic education. The problem of criterion exists at several levels. For the researcher there is the question of outcome measures for assessing the consequences of variations in observed approaches to teaching in the arts. Controversies regarding the proper measurement of educational outcomes abound in domains as ostensibly straightforward as reading and mathematics. How much more is it the case when assessing the outcomes of education in the arts?

The problem also exists painfully at the level of educational practice itself. By what standards is the classroom teacher to judge the quality of artistic performance by pupils or the aesthetic qualities inherent in particular episodes of instruction? Several times during these meetings we observed disagreements between subject matter specialists and teachers regarding the quality of particular instances of instruction in the arts. Arts specialists, however, were extremely reluctant to state the specific standards or criteria they employed to render their judgments. It was asserted that these judgments were subtle and complex, not capable of propositional formulation. Nevertheless, they maintained the expectation that teachers are obligated to judge their own teaching on the basis of these undefinable standards. How are teachers to employ standards they do not understand, have not been taught, and have not had an opportunity to learn?

As I discussed earlier, it is extremely difficult to communicate standards of practice that have not been clearly articulated by those who fashion them. Moreover, unexamined standards employed intuitively by experts are often in danger of being communicated verbally in one form while being employed by the experts in a very different way. Hence, many of the problems of teacher preparation in the arts rest on the difficulties we currently experience in specifying criteria for judging excellence in arts education. The elusiveness of the criterion, therefore, constitutes a crisis for the Academy rather than an indictment of the practitioner.

All teaching involves judgment. Since learning is typically defined as an internal change in learners which we infer from observable changes in behavior, the process of teaching demands continuous inferences or judgments from observed pupil behavior to inferred underlying states of mind, motive and emotion. Arts educators, researchers, and teachers must collaborate in a series of investigations to explicate those judgmental relationships between observables and underlying learning processes if we are to develop a durable program of research and teacher preparation in this field. We need programs of research in which the arts specialists themselves make the bases for their judgments of both products and instruction manifest and clear. Similarly, we need studies of teachers in the arts to clarify the nature of their judgments of instructional effectiveness. We can then begin to study ways of bringing the judgments of practitioners and those of experts in the arts into closer concordance.

We are likely to identify ways in which the judgments of experts are based on criteria far narrower than those of practitioners. The latter must take account of more than the correspondence between the processes and products of teaching and the standards implicit in the subject matter. They must also use criteria of active classroom involvement, articulation with school subjects taught simultaneously or serially, and other matters important for the accomplishment of successful classroom practice. Such a program of research could lead to more intelligent definitions of criteria than are current in most other subject fields.

Arts in the Curriculum

Much of the discussion during this meeting dealt with the place of arts in the total curriculum. Some argued that individual art forms should be taught separately and in their own terms. For some, the emphasis was on the performance of the art itself. For others, the greater emphasis was placed upon proper experience with, and appreciation, understanding, and critical evaluation of the various art forms.

Among specialists in the arts and arts education, the concept of integration of the arts into the other subject areas was distressing. They viewed the forms of integration as inevitably perverting the true character of the arts, rendering them handmaidens of the other curriculum areas. Yet the theme of coordinating and integrating arts education with the rest of the curriculum continued to appear. What forms might this integration take? One assertion was that the arts could build character and enhance the general quality of life. Another possibility was that arts instruction could serve to motivate and/or consolidate learning in the more traditional subject areas. The arts could also serve as a source of powerful methods or metaphors to increase the transfer of student learning in other subject areas. Finally, the arts might serve as a means for improving classroom and school learning climates through activities demanding large group involvement and cooperation. Naturally, complex combinations of these roles could also be envisaged.

It should be recognized that the arts are not alone in claiming these special virtues of enhancing creativity, character, curricular coherence, and communal cohesion. Most other subject areas—mathematics, science, social studies, for example—can also lay claim to these qualities. Given the unavoidable fact that the demands made on public education are increasing while the lengths of school days and years remain constant, educators in the arts must be ready to demonstrate that devoting curricular time to their areas not only serves to achieve the unique ends of aesthetic education but also enhances accomplishment of goals in other domains. Serious consideration of the integration of the arts into the curriculum seems therefore unavoidable. It may be necessary to do some injustice to each of the disciplines in order to make it possible to optimize instruction across all fields.

Concluding Remarks

Much of the dialogue during these meetings revolved around the question of what research on teaching could contribute to our understanding and improvement of teaching in the arts. In these closing remarks I would like to reverse that question. What can a developing understanding of education in the arts contribute to the general field of research on teaching? It is perhaps a selfish question, for my own commitments and obligations rest in the general field of research on teaching. Yet I feel it is important to recognize explicitly that the benefits of collaboration between these two fields are bilateral.

I believe that education in the arts can serve as a powerful counter-example to the currently popular studies of teaching in the "basic skills." While many educators express discomfort with the conclusions offered by Rosenshine on the superiority of direct instruction, the existence of and the popular faith in standardized achievement tests in those areas tend to prevail against those doubts. Researchers on teaching in the arts will not be able so blithely to employ existing instruments uncritically in their investigations. They will be forced to confront directly the purposes and processes of arts instruction as they wrestle with the problems of a criterion. I cannot imagine that simple conclusions regarding the effectiveness of direct instruction will be possible in the arts. Thus, through new programs of research in an area where the simpler methods of our current work will not be tolerated, we may ultimately develop strategies of inquiry that we can turn back on the basic skills to improve their investigation.

In current research on teaching in the traditional subject areas, the distinction between cognitive and affective outcomes is maintained with ease. Thus, although all practitioners recognize that the two aspects of learning interpenetrate in reality, researchers readily make the distinction for purposes of study. Enormous efforts are directed at calibrating instruments for measuring cognitive achievement, while the affective outcomes are either ignored or measured grossly. In aesthetic education, the fusion of the cognitive and affective is undeniable. To study properly the teaching of the arts, researchers will need to employ new methods which give proper attention to the manner in which cognitive and affective factors interact in learning and teaching. Since this interaction is just as important in reading, mathematics, and the sciences, what we learn from research on teaching the arts will be valuable for improving such studies in the other subject areas.

Finally, we should not ignore the power of apt metaphors for directing our thinking in research on teaching. Though I was critical of phrases like "the teacher as artist" earlier in this paper, there is no question that metaphors from the arts can serve a powerful heuristic function in guiding investigations of teaching in all domains. We must simply keep in mind that metaphors become most interesting at the points where they break down, and we must grow sensitive to the limits of our metaphor-making as well as to the aptness of the metaphors alone.

If there is a single lesson from research on teaching I would hope was conveyed to those investigating teaching in the arts, it is the avoidance of disciplinary dogma and doctrine in planning research programs and choosing among research methods. So much time and energy continue to be wasted in arguments about the relative effectiveness of quantitative and qualitative research methods. I believe we have learned that the problems of research on teaching are far too complex for any one research method. Those who wish to study teaching in the arts must be prepared to adopt a disciplined eclecticism as their general orientation toward research. The particular questions raised by research programs must dictate the selection of methods and combinations of method appropriate to the questions addressed. If research on teaching in the arts has developed later than research in other areas, this may become a virtue rather than a liability. Investigators in this field may profit from the experiences of those who preceded them, avoiding their errors and setting new standards for research in the future.

East Lansing, Michigan
February 1979

NOTES

[1]The alternative formulation, "the artist as teacher," is itself interesting. In arguing that one should strive for accord between two elements, it is often left unstated which of the two elements should define the terms for the accord. In principle, it seems as reasonable to call for artists to condition their efforts at aesthetic and expressive communication on the demands of education as it is to call upon teachers to perform in a manner consistent with the doing of art. Plato and Marx would have felt quite comfortable with the view of *art as teaching*.

[2]Ironically, careful analysis of the curriculum materials revealed that the accomplishment typically fell far short of the rhetoric (Shulman and Tamir, 1973).

[3]Algorithms are rules which *guarantee* correct solutions when correctly applied. Heuristics are more general strategies or "rules of thumb" which are *likely* to lead to correct answers when appropriately employed.

[4]Hawkins intended for the rare, outstanding teacher to be the only subject of this research genre. However, we find that it is not only the "good teacher" (if we can find him/her) who does good teaching. Most teachers can teach well under some conditions. Thus, our question is not "Who is the good teacher?" but "When is a teacher good?"

[5]The mirror question was rarely asked, though it is at least as important. How does the typically tacit knowledge developed in the minds of practitioners become accessible to the community of scholars? This "reverse dissemination" question is precisely the focus of wisdom-of-practitioner studies. Its importance is echoed by McLaughlin and Marsh (1978) in their report of the massive Rand studies of the spread of educational innovations. They observe ". . . in terms of knowledge about the practice of teaching, teachers often represent the best clinical expertise available" (p. 87). Their report is in general support of the arguments regarding dissemination offered in this section.

REFERENCES

Bussis, A. M., Chittenden, E. A., and Amarel, M. Collaborative research. This volume.

Chapman, L. H. The bearing of artistic and educational commitments on the teaching of art. This volume.

Clarkson, G. P. E. *Portfolio selection: A simulation of trust investment.* Englewood Cliffs, New Jersey: Prentice-Hall, 1962.

Cornfield, J., and Tukey, J. W. Average values of mean squares in factorials. *Annals of Mathematical Statistics,* 1956, *27,* 907-949.

de Groot, A. D. *Thought and choice in chess.* The Hague: Mouton, 1965.

Eastman, C. M. On the analysis of intuitive design processes. In G. Moore (Ed.), *Emerging methods in environmental design and planning.* Cambridge: MIT Press, 1970.

Efland, A. D. Conceptions of teaching in the arts. This volume.

Elstein, A. S., Shulman, L. S., and Sprafka, S. A. *Medical problem solving: An analysis of clinical reasoning.* Cambridge: Harvard University Press, 1978.

Erickson, F. What makes school ethnography ethnographic? *Newsletter,* Council on Anthropology and Education, Chicago, Illinois, 1973.

Erickson, F. Unpublished manuscript, Seminar on Conceptions of Conception, Institute for Research on Teaching, Michigan State University, 1979.

Finley, F. N. *Vertical transfer of instruction based on cognitive strategies for a sequence of geologic tasks.* Unpublished doctoral dissertation, Michigan State University, 1977.

Geertz, C. *The interpretation of cultures.* New York: Basic Books, 1973.

Getzels, J. W., and Csikszentmihalyi, M. *The creative vision: A longitudinal study of problem finding in art.* New York: John Wiley & Sons, 1976.

Groen, G., and Resnick, L. B. Can preschool children invent addition algorithms? *Journal of Educational Psychology,* 1977, *69*(6), 645-652.

Hamilton, D. *On generalization in the educational sciences.* Proceedings of the conference on "The Study of Schooling: Field-Based Methodologies in Educational Research." Research and Development Center for Individualized Schooling. Madison, Wisconsin, November, 1978.

Hawkins, D. Learning the unteachable. In L. S. Shulman and E. R. Kieslar (Eds.), *Learning by discovery: A critical appraisal.* Rand-McNally, 1966.

House, E. R., Glass, G. V., McLean, L. D., and Walker, D. F. No simple answer: Critique of the "Follow Through" evaluation. *Harvard Educational Review,* 1978, *48*(2), 128-160.

Kuhn, T. *The essential tension.* Chicago: The University of Chicago Press, 1977.

McLaughlin, M. W. and Marsh, D. D. Staff development and school change. *Teachers College Record,* 1978, *80*(1), 69-94.

Rosenshine, B. Classroom instruction. In N. L. Gage (Ed.), *The psychology of teaching methods.* Seventy-fifth yearbook of the National Society for the Study of Education. Chicago: University of Chicago Press, 1976, pp. 335-371.

Rosenshine, B. A response to Bussis, Chittenden, and Amarel: Describers and improvers. This volume.

Schwab, J. J. On the corruption of education by psychology. *School Review,* 1958, *66,* 169-184.

Shulman, L. S., and Elstein, A. S. Studies of problem solving, judgment, and decision making. In F. Kerlinger (Ed.), *Review of Research in Education, III.* Itasca, Illinois: F. E. Peacock, 1975.

Shulman, L. S., and Keislar, E. R. (Eds.) *Learning by discovery: A critical appraisal.* Chicago, Illinois: Rand-McNally, 1966.

Shulman, L. S., and Lanier, J. E. The Institute for Research on Teaching: An overview. *Journal of Teacher Education,* 1977, *28*(4), 44-49.

Shulman, L. S., and Tamir, P. Research on teaching in the natural sciences. In R.M.W. Travers (Ed.), *Second handbook of research on teaching.* Chicago: Rand-McNally, 1973.

Smith, L., *Accidents, serendipity and making the commonplace problematic: The origin and evolution of the field study "problem."* Proceedings of the conference on "The Study of Schooling: Field-Based Methodologies in Educational Research." Research and Development Center for Individualized Schooling. Madison, Wisconsin, November, 1978.

Sorokin, P. *Fads and foibles in modern sociology and related sciences.* London: Henry Regnery Co., 1956.

Tikunoff, W. J., and Ward, B. A. How the teaching process affects change in the school. This volume.

Woods, S., Resnick, L. B., and Groen, G. An experimental test of five process models for subtraction. *Journal of Educational Psychology,* 1977, *67*(1), 17-21.

Yinger, R. J. *A study of teacher planning: Description and theory development using ethnographic and information processsing methods.* Unpublished doctoral dissertation, Michigan State University, 1977.

Yinger, R. J. *A study of teacher planning: Description and model of preactive decision making* (Res. Ser. No. 18). East Lansing, Michigan: Institute for Research on Teaching, Michigan State University, 1978.

Conference Participants

Aspen, Colorado, June 25-July 1, 1978

J. Myron Atkins
Dean
College of Education
  University of Illinois

Arnold Berlin
Director
Norlin Corporation

Marion Blakey
Program Chief, Youth Programs
  Office of Planning and Analysis
National Endowment for the
  Humanities

Laura H. Chapman
Consultant
Senior Editor, Studies in Art Education

Edward A. Chittenden
Research Psychologist
Educational Testing Service

Geraldine Jonçich Clifford
Professor of Education
University of California, Berkeley

Edward DeAvila
DeAvila, Duncan, and Associates

Joseph F. Dominic
Senior Policy Research Fellow
National Institute of Education

Roy A. Edelfelt
Professional Associate
National Education Association

Arthur Efland
Professor of Art Education
The Ohio State University

Martin Engel
Arts and Humanities Advisor
National Institute of Education

Jan Greenberg
Director of Aesthetic Education
Webster College

Betty Hall
Research Specialist
Arts and Humanities Group
CEMREL, Inc.

James Hanshumaker
Professor of Music and Education
University of Southern California

George W. Hardiman
Professor in Charge
Art Education
University of Illinois

Gordon Hughan
Associate Director of Field Services
Agency for Instructional Television

Billie Jacobs
Principal
Daniel Boone School
St. Louis, Missouri

Charlette Kennedy
Institute for Research on Teaching
Michigan State University

Francis Keppel
Director
Program on Education
Aspen Institute for Humanistic Studies

Gerard L. Knieter
Dean
The College of Fine and Applied Arts
The University of Akron

Virginia Koehler
Assistant Director for Teaching and
  Instruction
National Institute of Education

Bette Korman
Executive Director
G.A.M.E., Inc.
New York City

Charlotte Lazar
Horton Elementary School
San Diego, California

Charles Leonhard
Professor of Music
University of Illinois

Richard Lewis
Director
The Touchstone Center for
    Children, Inc.
New York City

Richard L. Loveless
Associate Professor of Arts and
    Music Education
University of South Florida

Stanley S. Madeja
Vice-President
CEMREL, Inc.

Deborah Meier
Director
Central Park East School
New York City

Edward Mikel
Coordinator
Aesthetic Education Learning Center
    Network
CEMREL, Inc.

Donald M. Miller
Director of Research
Arts and Humanities Group
CEMREL, Inc.

Sidney G. Mollard, Jr.
Coordinator of Music
Montgomery County Public Schools
Rockville, Maryland

Jack Morrison
Executive Director
American Theatre Association

Sheila Onuska
Program Associate
Arts and Humanities Group
CEMREL, Inc.

Thomas D. Parker
Special Assistant to the Director
National Institute of Education

Bennett Reimer
Chairman
Music Education Department
Northwestern University

Shirley Ririe
Professor of Ballet and Modern Dance
University of Utah
Artistic Director
Ririe-Woodbury Dance Company

Wade M. Robinson
President
CEMREL, Inc.

Forbes Rogers
Director
Alliance for Arts Education

Bernard Rosenblatt
Director of Teacher Education and
    Dissemination
Arts and Humanities Group
CEMREL, Inc.

Barak Rosenshine
Professor of Educational Psychology
University of Illinois

Barbara Rowe
Coordinator
St. Louis Aesthetic Education Learning
    Center
CEMREL, Inc.

Mary Runge
Secretary to the Vice-President
CEMREL, Inc.

Barbara Salisbury
Consultant
Matteo Ricci College
Seattle, Washington

Martha Dell Sanders
Director
KEA UniServ
Paducah, Kentucky
Member
CEMREL Board of Directors

Maurice Sevigny
Associate Professor and Program
    Chairman
Art Education, School of Art
Bowling Green State University

Lee S. Shulman
*Professor of Educational Psychology
    and Medical Education
Director
Institute for Research on Teaching
Michigan State University*

Barbara Easton Smith
*Instructor
Art Department
Aspen High School*

Jane Stallings
*Manager of Classroom Process Studies
Education Research Department
Stanford Research Institute*

Elizabeth Steiner
*Professor of Philosophy of Education
    and Research Methodology
Indiana University*

Bennett Tarleton
*Coordinator
National Aesthetic Education Learning
    Center at the Kennedy Center
CEMREL, Inc.*

Patricia Thuernau
*Research Specialist
Arts and Humanities Group
CEMREL, Inc.*

William J. Tikunoff
*Director
Programs on Schooling
Far West Laboratory*

Barbara Truan
*Principal
Aspen Elementary School*

Dennis Verity
*Research Specialist
Arts and Humanities Group
CEMREL, Inc.*

Beatrice A. Ward
*Deputy Laboratory Director
Far West Laboratory*

Gene Wenner
*Arts Education Coordinator
U.S. Office of Education*

Discussion Groups

Group I

Barbara Salisbury, *Chair*
Consultant
Matteo Ricci College
Seattle, Washington

Arnold Berlin
Director
Norlin Corporation

Laura H. Chapman
Consultant
Senior Editor,
Studies in Art Education

Geraldine Jonçich Clifford
Professor of Education
University of California, Berkeley

Betty Hall
Research Specialist
Arts and Humanities Group
CEMREL, Inc.

Gordon Hughan
Associate Director of Field Services
Agency for Instructional Television

Richard Lewis
Director
The Touchstone Center for
 Children, Inc.
New York City

Deborah Meier
Director
Central Park East School
New York City

Shirley Ririe
Professor of Ballet and Modern
 Dance
University of Utah
Artistic Director
Ririe-Woodbury Dance Company

Barbara Rowe
Coordinator St. Louis Aesthetic
 Education Learning Center
CEMREL, Inc.

Elizabeth Steiner
Professor of Philosophy of
 Education and Research
 Methodology
Indiana University

Dennis Verity
Research Specialist
Arts and Humanities Group
CEMREL, Inc.

Beatrice A. Ward
Depty Laboratory Director
Far West Laboratory

Group 2

Gerard L. Knieter, Chair
Dean
The College of Fine and Applied Arts
The University of Akron

J. Myron Atkin
Dean
The College of Education
University of Illinois

Jan Greenberg
Director of Aesthetic Education
Webster College

Charlette Kennedy
Institute for Research on Teaching
Michigan State University

Bette Korman
Executive Director
G.A.M.E., Inc.
New York City

Charles Leonhard
Professor of Music
University of Illinois

Richard L. Loveless
Associate Professor of Art and Music Education
University of South Florida

Sidney G. Mollard, Jr.
Coordinator of Music
Montgomery County Public Schools
Rockville, Maryland

Forbes Rogers
Director
Alliance for Arts Education

Bernard Rosenblatt
Director of Teacher Education and Dissemination
Arts and Humanities Group
CEMREL, Inc.

Bennett Tarleton
Coordinator
National Aesthetic Education Learning Center at the Kennedy Center
CEMREL, Inc.

William J. Tikunoff
Director
Programs on Schooling
Far West Laboratory

Barbara Truan
Principal
Aspen Elementary School

Group 3

Maurice Sevigny, *Chair*
Associate Professor and Program
  Chairman
Art Education, School of Art
Bowling Green State University

Marion Blakey
Program Chief, Youth Programs
Office of Planning and Analysis
National Endowment for the
  Humanities

Joseph F. Dominic
Senior Policy Research Fellow
National Institute of Education

Roy A. Edelfelt
Professional Associate
National Education Association

Arthur Efland
Professor of Art Education
The Ohio State University

Virginia Koehler
Assistant Director for Teaching
  and Instruction
National Institute of Education

Charlotte Lazar
Horton Elementary School
San Diego, California

Bennett Reimer
Chairman
Music Education Department
Northwestern University

Jane Stallings
Manager of Classroom Process
  Studies
Education Research Department
Stanford Research Institute

Patricia Thuernau
Research Specialist
Arts and Humanities Group
CEMREL, Inc.

Gene Wenner
Arts Education Coordinator
U.S. Office of Education

Group 4

George W. Hardiman, *Chair*
Professor in Charge
Art Education
University of Illinois

Edward A. Chittenden
Research Psychologist
Educational Testing Service

Martin Engel
Arts and Humanities Advisor
National Institute of Education

James Hanshumaker
Professor of Music and Education
University of Southern California

Billie Jacobs
Principal
Daniel Boone School
St. Louis, Missouri

Edward Mikel
Coordinator
Aesthetic Education Learning
  Center Network
CEMREL, Inc.

Donald M. Miller
Director of Research
Arts and Humanities Group
CEMREL, Inc.

Jack Morrison
Executive Director
American Theatre Association

Thomas D. Parker
Special Assistant to the Director
National Institute of Education

Barak Rosenshine
Professor of Educational
  Psychology
University of Illinois

Martha Dell Sanders
Director
KEA UniServ
Paducah, Kentucky
Member
CEMREL Board of Directors

Barbara Easton Smith
Instructor
Art Department
Aspen High School